An Afghan Woman's Odyssey

Farooka Gauhari

An Afghan Woman's Odyssey

Foreword by Nancy Dupree

University of Nebraska Press
Lincoln and London

© 1996 by the University of Nebraska Press
All rights reserved
Manufactured in the United States of America

First Nebraska paperback printing: 2004

Library of Congress Cataloging-in-Publication Data
Gauhari, Farooka, 1947–
An Afghan woman's odyssey / Farooka Gauhari; foreword by Nancy Dupree.
p.   cm.
Originally published: 1996.
ISBN 0-8032-7116-6 (pbk.: alk. paper)
1. Gauhari, Farooka, 1947–   2. Afghanistan—Politics and government—1973–1989.
3. Human rights—Afghanistan.   I. Title.
DS371.2.G379   2004
958.104′6′092—dc22   2004015895

Excerpt on pages 187–88 reprinted by special permission. © 1988 Eqbal Ahmad and
Richard J. Barnet. Originally in *The New Yorker*.

Dedicated to the memory of my husband,
to my children, and to the silent majority –
the women of Afghanistan

CONTENTS

List of Illustrations
and Maps viii
Foreword ix
Preface xvii

BEFORE THE COUP
A Happy Childhood 3
Saleem 16
The Best Years 41

THE SEARCH
A Diary 63

EPILOGUE
253

ILLUSTRATIONS

Following page 124

Saleem and me with our children, 1972

Saleem's parents

Jaan, Mother, and Khalil

The Noon Cannon

Kabul, from Sherdarwaza Mountain

High school girls in school uniforms

A view of me in our back yard, 1964

Bibi Jan, Saleem's grandma, with Omar, 1966

Sahar, Ali, and me, 1970

Waterwheel and buildings on the Kabul University campus

The Darul Aman Palace

Ali, Sahar, and Omar, 1971

Saleem at Maxwell Air Force Base, 1971

My brother Jaan with Ali, Sahar, and Omar, 1975

The Blue Mosque in Marzar-i-Sharif

Lunchtime at a roadside stop on the way to Mazar-i-Sharif

Our first house

The new house Saleem was building for us in the spring of 1978

MAPS

Afghanistan xxiii

Kabul xxiv

FOREWORD

When societies are beset by calamity, be it loosed by nature or through men's machinations, women as well as men are physically and emotionally caught in the eddies of the upheaval. Yet seldom are women's voices heard.

In Afghanistan, since 1978, the populace has been seared by a coup d'état, invasion by foreign armies, and violence launched by their own contentious leaders. This war – its politics, its destruction and its refugees – has been described in a large body of literature in which women have their place, as groups of vulnerable victims, but seldom as individuals. Farooka Gauhari's personalized account of the human tragedy of these events is, therefore, an uncommon contribution. Her story holds meaning not only for the countless Afghan women whose experiences mirror hers, but also for those many women living through similar traumas in other parts of the world. But over and above its universal appeal, it offers many insights into Afghanistan's culture and also into its recent history, because Farooka Gauhari epitomizes this era of rapid change.

Farooka Gauhari's father was a liberal, and a civil servant in education.

The family thus belonged to the burgeoning urban middle class, which included the professionals, technocrats, bureaucrats, and administrators who, working mainly for the state, were charged with implementing the wide range of development schemes initiated during the 1950s by Prime Minister Mohammad Daoud Khan, cousin and brother-in-law of King Zahir Shah (1933–73).

From 1956 on, massive dams for major land-reclamation projects, hydroelectric plants, a greatly expanded road system, airports, natural gas exploitation, and industries as diverse as fertilizer plants and a winery changed the landscape, while the medical and educational infrastructure was expanded and reforms modernized the police, the army, and the air force. Social reforms included government support for the voluntary removal of the veil, signaling the end of seclusion for women. For Farooka Gauhari and her friends then on the threshold of womanhood, this meant that, with family approval, they could look forward to careers and active participation in the nation's surge toward new horizons. Farooka opted to become a teacher, a profession traditionally accepted for women.

The easing of strictures on the movement of women outside their homes also enabled Farooka to travel abroad, as did thousands of other young women and men. The development projects created a great need for workers with new skills and, more important, with attitudes compatible with efficiency, and the countries financing these projects – the USSR, the USA, East and West Germany, France, Italy, Poland, Rumania, Czechoslovakia, China, India, and Pakistan – eagerly offered them training.

Farooka Gauhari went abroad as a member of the faculty of Kabul University at a time when the steadily increasing student body began to take unaccustomed interest in social and political activities. Some had been inspired by concepts taken, either at home or abroad, from a wide spectrum of political philosophies; others championed values based on conservative Islam in order to challenge what they saw as a decline in moral standards emanating from the anti-Islamic ideologies of the left. Very soon both men and women at the university exerted political influence out of all proportion to their numbers.

The authoritarian nature of the state was a preeminent issue. The Afghan government consisted of a centrally directed bureaucracy subject to decisions made strictly within the royal lineage, the Mohammadzai, whose exclusive dominance had prevailed since early in the nineteenth century. Now, after a decade of rapid economic growth, the educated urban middle class represented a wide variety of social backgrounds outside the privileged Mohammadzai elite. Trained, articulate, and highly motivated, stronger and more numerous than ever before, the middle class felt thwarted because they were largely excluded from the higher echelons of significant decision making. Nor did Prime Minister Daoud Khan tolerate dissent, although change was clearly inevitable. Resentment against the primacy of the Mohammadzai ran deep; frustrations mounted; demonstrations escalated; and the prime minister eventually resigned.

Following Daoud's departure in 1963, the government launched an experiment in parliamentary democracy, heralded as *democracy-i-nao*, or the new democracy. King Zahir appointed a commoner, Dr. Mohammad Yosuf, as interim prime minister and in 1964 a Loya Jirgah (Grand National Assembly) wrote a new constitution that banned the Mohammadzai from participating in political parties and from holding office as prime minister, minister, member of parliament, or justice of the supreme court.

The new democracy was greeted by many with sense of euphoria but the pervasive secret police continued its harassment, thereby stunting the growth of a responsible opposition. Elections were held in 1965 and 1969, but vocal groups on the left and on the right instigated several periods of student demonstrations and a spate of labor strikes that kept the country in general unrest for three years.

The leftist groups purported to follow Marxist-Leninist ideologies, but, because there was no strong working class in Afghanistan, their membership consisted mainly of university professors and students, secondary school teachers, government civil servants, figures in the entertainment world, and, significantly, military personnel. Only one group with Maoist tendencies attempted to mobilize the rural areas. On the right, the guardians of Islam, influenced by the Egyptian Ikhwan ul-Muslimin, the Muslim Brotherhood, and the political Jama'at-i-Islami Pakistan party, were determined to eradicate the alien leftist influences they believed were undermining the society. There were numerous clashes in the streets of Kabul, the capital, and violent encounters at the university. Ugly attacks on career women wearing Western dress provoked Afghanistan's first women's demonstrations in 1970.

Western dress for men had been introduced by the monarchy in the 1880s; led by the ladies at court, women adopted Western styles for wear at home in about 1904. By the 1970s almost all urban educated families wore Western fashions outside the home. For men they were statements of sophistication; for women they symbolized emancipation.

In Kabul's spacious new suburbs families built single-family modern homes and decorated them with Western furnishings, as Farooka Gauhari herself describes. In addition, mammoth apartment blocks requiring further adjustments in domestic life-styles were built as the city's population surged in reponse to immigration from the rural areas encouraged by the expanded road system. Even so, a substantial portion of the capital's middle class still lived in the noisome Old City, in crowded extended-family households lacking basic amenities such as electricity, piped water, and sanitation. The disparity between this area, which had seen little change since Kabul became the capital in 1776, and the rest of Kabul was all too evident. Kabul was a divided city.

At Kabul University the combining of previously scattered faculties on a single campus in 1964 had an unintended result: with the students concentrated in one body, the university became a center of activist ferment. As a member of the faculty, Farooka Gauhari observed at first hand much of the turbulence, but she remained aloof from politics even though women were by now highly visible in public places. In largely avoiding political involvement, she typified the attitude of a majority of Afghan women who, despite their awareness of the importance of their roles in the development of the nation and their resentment of customs and attitudes that prevented them from taking decisions on their own, were still unwilling to participate in militant action in their personal lives and in the workplace. As a result women lacked the cohesive leadership necessary to enforce the new legal guarantees pledged to them.

Militant behavior goes against the codes prescribed for women in Afghan etiquette. Although the society by now accepted professional women in public forums and educated women expected to pursue careers, commitments to family universally stood first among their priorities. It is this strong sense of family which sustained women throughout the difficult period described in this book. Few social activities took place outside the family. Gatherings at each other's homes and family picnics or outings to shrines were the preferred forms of entertainment. Nevertheless, in Kabul the rising popularity of Western-style restaurants, a nightclub with dancing, a jazz club, and a bowling alley provided opportunities for unrelated men and women to socialize, a change in social mores the religious conservatives viewed as anathema.

If women generally shrank from political action, the overall political atmosphere early in the 1970s continued to be feverish. But it had no direction. The activists issued vociferous denouncements without defining viable alternatives, and the government, by procrastinating over the promulgation of the Political Parties Law, the Provincial Councils Law, and the Municipal Councils Act, failed to provide a structure for responsible political dialogue and offered no opportunities for regional participation in representative government. So, instead of furthering responsible political processes, the agitation fomented unrest.

To restore stability, Mohammad Daoud Khan staged a coup in July 1973, deposed the monarchy, and established the Republic of Afghanistan with himself as president and prime minister. The two main leftist parties, Khalq (The Masses) and Parcham (The Banner), initially supported Daoud's coup, but because the government continued its authoritarian style, they soon became disenchanted and unleashed a coup of their own on April 27, 1978. Daoud and his family and close associates were killed and the Democratic Republic of Afghanistan came into being under the rule of the People's Democratic Party of Afghanistan, the PDPA, led by Noor Mohammad Taraki.

Many in Kabul initially welcomed the demise of Mohammadzai rule and greeted the new regime with cautious optimism. This goodwill rapidly evaporated, however, under the new government's ruthless fervor. Having swept away "the tyrants of the ages," the PDPA proceeded to institutionalize repression to an extent far beyond the excesses of former regimes. The party claimed to have led a "people's revolution," but in fact the number of dedicated PDPA members remained inadequately small. Also, because they were overwhelmingly urban in their outlook, those who attempted to make contact with the masses proved insensitive to the value systems cherished by the bulk of the population, who lived in the rural areas. Farooka's puzzled observations on the life-styles of her rural relatives hint at the gulf that existed. Indeed, many Kabuli were genuinely afraid to venture too far outside their city.

Forays by the dedicated party cadres who fanned out into the countryside were disastrous. These young city men did not dress according to custom, nor did they sit or speak or pray properly. Their behavior was an affront to accepted form and manners. Antagonism, therefore, festered from the very first encounters.

Furthermore, being mostly illiterate, the rural populations could hardly be expected to comprehend the complexities of leftist dialectics. The villagers listened, but what they heard about agrarian reform seemed only to threaten their existing socioeconomic lives without providing an acceptable alternative. The proposed social reforms, they reasoned, would certainly erode their closely knit, kinship-based, family-oriented society. As a result, the rural populations refused to comply and their recalcitrance was met with brutal force. Pockets of local resistance grew into a nationwide jihad, holy war, led by many of the conservative religious student leaders once part of the ferment at Kabul University. Only an invasion by Soviet troops in December 1979 saved the new regime from foundering.

Power struggles within the PDPA leadership were equally destructive. Within six weeks of the 1978 coup, Khalq dismissed the Parcham leadership; within a year President Taraki was eliminated by his one-time protégé, Hafizullah Amin; three months later the Soviets invaded, eliminated Hafizullah Amin, and installed the ousted Parcham leader, Babrak Karmal. Propped up by the Soviets, Babrak lasted until May 1986, when the Soviets replaced him with Najibullah, formerly a Parcham student activist and avid supporter of Babrak Karmal. While chaos staggered the government and turmoil engulfed the countryside, the Soviets decided to withdraw. President Najibullah held fast after the last foreign troops left in February 1989, but in April 1992 his own party finally deposed him.

Farooka Gauhari left her country twelve years before the Afghan experiment in Communism ended and the rule of the Islamic State of Afghanistan began. Professionals by the hundreds had found the situation intolerable, for in their desperation to win acceptance the contending PDPA leaders had imprisoned and executed their perceived opponents and had smothered academic honesty and individual freedoms. For most, concern for the safety of family members was the overriding reason for leaving. As this account poignantly recounts, departure was not an easy matter. The clandestine disposal of homes and belongings required courage and ingenuity. The fact that women typically undertook these tasks testifies to the often underestimated strength of Afghan women.

Farooka and her family moved on to build new lives in the United States. Not all Afghans who left have been so fortunate. Because of their own power struggles, the leadership of the Islamic State of Afghanistan has proved to be equally inept in winning the confidence of their people. Over a third of the Afghan population still live as refugees in Iran and Pakistan; upwards of half a million urban displaced live in villages or tented settlements inside Afghanistan. The leadership of the Islamic State of Afghanistan has also failed to win the loyalty of their people. Their struggles for power generate spirals of conflict, causing the refugees to look at repatriation with extreme anxiety. They see no security for their families, no education for their children, no employment for professionals, diminished roles for women, and little in the way of basic shelter or services.

In addition, the years of discord have stretched taut the fabric of this society and left many lingering effects. National traits once respected, honored hallmarks of the Afghan character, are in jeopardy. Tolerance for others. Forthrightness. Aversion to fanatics. Respect for women. Loyalty to colleagues and classmates. Dislike for ostentation. Commitment to academic freedom. All have been compromised.

Thankfully, the spirit of courageous determination, amply evident in the pages that follow, is still strong. There seems no reason to doubt, therefore, that reconstruction can be astonishingly rapid.

But first there must be peace.

Nancy Hatch Dupree

Peshawar, February 1995

PREFACE

Do not ask me why I have postponed writing down my memoirs for so long. At first I was not able to write them all. Whenever I sat down to write, thousands of teardrops would fall and the paper would disappear behind the shadows of my mind. Even though more than fifteen years have gone by, it still hurts whenever I remember my past.

Today, however, I feel obligated to write. I am writing now because I owe it to myself, to my husband, to my beloved country, Afghanistan, and to my friends and others who have gone through their own silent and hideous inner battles caused by wars, executions, and simple human ignorance. This battle within me took such a toll that it cut years off my life; I used to constantly fall to my knees and only by sheer will power could I stand upright, holding onto that last vestige of pride and dignity. Only with great pain was I able to conceal my grief. I was perpetually afraid of losing my job, my mind, but above all the unity of my family.

My story is that of Saleem, the man I married. He came into my life on a spring day and was taken away from me on another spring day. I used to love springtime for giving new life to the world. Now spring makes me melancholy, because it has taken life away from my world. I feel such emptiness and loneliness that nothing can fill the holes in my soul and psyche. Saleem committed himself to his family until the last moments he spent with us. He always made me feel tall, proud, and confident whenever I was among others. He gave his love unendingly not only to us but to all of his friends and acquaintances as well.

My story is about my unrelenting, desperate, and unsuccessful search for my husband after the April 1978 coup. How deeply I wish that someone in this world could show me the place where he rests eternally. Today, on Memorial Days and similar occasions, I find myself in nearby cemeteries looking for a forgotten grave to put flowers on. There I sit for hours; I pray for its occupant and for my husband, who asked me once to pray for him at his grave.

My story is about a family who lived in Afghanistan, a family with deep love for their homeland, in many ways an ordinary family. It is about parents, brothers, and sisters who always gave me moral support. Whenever I felt lonely, they were there for me. Because of me they left their homeland under the worst conditions.

My story is about my mother, who still cannot adjust to life in the United States, who feels that we have trapped her in a cage by bringing her here, even though she is surrounded by her family and many good and friendly neighbors.

My story is about my children, my relatives, and my friends, who surround me and give me the assurance and confidence I still need. Finally, my story is about my husband and those I love whose whereabouts are unknown to me, of those with whom I can no longer communicate, but for whom I continue to pray.

My life story is not a heroic one. It is merely one of the many similar stories that happen every day around us in this hard world. Given the same circumstances and situations, most people would have acted similarly to me, making me far from unique.

I kept a diary, but it is not complete by any means. Whenever I had a bad day, I was too tired to write in the evening and hated to remember the events. Also, I was afraid to write down how I felt about things, because what if the diary had been discovered by the government's agents? The government agents were known to search houses at any time of day or night. Thus, my entire family and friends would have been put in jeopardy. Whenever my day's search yielded something positive, like someone saying that my husband was alive, I would sit down and take the time and risk of recording the events. In all such notes I was always very careful not to say anything against the government officials; on the contrary, I often praised them. For example, if there was shooting in the city, I would add, after briefly describing the episode, "I don't know why these WESTERN AGENTS do not let us live in peace, in spite of all our government's efforts to keep us happy!" I hoped that if my notes were discovered, the added statement would keep my family safe and secure.

If the following story touches you, do not be overly concerned about me, because I am only one survivor among many. I wish I had the power to shout loudly and clearly enough for all the world to hear: PLEASE STOP THE WARS! I have learned that in war there are no winners. In every war many are badly hurt – mothers, children, friends. Let me tell you that one can cope with natural calamity and deaths, but it is nearly impossible to contend with the unnatural upheaval which is the result of human greed and struggle for power.

My book is a cry against wars and executions. It strongly pleads for peace and justice – justice for those Afghans who have lost a member of their family in this miscalculated, senseless war. Peace be upon all those Soviet mothers and wives who opposed the invasion of a neighboring country, Afghanistan; were caught in this turmoil unwillingly; and have lost their loved ones. They were told that these soldiers were in Afghanistan on a friendly mission!

If I could, I would wipe away forever the tears and sorrow of all those brave Afghan women and their children who have suffered more in this war than anyone else though we hardly hear from them. They have lost their only breadwinners and are struggling hard for survival. No amount of money can buy their happiness and all the Gorbies, Bushes, Castros, and Thatchers of the world can never bring back the joy that has been taken away.

A question always comes to mind: Did Afghanistan spell the doom of the Soviet empire? Maybe not, but it certainly played a major role in the USSR's fall. The Russian leaders who were enemies of yesterday are our friends today. Let's not forget the crimes that were done by them and their puppets in Afghanistan; the flame that was ignited in this war will burn the country and the region for generations to come.

My book is already past due. There are reasons for the delay. First, it took me years to overcome my grief. Second, it was hard to decide whether it was worth the sacrifice of my family's privacy, and I had to struggle with the dilemma of whether or not my story would jeopardize my friends' safety back home. And many times I relinquished writing because of the thought "Who cares? It's my personal life."

Today I am convinced that if my writings are able to get the message across to five readers and stop a single man's death somewhere in the world, it will have been well worth my efforts, sacrifice, and the inherent risks as well. I sincerely hope, too, that my book will be an inspiration to all those educated Afghan women living around the world to record their side of the story and the disasters caused by this terrible war. Let the world know what a beautiful, proud culture and people we have, so that Afghanistan will no longer be considered an exotic and mysterious land to outsiders.

Finally, I hope this book will enlighten and inform readers who wish to know what is going on beyond the borders of their own country. I want to show how life can be unfair even though you have followed all the rules.

In writing this book I have tried to stay completely faithful to the facts as I perceive them. Most of the descriptions of events are based solely upon my personal perceptions and experiences and reflect only my point of view. I hope this account will not offend my Afghan friends; it reflects only a small portion of the society in which I have spent most of my life. For those of you who want to say something different, I value your views and thoughts and would like to see other aspects of Afghan culture exposed in public media to further confirm the multicultural, multiethnic nature of our native land.

To conceal the identity of people, I have changed the real names of many, except for a few top government officials. If any person described in this book resembles someone else, in Afghanistan or elsewhere, I sincerely apologize for the unintended resemblance.

Since there is no single system for the spelling in English of words taken from the languages of Afghanistan, I have used the spellings that seem to be most common or with which I am most familiar. In the "Diary" section of this book – actually a combination of direct translation from my diary and retelling based closely on it – the entries appear by date according to the Western, or Gregorian, calendar, followed by the Afghan date in parentheses.

My special thanks are extended to my family, whose patience and understanding made this book possible. Without their encouragement, criticism, and sacrifice I could never have made it to this point. I am greatly indebted to my sister who graciously typed almost the entire manuscript in spite of the fact that my views of the cultural aspects of our society do not always agree with hers.

I sincerely thank my good friends Emmajean and Fred Wupper for their encouragement and support during all these past fourteen years. Special thanks and gratitude are extended to Barbara O'Dell, who read the manuscript with great interest and spent endless hours proofreading and correcting the text. My book could not have been completed without the valuable help of Darrin Cheek, who corrected the first half of the manuscript.

I want to thank Professor Shaista Wahab of the University of Nebraska at Omaha Library for her valuable suggestions and insight and also for providing needed data and material. I am also grateful to Professors Melvin Bohn and Robert Runyon (director) of the University of

Nebraska at Omaha Library for their valuable advice and guidance.

The valuable advice, suggestions, and corrections of Nancy and Richard Newell, specialists on Afghanistan issues, are greatly appreciated, as is their unflagging encouragement. Nancy read the manuscript over and over many times and never tired of correcting and proofreading it.

Special thanks are included for the Reverend Darrel Berg of the University of Nebraska at Omaha Religious Center, who provided me the opportunity to present the manuscript at the Omaha Writers Workshop. I also want to thank our young paper carrier Gregory Wilson, who returned my diary from the street where I had accidentally dropped it from my car. Greg could not read my Persian handwriting, but obviously he had read the few lines written in English. After that whenever he saw me he asked, "That was some kind of a story! When are you going to publish it?"

I express my sincere appreciation to all my Afghan friends who graciously provided me with information and references on poets and some of the songs.

My sincere thanks are extended to my colleagues and friends in the Department of Biology, University of Nebraska at Omaha, for their enormous support. Special thanks are due Professor David Sutherland, who laboriously read and corrected the first parts of my handwritten draft, full of crossed-out and misspelled words, and later read the final copy. I am grateful to Professors William O'Dell, Roger Sharpe, Charles Ingham, and Robert Egan for their valuable encouragement.

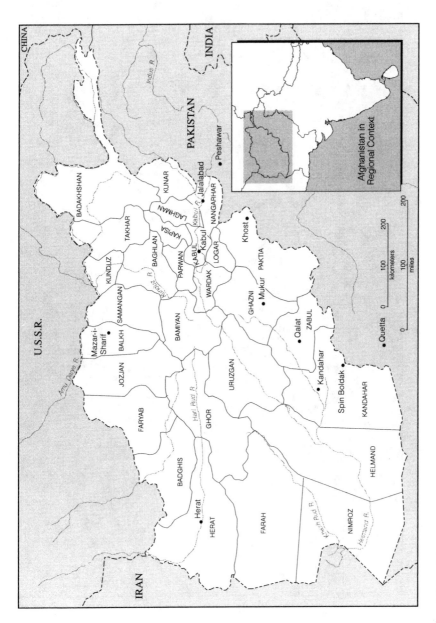

Afghanistan

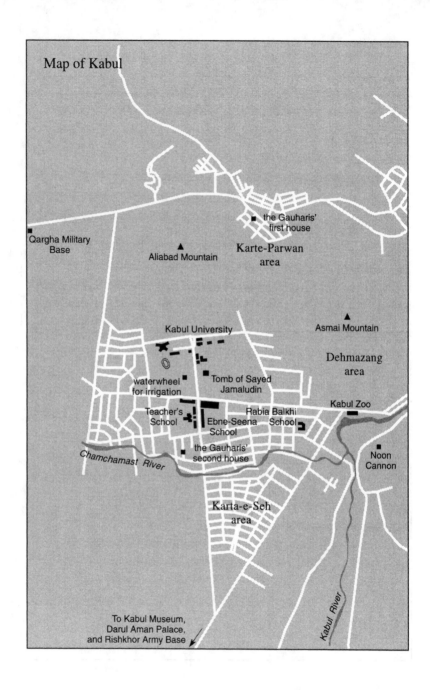

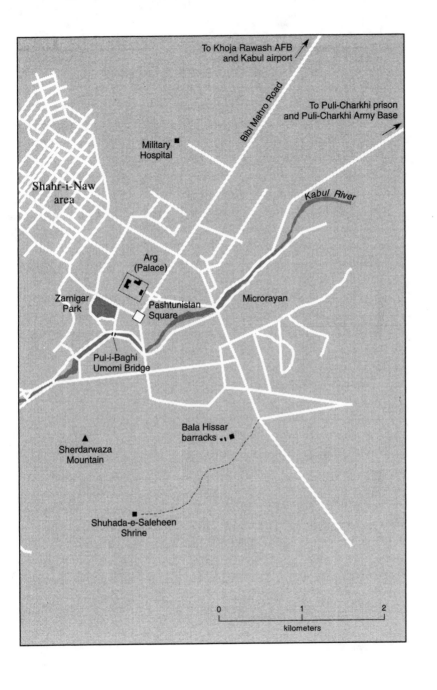

Before the Coup

A HAPPY CHILDHOOD

The roar of the Boeing 727 high above Afghanistan fills my ears and makes me very drowsy. Though I am exhausted I try to keep my eyes open. I want to see and treasure every detail of the landscape that passes below, so I press my face against the cold window glass.

I see a snow-covered land of mountains and deep valleys dazzling in the bright sun and contrasting sharply with the blue sky. Occasional clusters of squared patches of fields, especially along the valley floors, indicate human presence. Widely scattered groups of village houses stand out in the snow, looking at this distance like clusters of irregular dots put on a piece of white paper by the unsteady hand of a little child. A river flows through the landscape, tearing and weathering the rocks of its bed as it has for eons.

My heart overflows with mixed feelings and my head feels very heavy. I do not know whether to cry or burst with hope for the future. I seek freedom and beg God to grant me the courage to overcome the trials that lie ahead of us. My destination is uncertain, my future completely ambiguous.

I look to my left and my heart fills with joy as I see the happy faces of my three children, playing and laughing in their seats. I say to myself, "This is my entire world." I am completely responsible for them and must get them all they deserve. My God, we have already come a long way, but there are many more mountains and oceans to cross. I have taken a giant leap onto a course of no return!

Turning my gaze back to the outside, I watch the groups of houses come into view and then disappear from sight. I wish the pilot would tell us where we are, and I find myself reviewing my high school geography. This might be the town of Mohammed Agha in Logar province; that might be the Kabul River or one of its tributaries. Oh, this city ought to be Khost in Paktia province, but I am not sure. I try to figure out what peoples live down there; Afghanistan has more than fifteen major ethnic groups. I know that the Pashtuns dominate the southeast, but there are also small clusters of other ethnic groups scattered among them, each with its own customs and traditions. Now as I am leaving, I realize how little I know about them. There is a sad gulf of ignorance and prejudice between us, the city people and the villagers. How little time we spent trying to understand each other.

Wars have devastated my beautiful and tragic homeland many times in the past. I remember that once in class when we marked the death anniversary of one of our kings, I was very happy. The surprised teacher asked the reason for my happiness. I said, "Well, if he had lived longer, he would have made more wars and then I would have to memorize all those dates for your test!" The other students and the teacher laughed.

My husband's grandmother always prayed that *padsha gardishy ha*, or "change of kingdoms," would never happen. Horrible stories of mass murders, torture, riots, executions in jails, and forced exile followed most such transitions. At that time I had not seen such events and could not imagine the magnitude of such disasters, and I wondered why she included such a wish in her daily prayers. Today her prayers make a lot of sense.

The bell rings and the pilot announces that we are in Pakistan. Exhausted and sadder than I've ever felt before, I sit back in my seat and the long-frozen tears begin to melt and run down my face. Through half-closed eyes I see that people are moving around, but nothing interests me anymore. My mind rambles back in time . . . more than thirty years back.

Three persons have inspired my life: my father, my mother, and my uncle. I knew my father as a teacher who enjoyed his work a great deal. He always told us, "Education stays with you all your life but money does not, so try to concentrate on things that no one can take from you."

Mother, the second mentor in my life, was the only child of very wealthy parents and was raised by her grandmother after her parents died very early in her life. She married Father at the age of fourteen and thereafter followed devotedly in his footsteps wherever he went. The gleam of light, hope, and endurance in her eyes, radiating the message "Take it easy and look at the bright side of life," always made me forget my miseries. Her great efforts to raise the eight of her ten children still at home after Dad died suddenly of a heart attack in 1966, leaving no pension, just 450 afghanis in his pocket – less than enough for one week's food expenses for the family – are astonishing.

My uncle, a history professor and author of at least a couple dozen books, is the third person in my life who always encouraged my progress in school and championed education.

I do not remember clearly all of my childhood, but I do remember that I was a very normal healthy, active child. I always regretted, however, not being a boy. I liked to play the games set aside by society for boys only. For example, I loved to fly kites, ride bikes, and go out and shop as frequently as I wished without being asked where I had been or why I was late. I hated always being reminded that it was not my job. The words "Good girls never do that!" always hurt my feelings. Such distinctions between girls and boys were widely practiced in 1950 in Kandahar, a southern province where Dad had recently been transferred as a high school teacher. Teachers, doctors, and other professionals employed by the government were required to transfer every few years between the capital city, Kabul, and other provinces, in order to keep the education and health care levels there at par with Kabul's.

In Kandahar our family, which then consisted of my parents, my two sisters, and me, rented a house that had a huge, three-acre yard surrounded by a white picket fence. A large, clear stream ran through the yard, and I liked to wade in the sparkling cool water. In spring and summer the backyard was full of colorful cultivated and wild flowers. The gardener, Babba, with his large white turban, could be found among those flowers all day long. He seemed to enjoy being there. I always played in the yard, chasing butterflies and rodents, often waiting hours for a fox or a rabbit to enter the yard through the tiny openings under the fence next to the stream. Once I caught a rat by its tail after playing dead next to its hole for hours. Carrying it by its tail, I brought it happily to Mom. When she saw the wiggling rat in my hand, she screamed and called for Babba. Babba came and took me out in the yard and washed my hands many times as he repeated verses of the Holy Koran. After that I was not allowed to touch the family food or dishes for several days. Mother kept my utensils separate. She was a great believer in the germ theory; Babba, however, believed in the spiritual theory.

After two years Father was transferred to a different high school, miles from our house, so we decided to move to the section of town close to his new job. Our new house was in the old part of Kandahar city, where all the houses looked similar and were very old. Dad never seemed to like it – in fact we all hated this house – but it was close to his work. With no other options, we rented it.

The house must have been built many years ago, perhaps during a time of wars. The outer walls seemed as tall as a New York City skyscraper. These, along with the high walls of the neighboring houses, all framing the narrow streets, made a scene frightening to the eyes of those who walked there for the first time. A description of an old town I once read in a magazine – "Night never falls here, but it rises from these narrow streets" – characterized our street well. It took us a long time to adjust to our new house.

The house had two stories and a dark, sooty basement with two small windows. We never used the basement; in fact I was afraid of it. All the rooms had at least two windows that faced the interior courtyard. The ceilings were very high and the roof was constructed entirely of mud that reach several feet in thickness in some places. The thick walls and high ceilings kept the rooms very cool during the hot summers and warm in the mild winters of Kandahar. A long outdoor stairway connected the roof to the ground. During the summer months most people slept on the roof in the open air. There was a wall around the roofs to guarantee the privacy of each family. When all these walls – around yard and roof – were put together, the yard seemed very small. Whenever I looked up to the top of our yard walls, I always thought they met the edges of the sky. The sky seemed beautiful and crystal-clear blue, always beyond my reach, among those sun-baked red mud walls. On two sides of the court-yard were the bedrooms, a guest room, the kitchen, and several other rooms, which Mom never found any use for. My sister and I would play hide and seek there whenever we had nothing else to do.

At first I thought we were trapped in that house all day long; I dearly missed our previous residence. But finally as time passed I forgot all about our first house. My whole world as a five-year-old existed within these walls; actually, my hopes did not extend beyond them. Everything I needed seemed to be there. Large buckets of the tasty fruits of Kanda-har, lots of fresh vegetables, and simple homemade toys surrounded me. It was a beautiful small, self-sustained world. If there were any unfulfilled needs, I was unaware of them.

Kandahar summer days were very hot and humid. The summer nights, I shall always remember, were lovely and peaceful. After dinner we would all gather on the roof and Mom would tell us stories about the sky, stars, and clouds. I loved those stories; they took my imagination far away into those distant places where only a person's dreams can reach. I still love hearing Mom tell those stories. The way she puts them together is beautiful.

Summer evenings were also marked by muffled noises coming from neighboring houses. Close to sunset, people sprinkled water on the mud roofs in order to cool down the surface that had baked in the hot sun.

The evening breeze carried the cool, refreshing scent of mud mixed with water. The air smelled like the rains of spring. In order to keep drinking water cool, families put water-filled clay pots on top of the roof walls. The evening breeze cooled the water so nicely that one might believe it had been kept in a refrigerator. I think somehow this water tasted better.

In those days the government was just starting to build girls' schools in Kandahar. Father thought that their quality of education was not good enough. He wanted us to study at home until we could get back to Kabul, where the schools were much better. When I was barely five and my sister Farida less than seven years old, Mom and Dad decided it was the right time to start our education. We both studied the same books. Mom taught us how to read the Koran in Arabic, and at night Dad taught us the English language. In this massive campaign one of our neighbors wanted to express her goodwill to my parents and volunteered to teach us the reading and writing of Dari, a form of Persian that was one of the two official languages of Afghanistan. Dad approved her offer. Mother was happy that now she would have somebody to talk to every day.

The reading, writing, and memorizing assignments were very hard for me in the beginning; Mom, Dad, and the tutor expected us to learn everything after having told us only once. In spite of the difficulty, I learned reading and writing in no time. I read the entire Koran in the first year. At the end of the next year I had finished seven books of the Longman series for nonnative speakers of English. I still vaguely remember reading the English novel *The Vicar of Wakefield* in the last book. Today such books are taught in non-English-speaking countries closer to the senior level of high school.

Father also wanted Mother to learn English. It was funny to see Dad teaching her. Whenever Mom had trouble remembering the assignments of the previous day, Father would become upset. Then Mother would throw the book out the window. We often saw the book come flying into the yard as we played there. I would pick it up, smooth its pages, and take it back to Mom. A few minutes later it would be flying again.

Almost a year had passed in that house we all disliked. Mom felt depressed by the huge dark rooms, small windows, and tiny courtyard. At her insistence Father found another house and we moved in. The new house was not very different from the old one, except that it had a little bigger yard. During the first week Mom was told the rumors about it. Neighbors said the place was haunted; no one could live in it very long.

Mom was genuinely frightened, so Dad suggested that she get a maid who could help her around the house and would also be good company for her. Thus, Habiba, a girl in her late teens, was hired to come in from sunrise until evening when Dad returned home. Unfortunately, Habiba had lived in the area for a long time and was aware of all the stories told about the house. She wouldn't go into a dark room or outside into the yard alone, and after work she would sit down and tell Mom the tales that Mom may have missed hearing from the neighbors.

Nevertheless, our household fell into a normal routine. It appeared that its laws were made in heaven. The daily regimen was carried out at the same time regularly without any change or excitement. After breakfast early in the morning the dishes were washed and the house was cleaned before study of the Koran began at ten. Every morning Habiba made dough in a large clay pot and let it stand for few hours to rise. Then she made ten or twelve dough balls, each weighing at least a pound. She put them in a flat basket and took them to the nearby bakery, where they were baked into the large flat breads called nan. Later Mom prepared the food. Cooking was time-consuming work. First Habiba made wood fire in a small, U-shaped enclosed firepit. Then Mother sautéed onions and garlic in a generous amount of oil and browned the lamb meat with them. Later she added tomatoes and spices and various vegetables. After cooking, Mother took a nap in the basement, which was cooler than the first-floor rooms. In the evening when Dad came home he would have a cup of cardamom tea with us. Later we had dinner, then it would be time for our English lessons. After study, just before bedtime, if Father was in the mood, he would tell us what had happened at work or what was going on in the city. Other than the neighbors and Habiba, Dad was the only link between us and the outside world. We did not have a radio at this time.

Dad had found many friends. Almost every weekend they went to each other's houses and played cards till the early hours of the morning. It was strictly a party for men; there was no place for us children or for Mom. Every six or eight weeks Father would invite them to our house. Such occasions were very special for me because these were the only days that we didn't have lessons.

On the days we had company Mom and Habiba would go into the kitchen early in the morning. They would cook almost all day long. Food plays a big role in Afghan social gatherings. We believe that there should be plenty of food left after the guests have eaten; thus we often cook for twice the number of guests invited. Mother would make three or four different main dishes each time: a spicy spinach and lamb dish; fried eggplant in sour cream, garlic, and cilantro; and a meatball dish with cauliflower or other vegetables of the season. She also made lamb kabob, and rice pudding for the dessert. Since no Afghan party is complete without pilaf, she cooked the special Afghani *qabili*, a spicy brown-colored rice with lamb, topped with pistachios, almonds, raisins, and strips of sautéed carrots.

All the windows opened onto the courtyard, so it was impossible to keep us out of the guests' sight, a necessity because women must cover their faces when in public view (nomad and village women were an exception). While Mom and others were preparing the food, guests had to pass through the courtyard into the parlor and might catch a glimpse of the women. The only solution was to erect a screen in the courtyard. This was done by hanging bedsheets from a rope like a clothesline running the length of the courtyard. Dad always helped us, selecting the sheets carefully so that the colors matched. After the job was completed, the yard looked much more like a laundry than a residence.

While we were still living in Kandahar, my younger sister, Laila, had a persistent sore throat that none of the doctors could cure. Nothing worked. Father lost faith in all the doctors and wanted to take Laila to Kabul, where there were better medical facilities. One day a neighbor, Sharifa, suggested to Mother that they take Laila to a holy shrine, the tomb of a holy man that was considered by the local people to cure hopeless diseases. At first Father strongly opposed the idea and Mother agreed with him. But the good-hearted Sharifa persisted until Father finally relented.

The shrine was far away and there was no paved road leading to it. We'd have to walk several hours to get there, so Mother prepared to take enough food and water for all of us. Sharifa arrived early on the day of the trip, nicely dressed. She carried several large sweet breads, a bunch of leeks, and several other kinds of vegetables, all carefully wrapped in a sack. We started right away and soon found ourselves walking on a narrow trail among verdant farms. The air was fresh and the breeze carried a sweet herbal scent. Butterflies chased each other, competing for the colorful flowers. Bird songs broke the silence of the early day. I stopped often to look around, sensing the joy and freedom of our dearly missed first house full of flowers, but Sharifa's hand would drag me away. After two hours of constant walking, we sat down under a tree to rest. In front of us lay a vast desolate desert, for we had reached the end of the irrigation system. Sharifa pointed to a sandy hill on the horizon; the shrine was next to it. It took us almost another hour to get there.

The shrine was a small white building with a large-domed roof and a small window on the north side. Steep steps led up to the huge door. There sat a half-blind man called a mujaver who had a long stick with which he sorted the visitors' shoes into rows (visitors are not allowed to wear shoes in shrines). Mujavers are the caretakers of shrines. Some are probably descendants of the holy person buried there.

Once inside, we walked around the large tomb, which was covered with beautiful marble slabs engraved with verses from the Holy Koran. At one side of the tomb was a flag whose ten-foot pole was completely covered with bright, shiny satin material and strings of different sizes and colors. Sharifa explained, "Anyone who asks God to fulfill a request should tie a string there." Two mujavers sat by the tomb, at intervals reading some passages of the Holy Koran, which echoed through the building and added greatly to the spiritual atmosphere.

Sharifa moved expertly around the tomb, touching the marble slabs now and then, and tied a long string to the flagpole. Mother followed her closely. Then Sharifa went to one of the mujavers, said a few words, and bought from him a special knitted string that she tied around Laila's neck. She told Mom that the string must remain intact for a period of several months. It took Sharifa about half an hour to complete the rituals, which she had learned from her grandparents. Finally, Mom and Sharifa both put a few coins into the extended hands of several beggars and we left. Laila's sore throat persisted many months afterward, but one day she coughed and up came a badly deteriorated watermelon seed that had probably been caught in her tonsils. After that she recovered.

A few months later Mizhgan, my third sister, was born, and two years afterward Khalil, the first of my three brothers. Although Father always said there was no difference between his children, Mother was extremely happy when Khalil was born. Before breastfeeding him she always said prayers of thanks and for his safekeeping, a task that she never did for the rest of her children.

Father finished his teaching assignment in Kandahar. The Ministry of Education wanted him to stay longer, at least another year, but Dad refused because his children needed schooling now. We moved to Kabul in March of 1954. At seven, I entered school, where I passed the test for the fourth grade. Dad's income was sufficient to support a large family of seven very comfortably, but it did not permit savings. Monthly savings are almost impossible for most people in Afghanistan, so that did not bother us at all. Father always told us that all he had in this world was his children's education. And he was very proud of it, too. I recall that on the day my elder sister, Farida, received her B.A. degree, he was so delighted that he thanked God many times for his kindness and mercy.

My entire school days were full of happiness. Without any difficulty I was always among the top students in the class. Science was my best subject while sewing was my worst one. In fact, sewing was the only subject that lowered my grade-point average. Science classes started in the seventh grade, but we did not have science labs. Every year of high school we studied algebra, physics, chemistry, and biology two hours per week. Other subjects were history, geography, arts, religion, sewing, Dari and Pashto (the two national languages of the country), and English. All students had to take all of these subjects. We basically memorized everything. If students failed in one subject, they were allowed to take a make-up test. But with two or more failing grades, students had to repeat the entire nine-month school year. World history and geography were taught in great detail and we were expected to know a great deal about our own and other countries.

Grade reports were handed out to the students in special ceremonies. On such days all the classes lined up in rows in the school's front yard. The principal and teachers stood at the top of the steps leading into the hall. As the principal called out our names one by one, we walked up the steps and picked up our grade reports, which we took home for our parents to sign.

We also lined up, in pairs this time, when we went into the classrooms twice each day. When the school bell rang, we rushed to form lines, which the principal walked between to inspect our uniforms: black dresses, black stockings, and a small white cotton scarf around the neck. Makeup and long nails were prohibited. It was also forbidden to have any type of lace sewn around that white scarf. Years later, when a large number of schools operated in Kabul, all adopted the same black uniform but each school chose a different color for the collar. On rare occasions as the principal walked down those rows, we heard her slap someone who had not followed the school's dress code. After inspection, the students, led by an upperclasswoman, formally saluted the principal with a "Salaam!" and filed into their classrooms.

When I was in the tenth grade, in 1959, Mohammad Daoud, the cousin and brother-in-law of King Zahir Shah who served as prime minister from 1953 to 1963, proclaimed the voluntary emancipation of women throughout the country. This reform included the voluntary abolition of the veil. The new changes were received with great excitement in our school, where we gathered in large groups outside the classrooms and shouted, "Long live Daoud!"

I had been wearing the veil for almost a year before the reform came. Dad never told us to wear it, but society forced us to do so. My sister Laila resisted covering her face for a long time, but whenever she walked on the streets, passersby would tell her, "You look old enough to be my mother – and still not covering your face?" To an outsider, a veil looked like a veil, nothing important to it. But to those of us who wore it there were big differences. Some veils were chic and stylish, with special shorter cap designs. Veils also differed in the fineness of the eye mesh, the quality of the material, and the way the numerous pleats were set, narrow pleats being considered more stylish than wide ones.

Wearing the veil for the first time was very difficult for me but I came to find that it was not so bad. Under cover, our inner childish feelings came out, released from outside social pressures. In a country like Afghanistan, as soon as a girl enters her early teen years she is considered a mature young woman who must behave. Soon she learns that she must walk gracefully on the streets and not draw attention to herself. She must not ignore or question the preset rules of her society. Otherwise . . . otherwise people will talk about her and it will bring shame to her family. In Afghanistan a woman must carry the family honor. Of course it would be very unwise of a young woman to bring disgrace upon and destroy the good reputation of her family! Concealing your identity behind a veil and watching the world through a four-by-six-inch rectangle of fine mesh had certain advantages. It was a sign of respect, of growing up and womanhood.

SALEEM

By the spring of 1964 I was a full-time university student who taught part-time in a girls' high school. I also worked in the university research laboratory twenty hours a week. My studies and work kept me very busy, and this year I especially looked forward to the two religious holidays, both called Eid, when I would have the holiday break to catch up on things. The two Eids are seventy days apart and their dates change, determined by the lunar calendar.

Eid is important for many reasons. Friends and neighbors visit each other. This is the time to resolve old conflicts and make up for past wrongs. It is also the time to give thanks for friends and for the blessings you enjoy. It is a joyful time for all. Shops are filled with colorful toys, candies, cookies, and fruits. Every household buys candies and cookies for entertaining their guests during the three days of Eid. Wherever you go, you are offered tea, candies, and cookies. If you arrive at a friend's house at lunchtime, you are expected to dine with the family even if you have eaten only minutes before. It is considered bad manners for the host to eat alone in the presence of unexpected guests.

The timing of the first Eid holiday is related to that of the holy fasting month of Ramadan but was decided by the king or his advisers. Since

Eid begins with the first sighting of the new moon, we usually did not know the night before whether there would be Eid the next day or not. If the moon could not be observed in Afghanistan, the observation was left to the other Islamic countries. As soon as the moon was sighted, shots were fired from the cannon on a high ridge of Sherdarwaza mountain that was used to signal important events or times. Often when the moon could not be seen until the very late hours of the night, we went to bed not knowing if we should go to work or school the next day. In the morning Mother would ask others if they had heard the cannon the previous night. The second choice was to turn on the radio, which relayed the news at seven or seven-thirty, a late hour to prepare for work at eight.

Eid begins officially after the ten o'clock morning prayers that are conducted in the mosques by the adult male members of the families in Afghanistan. Women did not attend the mosque. The Eid celebration is of special interest to children. They receive presents or cash from their elders. Early in the morning the young children are dressed up in colorful new clothing and paraded to the nearby markets, where they find toys, merry-go-round rides, and other delights.

Girls had their own special way of spending the Eid holidays. They would get together the night before Eid and stain their hands, nails, or feet with henna – the dried, powdered leaves of the henna plant – decorating them with pleasing patterns. When henna was placed on the skin, it needed several hours to produce a stain. The girls wrapped their hands and feet in long strips of material and then went to bed. During the days of Eid, girls visited their relatives. They sang songs and played games with female friends or relatives. New clothes for Eid were important. I remember that when Mother hired a maid, she offered, besides a salary and meals, two new dresses, one for each Eid.

On an Eid day in the early spring of 1964, Dad started to go out to visit one of his friends. He returned home very soon, however, accompanied by a tall, nice-looking man probably in his early twenties, who had apparently come to see my father. Dad took him into the living room and offered him some tea. He did not know the young man and was puzzled by the visit. Father's confusion was not less than mine; when I looked at him while he was talking to Dad in the yard, I didn't remember seeing him before either. Soon after the visitor had left, Dad told Mother that he liked him and described him as a fine young fellow who had recently returned from abroad after completing his studies in a foreign country. He had also told Father that he was one of the neighbors who lived across the street from the bridge several blocks away.

Months passed and my memories of Eid had nearly passed into the history pages of my mind. School loads were getting heavier, but that was nothing to worry about; I was well prepared for the quizzes and tests to come. I enjoyed teaching at the high school very much. I loved my students so much that I always spent the last ten minutes of my classes preaching and giving them advice on women's rights. I told them about the other places to the east and the west, about the freedom and the family rights that women had, and also of their own important role in their society. I always said, "Let's try to change the old traditions of society in which half of the members are kept at home and are not fully participating in the progress of their land. The modern world advances exponentially and we move ahead too, but, unfortunately, numerically. That's why with each step we put forward, the world of science and technology has moved way ahead of us and the gap becomes bigger and bigger year after year. My dear friends, you don't have to go out and collect a big crowd and tell your story and concerns. Let us start this everlasting battle from our own home ground! Nobody gives you rights; rights cannot be given, but must be asserted." I pointed out the glories of our proud past and tried to build up their confidence. I asked them to compare Eastern and Western cultures without prejudice, then analyze and learn from their mistakes and experiences. All societies have good and bad things in them. Ignore the bad ones and adopt the good ones. Practice them here and build a different nation and name it Afghanistan.

My voice echoed here and there and was heard all the time, and repeated by the students. I wanted Afghanistan to be a land free from troubles and proud of its people and resources. What a dream! What a hope! My classes became famous among students and aroused the jealousy of a few other teachers, but I had the full support of the principal. Students liked such talk, perhaps because they were hearing it for the first time, or perhaps because it was coming from a person who was not very different from them – I had graduated just the year before from this very school and was very close to them in age.

I always left home early in the morning and returned home around six in the evening. One day, however, on my way to school, when I crossed the narrow suspension bridge over the Chamchamast River, I saw the man who had visited my father during Eid. He was walking along the street just across the bridge. He looked so different and very handsome in his navy-blue suit. But as soon as I had passed him I quickly forgot him, because in the next ten minutes I was in a zoology class listening to the professor describe the characteristics of sea anemones.

As the days passed I began seeing him almost every morning on my way to school. By a strange coincidence, as soon as I crossed the bridge, I heard the door bang as he came out of his house. It seemed that he always waited for me to appear on the bridge. In my heart I felt an admiration for him. During my childhood I was told over and over again not to talk to strangers, so I never dared to look straight at him. This was our lesson: "Good girls never talk to strange boys!" I must have learned that lesson well, because in spite of all my lectures to the high school students on women's independence and rights, I always responded in the way I was taught. One day as I was passing him, he called me by name. I stepped down from my bicycle. In a very low and cold tone I asked him, "Yes?"

He introduced himself as Saleem and said, "I apologize for coming to your house unexpectedly without Father knowing me." Very strange! He had called my dad "Father." I smiled and found myself out of breath. I also was surprised that he knew my name. Then the warning that was building up in my head became intense: "Good girls never talk to strangers." Wordlessly I nodded an acknowledgment of his apology. I didn't know what else to say, and he knew my position, so when I finally did look at him we both smiled. I found his face honest, warm, and full of life. To break out of my speechless condition, I said, "Sorry, it's getting late for school and I have to go."

"Yes, of course."

I rode off on my bicycle as he walked away, perhaps to catch the bus at the street corner. This incident was the beginning of a new, unknown feeling in my heart. Our university was coeducational and the boys and girls often worked together and helped each other with our studies. All such conversations, however, were of a routine business type and never about our feelings. Many of my girl friends had crushes and talked about boys, but I always found their conversation fatuous. Even though I believed in true love and marriage built upon truth, honesty, and faith, my mind was fully occupied with studies and work. Several of my friends had proposed marriage, but I had rejected them. They were very good individuals, and in order not to offend them, I told them simply that I wanted to pursue an education and that marriage at this point might affect my studies abroad (I was one of the candidates selected by our school for doctoral studies at the University of Bonn after graduation).

On this day, however, everything was different. My heart pounded; my face blushed; I had warm feelings all over my body that were unfamiliar to me. In class the professor's voice seemed to come from a distant world; I could hear only the echoes of his words. Physically I was in class but mentally I was wandering outside. I said to myself, "Forget about arthropods and mollusks! Who cares!" Wherever I looked that day, I could not get Saleem out of my mind. I felt him deep in my heart and his gracious smile was always there.

After a month, during which I did not see or hear from Saleem, he sent his two young brothers, Yosuf and Khalid, and his mother to our house without telling me what he had in mind. In those days, if a mother of a young man saw a girl on the street that she liked for her son, then the mother would come to the girl's house and ask the parents for the girl's hand. Sometimes one of these women unknown to the girl's family would unexpectedly enter the open door of the courtyard in the hope of seeing the girl up close. When asked what she wanted, she often replied, "Do you have a house to rent?" or "I am looking for a place to buy." In our family it was a joke between my sisters and me. Whenever someone came to inquire about renting the place, we would say, "Let's see – who is in line now?" Then we would all laugh. In fact my parents did have two houses to rent.

Anyhow, neither Saleem nor his family members came in such a manner to our house, and his marriage proposal and the way he visited my father for the first time were unique. Saleem was not sure what my answer would be, but Mom and Dad's feelings toward him were completely positive. In fact, Father liked him very much and admired his honesty and character. Dad probably spent long hours investigating his background. Although he never told me how he got all the information he had about Saleem, Father knew more than I did. After several visits from Saleem's relatives, Dad finally approved of Saleem's proposal and asked me if I agreed too. My answer was clearly affirmative.

In those days it was not considered good to accept a marriage proposal on the first meeting. For a girl's family the prestigious act was to let the boy's family go back and forth as many times as possible; then the bride's mother would brag to her friends and relatives that the boy's family was very persistent. According to the customs of that time, the bride's family, upon their acceptance, would give the groom's parents a tray of candies and sugar-coated almonds, so at a special gathering of a few close friends from both sides, Mom and Dad gave Saleem's mother candies. During all the rituals and endless ceremonies, the prospective groom does not join his parents and friends. He only extends his proposal through others.

After Saleem's family received the answer, they went home. That evening Saleem came to our house. I do not remember now what my actions were. Probably I was totally at a loss and blushed when I saw him so close for the first time in the living room with our friends. After we became engaged, Dad never cared where we went. Mom, however, was very careful, even a little too cautious. She always told us not to be late. Strangely enough, in spite of all her concerns we always found some time to spend together alone. There was no movie in the whole city that we did not see nor any street in Kabul that we did not walk.

I found in Saleem a very compassionate and sincere person. His heart was big and the entire world had a place in it. He cared for others and went out of his way to help those who needed him. With children he played like a child and with grownups he was well liked and respected. He always made me feel tall and proud. Saleem was a religious man who prayed only because he believed in prayers and never misused his prayers to impress others. He was tall, handsome, and a devoted air force officer for his country who had spent almost six years studying in the United States before I met him. He had three sisters and three brothers, all married except his two youngest brothers, who were in junior high and high school. His sisters lived in the provinces. Because of the lack of student jobs in Afghanistan, Saleem had attended the air force academy to reduce the burden on his family. In the air force the government paid all the educational and training costs.

One day out of curiosity I asked Saleem how he had found out about me and had decided to come to our house to visit my father. He laughed and said that once he had made up his mind it was easy.

"Easy?"

"I knew you would fall in love just by looking at me!" He laughed.

"Well, I am just curious. There is a big distance between Air Force Headquarters and Kabul University."

Saleem laughed again. He said, "Honey, I think no one can say no to me!"

I knew he just wanted to be funny that day, so I laughed at his comments and said, "Well, if you hadn't slammed your door and hadn't dressed up in colorful clothes like a peacock, I would not even have noticed you near the bridge."

My mother-in-law was listening to our conversation, laughing. Finally Saleem told me that he had seen my picture in the home of a friend whose wife was one of my high school students and that he had heard a lot about me from her. It was a photo taken with my students the year before. Then Saleem looked at me, laughed, and said, "Honey, I think that picture was quite o . . . l . . . d. If I had seen a recent picture of you, I might have changed my mind right away."

"Get out of here!" I said. We all laughed.

We set the date for the wedding for the early summer of 1964. It would take place in a relatively small hotel, with over a hundred guests invited. Dad believed that such expenses were a waste of money. He wanted a small party with just few close friends, but Mom . . . Mom insisted upon inviting almost everybody she knew. So we decided to have a rather small party at four o'clock where the mullah (priest) and some friends would come and the marriage papers would be signed. This first group of guests were all male. I was at home getting ready for the evening party. At the signing of the papers I was represented by a person I had selected from among my husband's relatives. Such a ceremony, called Nikah, is the first requirement of every Moslem's marriage. The evening party is only for celebrating the event.

During Nikah the bride's representative settles the amount of money that will be given the wife in case a divorce happens later. Normally the bride's family tries hard to negotiate as large an amount as they feel is fair. Most often it becomes a bargaining session in which one party or the other gets upset. Such money is called haqmeher, and it could be as little as thirty afghanis (equal to thirty cents at that time) or as much as several hundred thousand, depending on the groom's income and wealth. Haqmeher is one of the required parts of Moslem marriage. It has to be mentioned in the marriage papers during Nikah. Divorce is rare in Afghanistan and I have not heard of a single case in which a woman received her haqmeher.

Bride's wealth is a different thing. This custom is fading out nowadays, especially among educated groups, and is not required by Islamic laws. A bride's wealth is requested before any marriage date is settled. It is the money that the parents of the bride request from the groom's family and is used partly for the bride's dowry. Negotiating bride's wealth gets very ugly at times. I personally think that it is a great insult to the bride, but some people believe that the groom's family, by presenting such money, are showing respect to the bride, and take it as evidence of the groom's pledge that the marriage will work. So a tradition that signals respect to some is considered an insult by others.

Saleem told me later that one of Dad's close friends thought I might choose him as my representative, so he tried to bargain ahead of time for the haqmeher. His act had disappointed Saleem and his family a great deal. I did not want our marriage to be supported by a large sum of money, nor did I think that money could buy me any happiness in life. Perhaps one of the reasons was that I wanted to work and be independent; also, I was sure that I would be able to get a job with my educational background if something went wrong with our marriage.

On our wedding day two witnesses (I do not know who selected them) came to our house. They said Persian words with special rhymes which I hardly understood. Not knowing that Dad's friend had already attempted to represent me in the haqmeher negotiations, I selected Haji, a relative of my husband. The witnesses returned to the hotel with the message that I had chosen Haji as my representative. This embarrassed Father's friend.

The afternoon ceremony finished at about six and the guests were entertained with refreshments. The evening party started at seven o'clock and dinner was served around ten. In the interim the guests were entertained with music and dance. Saleem, together with his brothers and close friends, joined the guests while I waited in the back room until the dinner was served. After dinner, Saleem and I, plus a few close relatives from both sides, walked through the party hall while one of the relatives held the Holy Koran above my head as a symbol of the blessing of the marriage and the musicians played a special song. The guests all stood as we crossed the room to a special sofa at the front, which was covered with pretty silver-lined material. As Saleem and I sat there, a large shawl was lowered in front of us and we both kissed the Holy Koran and looked at each other in a mirror wrapped in silver cloth. After this traditional ritual, which dated back to the time when all marriages were arranged and the couple first laid eyes upon each other through a mirror at their wedding, henna was put on our palms and we exchanged rings. Our guests and family members completed the evening's celebration with dancing.

Since I was the first child of my parents to leave home, it was very hard for them to see me go, especially the night before my marriage. I saw tears in Dad's eyes, something I've vividly remembered in the years since.

Saleem and I rented a fairly large house close to my parents' home. His father had died long ago and his mother had spent all their money on food, education, and doctor bills. Whatever was left was hardly enough to raise her younger children. So they all lived with us: my mother-in-law and two young brothers-in-law. Once in a while I felt that Saleem wanted my opinion about his family living with us, but he never mentioned it openly. One day when we were at the movies I told him, "I never want to see our marriage ruin your family unity. I enjoy having your brothers and mother with us. I hope that your brothers get the best possible education."

Saleem became very excited and happy. I had not seen him so happy before. "You really mean it?"

"Yes, I would love to see it happen!" I replied.

My husband had a wonderful family. I liked very much his two well-behaved younger brothers, Yosuf and Khalid. Although there was not much difference in our ages, they were in the seventh and ninth grades at that time. As time passed, I enjoyed their progress in school, helped them with their homework, and was very proud of them. I always thought that if I ever had a son, I surely would try to bring him up exactly like them. My feelings were like those of a mother watching her own children grow. There was lots of love and caring in the family. My house was full of joy and laughter in the evenings when we all got together.

Daily life in Afghanistan, in our household, was very different from that in the United States. Because of the lack of weekend or night jobs and the absence of night schools, we all gathered together at home in the evening. We sat and dined together. Our frequent contact and sharing of time with each other brought us very close. Life was very simple, relaxed, and less stressful. Here, during my life in United States, I hardly remember the few days when my children and I have dined all at the same time. Because of our heavy workloads and different schedules we would all come home at different times and dish out whatever food we found and eat by ourselves.

In Afghanistan good job opportunities for students were very limited. Jobs such as working in restaurants were not considered suitable. Most families did not like to see their children washing cars or dishes or cleaning tabletops. Students relied mainly on their parents. This was the case in my household, and my brothers-in-law did not even try to seek a job, nor did my husband and I expect them to do so. But the situation was different in Mom's house. When Dad died in 1966 as the result of a heart attack, he was survived by ten children. Of these only my sister Farida and I were married. The rest were at home and their ages ranged from eighteen years down to sixteen months. Besides keeping up their schoolwork, my sisters held jobs, not in restaurants, but writing articles for journals, or as a news announcer for Kabul Radio. Thanks to free education in Afghanistan, there were no school fees to worry about.

In February of 1965 Omar, our first son, was born while I was in the third year of college. He was a very healthy and handsome child. My mother-in-law supervised the babysitter who took care of him during

26

the day while I was in school. When Omar was a few months old, we decided to visit one of Saleem's sisters whom I had not met and who lived in Qalat.

Being a city girl almost all of my life, I was very excited about this trip because I had not been outside Kabul for many years. Since my own family did not have relatives in the provinces, we did not travel much. Now, with my husband's relatives living in Qalat, Kandahar, Laghman, Jalalabad, and Herat, I had the opportunity to visit those places. I thought of these trips as an educational challenge to learn things that I would never know by reading the very few books that mentioned anything about our countryside. Many adventurous foreign writers, most of whom were in the country only briefly, had written about certain villages in Afghanistan, and almost all of them had described the culture as the most inexplicable and strangest they had ever encountered, but of course such books were not published in Afghanistan and I had not read them. My unwavering high spirit was ready for adventure.

At first I started these trips with the idea that Kabul represented Afghanistan. Surprised many times and occasionally shocked, I came to realize that Kabul made up only a very small fraction of the country and certainly did not represent the people as a whole. After several visits into far provinces over a few years, I changed; as my father said, traveling makes a person mature. I learned a lot. Now, whenever I encountered a different custom or tradition, instead of criticizing, I would mentally step into the shoes of those people and walk with them through time. I always came to the same conclusion: that probably I would have reacted exactly like them under the given circumstances. In fact, all those customs were based upon time-tested experience.

Qalat is the central district of the south-central province of Zabul, which at that time encompassed several hundred villages. Zabul's economy depended mainly on agriculture and livestock raising. Qalat was famous for its watermelons and other fruits, and for its mild, pleasant summers and bitterly cold, windy winters.

We took ten days off from work and Saleem reserved four seats on a local bus that belonged to a small private company. The bus looked very comfortable and colorful from the outside. It was painted bright red and blue and had beautiful scenes of gardens on the sides. Our seats right behind the driver were supposed to be the best. When we got on the bus, however – my husband; my mother-in-law; my four-month-old son, Omar; and I – we found that the seats had little foam underneath and felt like a hard wooden floor. There was not enough legroom for my husband, and the backs of the seats were connected to the base at an almost ninety-degree angle, making us feel very uncomfortable.

As the bus left the city limits, it began picking up passengers from the roadside. Within the next few hours all the inside seats were filled to capacity. The greedy owner, who was also riding with us and collecting the fares from the roadside passengers, would not give up. He kept adding more and more people on the bus roof, next to the luggage.

The bus moved slowly as the engine screamed and screeched under this heavy load. A trip that was supposed to be made in four hours took some twelve hours to complete. We drove all day. In the evening the bus stopped for an hour at a small roadside teahouse in Moqur. We all got off and seated ourselves in a far corner, outside the teahouse, under a tree. Saleem ordered kabob and some tea. My poor mother-in-law was very tired. She cursed the owner of the bus for the uncomfortable seats. My husband and I tried to cheer her up. At one point I heard her curse my sister-in-law's husband for living in Qalat. On hearing this I could not help but laugh out loud. "Mother, what did you say?" I asked.

"That big ape! Why did he have to bring my poor daughter into this desert? From the beginning I was not happy at all to give my daughter to this shim-shan-zee!"

Saleem and I both broke into laughter. We laughed so hard that she began to laugh also. Saleem explained, "Mother, it's not 'shim-shan-zee'; please say 'chim-pan-zee.'" We ate in a happy atmosphere of laughter and forgot all about being so tired.

Not long after the bus got underway again, the headlights failed. It was almost dark by this time. The driver and the owner worked under the hood for an hour without success as the passengers became more and more impatient. My mother-in-law's low muttering could be heard from time to time. There were no nearby lights; we were far from any towns. The bus conductor had apparently faced this problem before. He climbed on top of the bus, dug into the luggage, found a small kerosene lamp, hung it to the right of the windshield, and told the driver to proceed. The road lay like a murky shadow in front of us, but the driver drove on slowly without fear.

The situation reminded me of a story I had read years before in high school: A blind man had a lantern in his hand and was walking with a cane on a narrow street. A person passed by, laughed at him, and said, "You are blind! Why are you carrying that lamp?" The blind man replied, "It's not for me, it's for you and people like you who are blind inside and cannot see others!" Of course our driver could not see the road clearly. The dim light of the lantern was for the others to see him.

After another three or so tiresome hours we arrived without incident in Qalat. The small city of Qalat stood near the main highway. Half a dozen shops were still open and their powerful gas lanterns lighted the surrounding area. In the distance a few dome-shaped farmhouses were silhouetted aesthetically against the dark. We did not know the exact address of our relatives, so after unloading our luggage, my husband asked at the first shop the address of his sister, using her son's name, Farid. A little boy who was standing there came forward and asked, "Do you want Farid's house?"

Saleem replied, "Yes, do you know him?"

The little boy nodded his head and we followed him. He walked so fast, without saying a word, that it was hard to keep up with him. We almost ran, afraid of losing him. We hurried through narrow streets with high walls on both sides. Finally we came to Farid's house. Gul-jan, my sister-in-law, was very happy about our unexpected visit and her daughters surrounded us in no time. Even though it was late and we had already had dinner, she insisted on preparing us some food.

A few minutes later Guljan's husband, Khan, came in. At first glance I could hardly keep from laughing as I remembered my mother-in-law's curses. Indeed he was a tall, huge man and well built.

It was past midnight when dinner was ready; then we talked and talked about everything. Omar was passed from arm to arm and the girls took turns playing with him. Noticing that the little boy who had given us directions was standing in the yard, my husband asked, "Is that the nice little boy who brought us here? Why is he still here?" I thought he was most probably waiting for some reward for the work he had done. Guljan laughed and said, "He is Ahmad, my youngest son!"

My mother-in-law never liked Khan, probably because Guljan was married to him while she was very young, in her early teens, and her husband was forty-five years old. Their age difference was thirty-one years. The marriage had been arranged; my father-in-law had agreed to it, but my mother-in-law had objected. Arranged marriages were common at that time, so this one was not prevented even without consent from the bride or her mother. It was strange that my mother-in-law always blamed Khan for marrying her daughter and never said a word about her husband, who had agreed to the marriage. Then, too, my mother-in-law would have loved to see her married daughters living close to her in Kabul, but since Khan had some farmland in Qalat, they lived far away.

Qalat was very beautiful in many ways. The people; their dress and customs; the land; the small bazaar with its narrow, powder-dusted roads caught my imagination. The farmhouses were small and domed, often with a single door and a small window. One day I walked around until I reached the vegetable farms. Wherever I went I was the center of attention – something I tried to avoid, but it seemed impossible. People looked at me inquisitively because my dress appeared strange to them. I was interested to see how these people lived, and I tried to get a conversation going, but somehow I was not able to.

Back at Guljan's home, I learned that we were invited to Karim's house. As a young boy Karim had worked at my mother-in-law's house. Now he had a business of his own; he was a coppersmith who made copper pots and pans. The market for such copper things was very good. People were known to buy them as an investment. Such things doubled in value in a few years' time. So Karim was a rich man.

My husband accepted his invitation and the next day we all went to Karim's house. At the front gate we were somehow automatically separated and went in different directions. The men went to the farthest room and ladies into the nearer one. Feeling somewhat confused in this sorting-out process, I nevertheless ended up in the right line along with the other women. Then it occurred to me how quickly we human beings forget our past. Several years earlier, in Kabul, the same situation had existed, until veils were abandoned. People had two living rooms, one for each sex, although close relatives, cousins, and friends all sat in the same room together. In our house, when nonrelative guests came over with their spouses, my husband and I both entertained them. On the other hand, if my husband's friends came without their wives, most often I did not go into the guest room.

The living room we entered was decorated beautifully. It was completely carpeted and the curtains matched the brown carpet. There were no sofas, chairs, or tables, but how attractively a room can be furnished with rugs and cushions! Long red velvety cushions were placed all around the corners, with lovely large green pillows scattered here and there. The two old discolored frames on the wall held inscriptions, one in Persian, the other in Arabic: "Our Guests Are God's Friends" and "God Loves Those Who Are Patient." A Koran carefully wrapped in many layers of cloth was kept on a shelf. People believe that unwashed hands must not touch the holy book. As we all sat on floor mattresses, my mother-in-law in the far corner of the room, my sister-in-law next to her, and me close to the entrance door, I looked around the room and admired the good taste of the hosts.

A little girl brought in cardamom tea and cookies and put them in front of her mother. The fragrance of cardamom filled the air. With special care our hostess rinsed each cup with a couple of tablespoons of hot tea, poured the liquid into a separate cup, and then filled all the teacups. She set the cups along with a teapot and a plate full of cookies in front of us. My mother-in-law was busy talking with Karim's wife about their old-time friends and relatives whom I did not know. At this point a woman entered and, after greeting us, sat directly across from me in the opposite corner of the room. She was very attractive, probably in her late twenties, dressed in beautiful bright colors that complemented her golden necklace perfectly. Her heavy necklace was made of at least a dozen antique coins polished with great care. The several gold rings on her fingers were ornamented with turquoise. On special occasions people often wore all their gold jewelry, showing off their wealth. The red marks of henna on her palms and her feet were very obvious. The black color of *surma*, a powdered antimony stone used as eye liner, added to her beauty. Since I liked art and painting, I studied her wonderful way of putting the bright colors together. I don't know how many times or how long I stared at her until I noticed that whenever I looked at her she would avert her eyes with a half-dead smile on her lips. Each time I responded by smiling back at her. We did not exchange a single word and I thought she was very shy.

After an hour or so my sister-in-law's youngest daughter brought my son and I filled the milk bottle to feed him. I also changed his wet clothes. The woman opposite me left, and later I was told that she had thought I was a man. I think that when she saw I was changing my son's diaper she had realized that she was mistaken about me. My short haircut and European-style dress (the way we dressed in Kabul) had confused her. Nor was I wearing any necklace or earrings or makeup. Certainly she must have thought me a very rude man who would not quit staring at women! Guljan laughed many days afterward whenever she remembered this.

Late in the afternoon the food was ready. The customary large white cloth was spread on the floor and adorned with large platters of rice and meat and many side dishes. There was at least four or five times more food than we could eat. The room was filled with the aroma of the food. When plates, cups, and soft drinks were distributed, the white cloth was almost entirely covered. Then a little girl came in with a couple of towels, a brass basin and ewer of water, and a bar of soap. She went around the room and poured the water as we washed our hands. This done, I sat there with my relatives waiting for our hostess to join us. To my surprise, the door was closed and we were left alone. We waited for a while, then I asked Guljan where our hostess was.

"I think she has left us alone."

"Alone!" I exclaimed.

Guljan replied, "Here they do not eat with important guests. In order for the guests to feel free, the host or hostess leaves them alone to dine."

I looked at my mother-in-law and she added, "They feel that it's a way to respect the guests."

Guljan picked up a plate and said, "Well, let's get started then."

"Yes, I am very hungry," I replied.

After an hour the hostess returned to collect the dishes. The little girl came once more with ewer and basin, soap, and towels. We washed our hands and ended the day by drinking several cups of hot tea.

When I returned home, I told my husband about the way that Karim's family had left us alone while we ate. He said, "They tried to do the same thing in the other room, but I insisted that they eat with us, so they did." By asking them to dine at the same food-spread, Saleem wanted to tell them that there was no difference between them and himself, and that they were his friends, not former servants.

The days passed quickly and our vacation was over. We returned to Kabul, this time not in a private bus but by a more comfortable bus of the government-owned travel agency. The memories of Qalat remained with me and would last forever, like those of other trips outside Kabul that we would take in the future. One of the most memorable of those later trips was to to the area of Jalalabad, capital of the eastern province of Nangarhar, which borders Pakistan and shares with it the famed Khyber Pass on the ancient trade and invasion route from central Asia.

My husband, my mother-in-law, and I were invited to visit at the home of a friend, Abdul, in Kama, a village near Jalalabad. I'd heard from Saleem that Abdul had, a few years before, married a nomad girl named Kouchi, who lived with Abdul and his first wife, Zari. Zari and Abdul had five children ranging in age from seven to twenty-one, and Kouchi and Abdul had two small daughters, one and two years old. Saleem, who had known Abdul from high school days, also told me that Abdul was a khan, or tribal leader, who had inherited a large farm, a couple of fortresses, and thousands of head of cattle and sheep.

On arriving at the bridge on the road between Jalalabad and Kama, we saw two armed men waiting for us on the far side of the bridge. Since we were esteemed guests, Abdul had sent two of his men to protect us and guide us to his fortress. When we arrived at Abdul's home, a fortress similar to the houses I had lived in as a child in Kandahar, but set on extensive grounds, several men, including Abdul, came forward and welcomed Saleem with an embrace. Then Abdul greeted my mother-in-law and me and helped us with our luggage. He was a small, dark man with a good sense of humor. I found him very sincere and pleasant.

Near the front gate was a structure containing several rooms used as a men's parlor. Saleem entered it while my mother-in-law and I followed Abdul to the fortress, where he lived with his wives and children. The grounds encompassed several acres and were surrounded by a mud wall some six feet high. A small, clear stream provided enough water for household use and for the vegetable and rose gardens that dotted the grounds. Everything looked green and fresh. Later I found that each of Abdul's wives and daughters had separate gardens for the vegetables and flowers they grew.

The fortress, enclosed within a second high wall, was constructed around three sides of a barren courtyard that contained a water well. A narrow stairway led to the roof, where a long clothesline sagged deeply under its heavy load. Several small children stared at us from open windows, giggling and trying to hide behind each other. The household included not only Abdul and his two wives and unmarried children, but also Abdul's two married sons and their wives. At the door, Abdul left my mother-in-law and me with Kouchi, who kissed us each on both cheeks. Then Zari and her two daughters and two daughters-in-law came one by one and we exchanged kisses. After this first round of greetings was finished, we started the second one, a series of mutual inquiries about each other's health and the health of each other's children, husband (even though we'd seen Abdul just minutes ago), and parents. The repeated rounds of questions and answers went on for thirty minutes, when suddenly we heard several shots outside the fortress. Kouchi, noticing my fear, smiled and explained that it was only to announce the arrival of their honored guests to the rest of the villagers.

Later Abdul's two oldest sons came in and told us how pleased they were to have us in their home. They were both attired in their customary national dress topped with vests and carried weapons at all times. Their cartridge belts were well filled. Whenever they were home they seemed to occupy themselves in cleaning their firearms, and whenever they left their village they were accompanied by at least one armed guard, who walked a couple of steps behind them.

In Kama I seldom saw my husband during the day. He left with Abdul and his sons early in the morning, right after breakfast, and returned with them late at night. Saleem seemed so out of reach that I began to miss him. That dear, caring husband who didn't spend a single moment after work away from his family in Kabul was now totally changed. I thought he'd fallen under the influence of the male-dominated life of Kama. One day I told him he needed to get rid of that "maleness ego" of his as soon as possible. He laughed and said, "Well, it's good to know that someone realizes by now how important men are in women's lives!"

When I teasingly chased him out of the room, he whispered, "Honey

. . . honey, everyone is watching us!" I almost froze when I saw that Abdul's wives and daughters were looking at us. Afghan village women have immense respect for their husbands, and Abdul's womenfolk must certainly have been surprised to see me throwing Saleem out of the room.

It was hard to keep a conversation going all day long with people I didn't know and who had quite different tastes and interests. My mother-in-law was a great help, as she always came to my rescue and kept up the conversation for hours.

One day I asked Saleem why Abdul's sons were always armed and didn't it bother him. "No, not at all," he replied. "It's their way of life. They are cautious about their old enemies."

"Who are their enemies?" I whispered, trying to keep my voice low so no one else could hear me.

"Several generations ago Abdul's forebears killed someone from another village. Here tribal feuds last for generations." He laughed and added, "Don't worry; they would never kill women. Honey, you are out of their reach. Here is one tradition that you benefit from!"

"And what is that?" I asked, thinking he was trying to be funny.

"These people have great respect for women. It's very hard for the outside world to understand, but they would never attack a woman even if she were from the enemy's side," Saleem explained. "When a fight breaks out between rival groups and the men cannot go out because their enemies have them surrounded, the women are allowed to walk about freely and to keep their households running. In the Pashtun code of honor it's a big disgrace to shoot at a woman. It would never be forgiven, even if the woman were armed."

One evening we all, including Abdul's entire family, were invited to visit neighbors who lived across the farmlands. Near dark the host sent for us with two large trucks that had no license plates. After a twenty-minute ride we arrived at their house. The women were escorted to the third-floor room, which was lighted brightly by several powerful gas lamps. It was close to midnight when we ate. Colorful dishes were arranged on the usual white cloth spread on the floor. As we started eating, I noticed that none of the hostesses had joined us; instead, six or seven women, each holding a large dish in her hands, stood quietly behind us and watched us. I asked them to join us but no one moved. Surprised and disturbed, I asked Kouchi why. She smiled and whispered that I should eat my food and forget about it.

Whenever someone's plate was half empty, one of the standing women came forward and offered more food or simply refilled the plate. After dinner they brought us tea and small plates of candies. Around two in the morning we returned to Abdul's place. Then Kouchi told me about the customs of these people. "Out of great respect for their distinguished guests," she said, "the hostesses stand there, ready to serve the guests, and never dine with them." So in Qalat and Nangarhar provinces, just south and east, respectively, of Kabul, and not very far from each other, were two completely different customs. Each made sense in its own way.

As time went by, Abdul's family felt more at ease with me and I found them very friendly. Whenever there was free time during the day, Zari or her daughters and I would walk around the grounds to look at their gardens. On such walks I learned from Zari that Kouchi was Abdul's favorite wife and had responsibility for all the household financial and social affairs. Zari was very unhappy at having all the kitchen work and drudgery while Kouchi entertained the visitors. Yet one day Zari surprised me, after I explained what I did in Kabul, by saying, "You poor thing! You have a very bad life, more difficult than mine."

"How come?" I asked.

"Well, no veil, no respect! Working outside the home and also taking care of the family." The simplicity of her thought affected me a great deal.

In the summer of 1967 some thirty-five of Saleem's relatives rented a bus to attend the wedding of one of Saleem's cousins in Koh-Daman (also called Kohistan), a beautiful region just north of Kabul famous for its vineyards and orchards. It was an opportunity to see a large number of villagers and different traditions and customs. There were huge cultural differences and misunderstandings that separated us. We arrived at the village in office dress, having come straight from work, and were greeted with the villagers' stunned remarks and questions. A couple of people asked us women why we did not cover our legs, and one courageous village woman came forward and asked, "Aren't you afraid of God and the Judgment Day?"

Still, I liked the trip. Besides, we had never before gotten together with almost all of Saleem's relatives and spent the night under one roof with them. We talked about many things all night long: about village life, city life, funny stories, and unhappy occasions, too. Saleem's grandma talked about her young days when the family owned slaves.

Saleem's grandma, Bibi Jan, was a very special lady, probably in her early eighties at that time. She never liked to talk about her age; in fact, she didn't know how old she was. Once in a while, when my brother-in-law Yosuf wanted to tease her, he would ask her about the olden times and the kings she remembered. Bibi Jan remembered King Habibullah (1901–19) very well. According to her, she had been about fifteen years old when he came to power. Then Yosuf would go into the study room and bring out a history book. In front of her he would sit down and begin to calculate her age on his fingers, loudly. Then he would confirm the numbers with me. As soon as his count reached the seventies, Bibi would get upset and say, "Go away! Get lost from my sight!" After a deep breath she would add, "Oh my God! I have never seen such a devil in my life!"

Then she would ask me or the nearest person in the room to go and get her some lighted charcoals for burning a few seeds of *ispand*, a species of rue, a desert plant, which, when put on the fire, burned with a loud popping noise and produced heavy smoke with a distinctive odor. Bibi always carried the seeds with her wherever she went. She believed that they repelled the effects of the evil eye. When the hot charcoal was brought to her, she put a few seeds on it. After loudly reciting a poemlike incantation, she passed her hands, her head, and her clothes through the column of heavy smoke coming from the burning rue seeds. Finally she would call the servant and ask him to put the ashes in the river, which was miles away. She stressed the words "river only" because she thought it also would bring her good luck. She burned these seeds not only to neutralize the evil eye's effect; she used them generously for other occasions, too, even when she took a shower or wanted to go out of the house.

Grandma had strange ideas. There were special days in the week for washing her clothes. Her wash day was a bad day for all of us because no one was allowed to walk in that half of the yard where her clothes were hanging in the sun. If she was sick, we could not go and visit her on Wednesdays, because she believed that anything you do on Wednesday will be repeated. She believed that yellow flowers would bring misery to the person you gave them to, and one should never wear a yellow dress when going to visit a patient. Grandma also believed that a spoon must not be placed on the lid of a cooking pot because it would take the taste away from the food. She would get very nervous if one swept the floor with a broom or took a tablecloth and shook it outside to get rid of the food crumbs after the sun went down. In her opinion both of these actions had to be done in the daytime; otherwise they would bring misery and poverty upon the household.

Watching the new moon was a special event for Grandma. If she saw the new moon on its first or second evening, she took it as a sign of good luck for the rest of the month. As soon as her eyes fell upon the moon, she started praying and made a wish, then closed her eyes and turned around. If she saw a person she liked when she opened her eyes, she considered it a good omen and became happy. But she thought it bad luck to look at the new moon on its third night.

Grandma lived among five generations of her relatives and had more than a hundred close relatives to visit. She came to our house every two months and stayed with us for a couple of days. Two days were long

39

enough for her to stay in one place at one time. Her memory was so sharp that even after several months she remembered exactly what she had eaten on a specific day or what she had heard. Whenever she came to us, I tried very hard to keep her happy; otherwise for the next two months our story would be told everywhere, along with her curses or prayers, depending on what her feelings had been when she left us.

THE BEST YEARS

In the summer of 1966 my second son, Ali, was born. It was soon clear that we needed more room; the two boys were both growing fast. They added a lot of excitement around the house and kept Saleem very busy when he came home. He loved to play and wrestle with them. At times I worried and told him to leave them alone, fearing they might get hurt, but Saleem would laugh and say, "Don't worry, honey! My sons must be physically and mentally strong to face this wild world."

In April of 1967, when Omar was two years old and Ali nearly one, Saleem started to build our own house. It made me very happy. I was tired of moving from one rented home to the next almost yearly. I remembered moving from one house to the next as a child, and with our marriage the whole cycle seemed to have started all over again. Saleem had told me that we owned a small lot around the side of the mountain, but I didn't know exactly where it was. He didn't want me to see the property before the house was built. His idea was that I should see the house only after it was completed, since a dry lot on a mountain slope would not be a very pleasing sight.

One day without telling Saleem I took the bus and went out to our property. It was about seven minutes' walking distance from the nearest bus stop. Although it was only half completed, the sight of it pleased me greatly because it was our house. It seemed like heaven! I approached the house slowly, trying to surprise my husband. But Khoja, the mason, saw me from a distance and said, "There she is. I told you she would be here very soon!"

Saleem dropped the bricks he was holding and almost ran to me. He put his arms around me and laughingly pulled me toward the house to show me the rooms inside. "Honey, this is our bedroom. See the large window? We can see the whole city from it! Here is our dining room. This is Mother's bedroom. Oh! Here is our bathroom. Look how large it is! I want it to have enough shower space." He went on and on, so happy and delighted. I had hardly ever seen him so proud. Khoja and the rest of workers laughed as I passed by them. I think Saleem had told them that he wanted to work fast to finish the house as quickly as he could to surprise his wife. But now since I had caught Saleem off guard, they were laughing at him. Finally Saleem stopped and asked me, "Do you like it?"

"Of course!"

I looked around. The window frames were completed but there was no glass. The interior walls were plastered but not painted. The exterior walls lacked stucco; the red bricks were bare. The yard looked a mess, dotted with huge piles of sand, gravel, stones, and even piles of dirt with which to fill the ditches. There were walls around the yard on three sides. The front one was not built yet. I thought to myself, "Oh my God! It's so beautiful."

I told Saleem, "It's one o'clock; I will move in today and we will sleep here tonight so you will not have to make the trip every day to get here anymore."

"Honey, it's not ready yet," Saleem objected.

"That's all right. We can both make it ready when we're moved in," I insisted.

Just that morning Saleem had had an argument with his sister, Latifa. We had rented her house during the past year after she moved to an outlying province with her family. The previous week she had returned to Kabul unexpectedly and had been staying with us along with her six children and her husband. Things were so bad at home because of the overcrowding that we were all frustrated and tired.

Remembering the morning's unpleasantness, I was determined to move that very day. Saleem did not know how tired I was of changing houses and of nagging landlords. I could hardly wait to live in the house that belonged to us. I would have all the freedom of how to make use of it, to remodel it, or to put as many nails as I wanted in the walls, wherever it pleased me. I would never worry again about the landlord's long face and upset looks. Determined, I repeated, "Yes, I am going to move in today."

Khoja and Saleem did not believe me; Khoja said, "Okay, if you move in here today I will prepare you a nice shorba [soup] for dinner."

"Well, then start cooking it, because it's getting late. I will be here at five o'clock!" I exclaimed.

Saleem reluctantly assigned two workers to clean the rooms while I rushed back home. This time I took a taxi, and I also took Abbas, our servant, with me to help. When I arrived home, I asked my brother-in-law Yonus to obtain a large truck for hauling things. Then I told my mother-in-law to get ready. At first the poor woman didn't believe me, but she soon saw that I was completely serious.

The truck arrived an hour later. We all packed whatever we could find, and in two or three hours the truck was loaded. At five o'clock we arrived at our new home. Khoja was still working on the roof. As I approached the house, Khoja quit his work and came forward saying, "I can't believe that you did it so fast!"

"Well, Khoja, I am here and, remember, very hungry too!"

The workers stopped what they were doing and came to unload the truck. Saleem and a couple of neighbors assisted in hanging bedsheets over the window frames until we could buy glass panes. The floors of the two completed rooms lacked the final layer of concrete, so we spread carpets on the uneven surfaces. Completely exhausted by evening, I sat down on a pile of unopened cardboard boxes to rest. Abbas brought in two large trays of hot food and a large teapot full of tea sent unexpectedly from one of our neighbors.

That night we slept here and there all over the floor. Before sleep, however, I thanked God for giving me the house of my dreams. I owed nothing to anybody for this house. It was my land, my property, my kingdom, and my family. I cannot express in words my feelings at that moment, even though the mattress on the floor was not very comfortable. Everything seemed so peaceful and calm. Even the bumps of the floor under my body gave me the satisfaction and peace of heaven. This was the Mecca of my dreams!

The house was completed slowly. Every month, from our paychecks, we bought something for the house, and rooms were added slowly, one by one. We spent altogether about nine years on this house. Actually living in it made us realize some of its problems. First, the house faced the north, making it very cold in winter and deadly hot in summer. Drinking water was a major problem. Every day a big truck came and filled one or two water barrels left at the side of the street by each of the homeowners. We used this water only for washing and for watering the few plants we had. Our drinking water came from a city faucet that was almost dry throughout the day but had water after nine in the evening. The water pressure was so low that there was always a line of children and homeowners with pots and pans, waiting their turn at the public faucet. Abbas spent a lot of time every day at that faucet. Another problem was the bathrooms. The water pressure was very low, and because the house was built on rock, underground pipes could not be laid. Nevertheless, it was still our very own house and I cherish the days we spent there.

A few months before our move to the new house, in December 1966, I had graduated from Kabul University with good grades and still eligible for the scholarship in West Germany. While the paperwork for graduate study at the University of Bonn was being completed, I worked at the Faculty of Science as a biology assistant and continued my job at the

Kabul Zoo, where I had worked during my student years as a research technician.

Soon it was time for me to start the next semester in Germany. My passport and airline ticket were ready; the flight was scheduled for the Tuesday of the first week of January. Somehow confirmation of the dates of departure and the beginning of school abroad made me very depressed. It meant leaving my family for five or six years. Realizing that I had made a grave mistake by accepting the scholarship at this time, I returned all the documents to the dean of the Faculty of Science just two days before the departure date. I also resigned my position at the university because I did not want to work under my classmates who would return with Ph.D. degrees later. Depressed and angry, I stayed home the entire month of January and made it hell for everyone around me, although when I told Saleem what I had done, he was quiet and supportive.

A month went by very slowly. Since I had worked all my life after high school graduation, I got tired of staying at home. One day I went to the Ministry of Education and applied to teach at Rabia Balkhi Girls' High School, the school where I had taught during my first two years of college. Two weeks later I received permission to start teaching in March.

I taught at high school throughout March, but when payday came at the end of the month, the school officials told me they did not have my money (salaries were paid in cash and we did not use checks or credit cards in our daily purchases). A few days later I was asked to contact the Ministry of Education. There I learned that Kabul University had kept all my credentials and the university's vice president and dean of the Faculty of Education, Dr. Mohammad Siddique, wanted me to get in touch with him as soon as possible.

So far, I had avoided seeing anyone, even my friends from the university, since resigning from the Faculty of Science. I had not even returned their numerous phone calls. Reluctantly I went to the campus and met Dr. Siddique for the first time. He greeted me pleasantly and showed me to a chair opposite him. I sat down wordlessly as he looked at me, then shook his head and said, "Frankly, I do not understand why a person has to give up the scholarship and also resign a university position at the same time." He added, "Both of these are highly competitive and there are not many lucky ones who have both." I had not said a word so far. He probably thought he was talking to a mute person. "Could you tell me what went wrong?" he asked.

From his words I assumed that he thought someone at the Faculty of Science had agitated me. Therefore I assured him that my decision was based solely upon my personal problems and had nothing to do with the university people. Dr. Siddique asked his secretary to bring him my records, which he paged through though it seemed that he already knew my background. After a couple of minutes he said, "We need you at the Faculty of Education in the Math-Science Department."

I told him of my application to the Ministry of Education and the month that I had taught at the high school. "That's no problem; we will take care of it. The university will pay you from the day you left the Faculty of Science."

He looked at me and asked, "Do you need to consult with your family?"

"No; the decision is mine. Whatever I decide is all right with my family."

"So?"

I thought about the offer for a few moments and then replied, "All right. Now, what do you want me to do?"

Dr. Siddique, pleased with my quick decision, smiled and signed the bottom of a few pages in my records. Then he looked at me and said, "I will never be able to figure out women!"

Then he told me, "If you go to the Math-Science Department, they will direct you to your office." We shook hands as I stood up to leave. "From here on, you are on your own," he added. "I have great confidence in you."

From the central administration building I went directly to the Faculty of Education. There I learned that this recently founded faculty was affiliated with the Columbia University Teachers College. A few American advisers were on campus to help with its programs. The Math-Science Department had very few Afghan instructors. The first person in the department I met was Mahmood Sooma, who stood up politely when I entered the room. A recent M.S. graduate of Teacher's College, Columbia University, he was a tall, dark-haired man with a mustache, probably in his mid-thirties. His big black-rimmed glasses overshadowed his facial expression. After I introduced myself, Sooma explained that he was in charge of the chemistry courses and I was the only full-time person in the biology section, which I would be in charge of. He also explained that there were instructors from the Institute of Education and other schools who worked as part-time teachers in the department.

Sooma and I shared an office on the second floor of the Faculty of Education. He was from an eastern province, Paktia, and spoke Pashto but could communicate fluently in Dari also. We both worked hard, often into the evening, to meet the needs of our students. In the first few months we worked with the foreign advisers to set the goals and curriculum guidelines of this newly established faculty. Later other faculty members were hired. Our main problem was the lack of university textbooks in Dari, the language spoken in Kabul. At that time we had to translate basically all our classroom materials from English-language textbooks.

One day during my first few months of teaching at the Faculty of Education I received a message from the central administration office that I should keep a close eye on Sooma's activities and report to them the nature of his conversation and his visitors. This message upset me tremendously. Without further thought I told them angrily that they had better hire an intelligence agent, not a teacher! Everything they requested was against my personal ethics. On the day I graduated from the university, I made an oath to myself that no matter how big or important a job I might hold in the future, I would never misuse my power to harm anyone. This was my solemn oath to the people of my country.

I did not say a word to Sooma about the central administration's message, but after that just out of curiosity I paid close attention to his visitors. Once in a while a few came to him who certainly did not have the appearance of college students. Most of these visitors were from Paktia, like Sooma himself, and spoke Pashto with the Paktian accent. I thought Sooma probably belonged to a leftist political party that I had not heard of at that time.

Political activity was not very obvious at the university in the mid-1960s. All I knew was that King Zahir Shah's "New Democratic Reform" of October 1964 included freedom of the press, freedom to organize political parties, the holding of open elections, and the establishment of a parliament and a constitution. It also said that members of the royal family could not hold the positions of prime minister, minister, supreme court justice, or parliament member.

As a result of this reform, small political groups sprouted up all around the country. By 1967, however, it was apparent that these newly established small, disorganized political parties had no power, nor would one expect them to bring any significant changes in the country. Thus I did not understand why the government was interested in people like Sooma. I had previously largely ignored politics, being simply too busy for it or just not interested in the unfulfilled promises of politicians, and I had not paid much attention to the country's internal affairs. Now, being around Sooma, I began to think about the present situation.

I recalled an incident in 1965, the student riots that followed the introduction of the "New Democratic Reform." When the first meeting of parliament was held, on the king's birthday, October, 24, 1965, a large number of students entered the Parliament House. They tried to prevent parliament from approving the second term for the interim government of Mohammad Yosuf that was proposed by King Zahir Shah. It was reported that during the ensuing clashes between students and the government forces, at least one person was killed. Some of the students claimed that three persons were killed. Students continued to demonstrate afterward, demanding the prosecution of the persons who had ordered the police to fire. As a result of the demonstrations, parliament voted in closed session for a second term for Mohammad Yosuf the day after the king's birthday. In fact, the proposed government received the overwhelming approval of parliament. The students continued to riot. As they marched in the streets, they were joined by a large number of high school students. They stood all day long in Zarnigar Park near the palace, protesting and condemning the government's injustices.

Finally, after four days of student protests, the newly approved government resigned. The students, intoxicated with the discovery of their new power, not only continued to demand the indictment of those responsible for the shootings on October 24, but also sought further changes in the system, including a lowering of the university's passing grade from 60 percent to 50 percent and the elimination of its policy of mandatory daily class attendance. The newly formed government of Prime Minister Maiwandwal promised to investigate but quietly dropped the subject afterward. In succeeding years the anniversary of this event was celebrated with huge student demonstrations and provocative speeches condemning the government for the killings and coverup.

Now I was curious who was behind these political groups. People said it was agents of the Soviet Union. Obviously students did use Communist slogans, and Soviet influence was evident in the military: during Jeshn (national independence day) parades one could see the Russian-made tanks, artillery, and airplanes. As a matter of fact, years earlier, in 1947 and 1954, when Afghanistan's appeals for United States aid to modernize its military forces were rejected, the country turned to Moscow for help. The Russians welcomed the opportunity, and large numbers of Afghans, mostly in the armed forces, were sent to the USSR for training.

I remember the day in 1966 when my brother-in-law Yosuf graduated from high school and was selected by the Afghan government to go to the Soviet Union for five years of military training. Yosuf did not want to go there, but Saleem talked him into it. Saleem and I both thought that gaining knowledge was important and that it didn't matter from which country it came. There were rumors that a few of the students who came back from the Soviet Union were brainwashed and acted pro-Russian. They often could not express their ideas publicly because of the deep hatred that existed in Afghanistan for infidels, but most people like me had not heard of such pro-Russian activists in the mid-60s.

In 1967 I received a scholarship from the U.S. Agency for International Development to participate in the English-language program at the American University of Beirut in Lebanon, for the 1967–68 academic year, then to continue graduate work in Long Island, New York, in ecology. My family stayed behind, for the grant did not cover their expenses.

Lebanon was at that time, before war tore it apart, one of the most beautiful countries in the world: houses with red-tiled roofs were surrounded by forests of pine trees and citrus groves on a line of rolling hills as far as the eye could see. The deep-blue sea and beautiful beaches with tall houses in the background were breathtaking. The famous St. George Hotel, built by the French in the 1930s, gracefully stood near the campus next to the seashore. Beirut reminded me of that peaceful "Land of Gods" where no human hand could disturb its heavenly calmness. Unfortunately, it was far from that.

I soon found that Beirut was burning quietly, deep down, with an ugly war hard to detect at first. Just a few months before my arrival in Lebanon, the university was hit by a number of rockets aimed at the American embassy across the street from our campus. At that time all the students were evacuated and the foreign students were sent back to their homelands. Now the university was reopening for the fall semester. During my stay I never saw war scenes myself, but there were times when one could feel the animosity between the Moslems in West Beirut and the Christians in the east sector of the city. Conflicts often broke out between them. The sad thing was that it was a war between neighbors.

By the end of the second semester in Beirut I felt very homesick. All the forms for my graduate work at Long Island University were completed but I did not want to go. I was afraid to tell the university officials for the second time that I was turning down a scholarship. It would be easier for me if the teachers told them I could not go. So, when I took the final language test, I purposely gave the wrong answers. Mrs. Mellecky, our language teacher, was surprised; she wrote to my adviser in Kabul that I knew far more than my final exam had indicated and that I was certainly ready for the proposed graduate studies.

I finished my studies in Beirut and chose to return home in May of 1968. I had always made good, solid decisions in life, but whenever it came to a choice between my family and my education, I was confounded. I loved both of them. Unfortunately, my children and my study place were always at opposite ends of the world! Once back in Kabul, I found that my family was completely all right. Omar and Ali had grown up quite a bit; it surprised me to see them as miniature figures of very handsome men.

At school, student demonstrations continued, incited largely by a small number of relatively unheard-of political groups. Most of the participants refused to go to class and stood around in groups all day listening to the leaders harangue each other. The majority were there only to see who was in the opposing groups and to accuse each other of aberrations and deviations based mainly on their personal conflicts or their leaders' desire to control the party. The attacks were so personal and perturbing that after I watched them once, I thought it was all a bunch of blather, and a complete waste of time.

One of the most vocal leftist political parties was Khalq (People or Masses), or People's Democratic Party of Afghanistan (PDPA). It was founded in 1965 under the leadership of Noor Mohammad Taraki, a self-educated writer and a poet. Two years later PDPA split into Parcham

(Banner) and Khalq factions. The Parcham party, headed by Babrak Karmal, was made up mostly of non-Pashtun, Persian-speaking students. The majority of the Khalqis, on the other hand, were Pashtun students who spoke the Pashto language and originally came from the provinces. Khalqis and Parchamis did not like each other. Since Karmal came from a well-to-do family, his party was seen by the Khalqis as being the "royal family's Communist party," composed of bourgeoisie who were oblivious to the workers' problems.

The protests intensified after the king appointed a Senior Committee, which included several cabinet members, to control university affairs. In a second inflammatory event, in May of 1969, a student by the name of Assyle was injured in a student clash with police and died in the university hospital. Rumors spread that Assyle had been killed in the hospital by one of the leftist political groups to arouse hatred against police and the government, while the government claimed that he had died of natural causes. Assyle's body was kidnapped from the hospital by students, who carried it through the streets the following day, shouting antigovernment slogans. They tried to return his body to his home province for burial; but on the way, government forces, afraid of further disturbances, took the coffin from the students and forced them to return to Kabul. Not a word was said about what happened to Assyle's body thereafter.

After months of demonstrations, the government forces, which the students called Ghund-e-Zarba (the Whacking Battalion), finally got impatient and attacked the university. I remember the day in May of 1969 when the university was invaded by both army troops and police. I was sick that day and had left the office at ten in the morning. I walked toward the farmlands adjoining the university and the Tomb of Sayed Jamaludin Afghani, a famous landmark on the campus, to catch the bus. Still about a kilometer away from the tomb, I saw a huge crowd of students standing in the middle of the main street. They were trying to go downtown, but the police had blocked their way. A couple of minutes later, as a friend and I approached the cafeteria, I saw students and police start attacking each other furiously. Scores of hands clutching sticks and batons flailed the air. Students at the far end of the crowd started running away. My friend shouted, "Run!"

I stood there, stunned, watching them. My friend, who had run a few steps, came back and pulled my hand to run with her. The crowd was still far from us. The wisest thing for us was to run back to our offices. Many fast-running students passed us. I ran through the two long hallways of the Faculty of Education and finally, out of breath, approached my office. I unlocked the door and entered. The police had arrived and their footsteps resounded just behind me in the hall. They were chasing everyone in their path and indiscriminately hitting them with batons. Once inside my office, I realized that an extremely worried Sooma was sitting on the floor, afraid of being seen from the large windows of the second floor. I couldn't help laughing at the sight. Going to the window, I saw a group of students throwing rocks at police who were chasing them. Rocks and stones filled the air and covered the walkways. One of our friends was running very fast at the front of the crowd. I laughed and said, "Sooma, look! Ahmad is running away as fast as he can. When he gets here, he'll say that he fought the police!"

Ahmad opened the door and entered. Before we could say a single word, he said, "Look at those jerks!" (He meant the police.) "I rescued several girls from them. They are so stupid and inconsiderate!"

I looked at Sooma, who was laughing. Still standing behind the large windows of the office, I saw four students who had hidden in the corner of the roof of one of the buildings across from me. By this time most of the action was over. A lone high-ranking police officer came by and checked around to see what was left after the attack. As he approached the building, the four students jumped down from the roof and caught him by surprise. He fell face down on the ground. The students ripped off his emblems and tore his clothing. Then they took him to the stream that ran behind the building and threw him in the dirty water. They ducked him a couple more times till his uniform was covered with mud.

53

I watched with great interest, still upset at the police brutality toward the students. Finally the four students let the officer go. He walked away, his clothes tattered and his ripped-off hat in his hand. I always wondered what the reaction was when he confronted his subordinates later.

Although the protests continued after the police invasion, the cost was heavy for many students because the university was closed for the next six months. The minister of education resigned.

In August of 1970 my third child, a beautiful little girl we named Sahar, was born. Saleem and I both thought our happiness was now complete and that we should concentrate on raising our three little children the best way we could. A few months later, in November of 1970, Saleem went to the United States to complete his higher education on a scholarship. I was left at home because his scholarship could not support the expenses of his family.

One day as I was about to leave my office after lunch, I noticed a huge group of people going into a large classroom. One of my school friends was in the crowd, and I asked her what was going on. "It's the first test for the Fulbright-Hayes scholarships," she replied.

"Who is eligible?" I asked.

"Anyone who passes the tests."

"Can I take it, or is it too late to register?"

"I don't know. Let's go in and ask whoever's in charge of the test."

We entered the room and asked one of the proctors, who added my name to the bottom of the list.

So, without any specific aim in mind, I joined the crowd, only because it had been years since I had taken any English-language test. Frankly, I didn't care about the scholarship, knowing that in the past I had rejected so many of them. I only wanted to know my English-language standing.

In the testing room, about 150 people, including a few professors of mine who had spent years in England, and other faculty, staff, and students were gathered. I took the test with them and a week later the results were posted. My name was in the top five of the seventeen of those selected for the second test.

During the next few months I took the second, third, fourth, and fifth screening tests, some in general knowledge, others in sciences, and the last one specifically in my area of studies. The list of candidates became smaller and smaller after each test. I made it to the last list and was selected second out of the top five candidates, till finally I was a recipient of the scholarship.

The Fulbright office gave me a choice of universities abroad. I chose Auburn University, the one that was closest to my husband's school, Maxwell Air Force Base in Montgomery, Alabama. I joined him six months later with my two sons, leaving my daughter at home in my mother's care. My in-laws stayed in our home and their expenses were paid out of my husband's salary. The Afghan government paid in full the salary of a person who went for studies outside the country.

Living in an extended family has its advantages and its disadvantages. For example, I never had to worry about my children or the misbehavior of babysitters or child abuse; I always got support from my family. But relatives could be too much concerned about things that were none of their business, especially some women who had too much time on their hands.

Leaving my daughter behind was very hard and I felt miserable and sick for the first several weeks in the United States. After school started in September of 1971 I was overwhelmingly occupied with my studies and thought less about Sahar. I tried very hard to finish my education as quickly as I could. At school my main problem was to finish reading the big textbook of invertebrate zoology from page 1 to the end. I didn't know what to read; I even read all the reference pages too! Of course this was not the only class I took. I enrolled for thirteen credit hours the first quarter, fifteen credit hours the second quarter, and twenty-one credit hours (including the research for my thesis) the third quarter. Finishing two years' worth of schoolwork in seven and a half months was very hectic, especially with my limited English-language abilities.

My other problem was commuting between Montgomery and Auburn, seventy-five miles away. I basically spent three hours every day on the road. Saleem was very helpful. Besides taking care of Omar, Ali, and his own studies, he did the cooking and housecleaning when I came home late in the evenings for the first five months of my studies.

Since Saleem was in the air force, he was transferred from base to base every few months. I stayed with my sons in Alabama when he went to Boulder, Colorado, for further training. As soon as I finished my coursework and field research at Auburn, we joined him at Chanute Air Force Base in Rantoul, Illinois. I finished writing my thesis there, then returned to Auburn University for two weeks to defend my research work.

After learning at five in the afternoon that I had successfully completed all the M.S. degree requirements, that evening I took the eight o'clock Greyhound bus for Illinois. I slept on the bus for more than twenty-four hours straight, thinking that there was nothing in the world to worry about. Oh God, I had tried for this degree so many times and it was so hard! When the choice came between my education and my family . . . I always went with tears in my eyes to my family.

At the end of 1972 we returned home, having completed our studies. On our way back we bought a car in West Germany from the savings we had accumulated during our time abroad. It was difficult traveling east toward Afghanistan in the early mornings because of the sun's position, so we traveled slowly and rested overnight in hotels – expensive hotels, just to be on the safe side. People had warned us that car thefts as well as unpaved passes made traveling in Turkey and Iran both dangerous and arduous.

When the Afghan border came in sight after two full weeks of driving, we all started shouting. Here, finally, was home – OUR HOMELAND! Although the land was naked and desertlike to the eye, we loved its bare, rocky ground! To us it was beautiful. All the comforts of the West began to disappear from our minds. The joy of being home was so great that Saleem, after observing the tall fifteenth-century minarets of Herat city on the far horizon, stopped the car on the roadside, got out, and, kneeling, touched his head to the gravel. He thanked God to be home again. Here we were not aliens; no one would call us foreigners.

In spite of the attractiveness and comforts of other countries, we always preferred to be home and live with all the good and bad things of our own land. Saleem always thought that he owed his countrymen a lot. All of his education expenses had been paid for by the government. Now it was his obligation to take part along with others in the progress of Afghanistan toward its dreams.

Kabul had not changed a bit: the same streets, the same buses, the same houses, most often the same familiar colors, except that now the paint was a little more weathered and worn. On the surface it seemed that daily life in Afghanistan marched by very slowly and leisurely, resisting all the new ideas and changes.

The best years of my life, which, unfortunately, did not last very long, were the years between 1972 and 1975. Saleem and I, after spending the better part of four long years in studying overseas and attending meetings and seminars, most often away from each other, finally were getting closer to our goals. The future seemed bright; all our hardships were history by now and financially we were in good condition. Above all, our fast-growing children completed our happiness and added a lot of joy and excitement around the house for both of us. We no longer supported a large family. My brothers-in-law had completed their studies, married, and lived on their own. My mother-in-law decided to live with Yosuf, thinking that his new bride, Mariam, needed her help more than I did.

During this time we met a fine couple, Zalmai and his wife, Naheed, with whom we became good friends, sharing mutual interests and spending most of our weekends and holidays together. We traveled at every opportunity, visiting the most remote parts of Afghanistan. Financially better off, we no longer needed to stay with relatives or friends when traveling; instead we stayed in hotels. This was better because it allowed us more freedom to see places of interest, or to play cards in our free time, which we did by the hour on such trips without ever tiring of it. Typically, over the weekend, we would drive to a nearby village early in the morning, cook out, and play cards the rest of the day, returning home late at night. On longer holidays we traveled to farther provinces such as Balkh, Mazar, Kandahar, Herat, Samangan, Jalalabad, and Logar. But there were many other places, such as Bamiyan and Nooristan, that we did not see. In fact, we thought we would have all the time in the world to see such sites later. Little did I know that the travel we enjoyed then would in the next few years become a necessity in order to save our very lives.

One interesting conclusion that I reached from all our trips was that Kabul was not Afghanistan. There was a big difference between Kabul and the rest of country. The innate hospitality of the village people was worth admiring – a beautiful tradition of Afghan culture, which, unfortunately, was fading away in the large cities, especially among the younger generations. For people in the provinces, the love of God, love for their independence, and the love for family runs through their veins. It reflected the core of all Afghan society's philosophy and outlook.

Another obvious fact was that the countryside was so serene, compared with Kabul and its political unrest. One thing was very clear: the Afghan nation was not tolerant of Communist ideas. I was sure that the few Marxists in Kabul – the Parchamis and the Khalqis – could by no means alter or represent the beliefs of the majority of the country. Afghanistan was not ready for such foreign ideas, not now and not for many more years to come.

At the university in the mid-1970s, the government wanted to reduce the duplication of departments that existed within the various faculties. For example, the Math-Science Department in the Faculty of Education and all its staff and teaching members were transferred to the corresponding departments of the Faculty of Science. Thus, I was transferred back to the Biology Department of the Faculty of Science, where I had graduated several years before. My last overseas trip, from January to November of 1976, was to the University of Nebraska at Omaha, where I served as a visiting professor and also attended some classes and did research on the Protozoa of Kabul, using the university facilities. As before, Saleem took care of our children at home.

For an Afghan husband, it was very hard to see his wife go away for months, leaving the family behind. In a society where men never worked inside the house and their food was always ready, their clothes washed, their shoes shined and brought to them to wear, it was very hard to do the housework in the absence of a woman. But Saleem was an exception. He always took good care of the children when I was not around, although I knew it was extremely hard on him.

Personal loans to finance the purchase of real estate, cars, and other big items were not available in Afghanistan. One had to have cash on hand before buying anything. Saleem and I both had good jobs and had saved a considerable amount of money. With our cash we bought a house in the middle of town with a large backyard and sold our first house, the one built on the mountainside. So now we had a big house, a new car, several servants, and enough money to enjoy the life ahead of us. In Afghanistan a car was a luxury rather than a necessity as it is in America. It was not needed for work because the government provided transportation to and from work for most. Besides, the public buses ran in every part of town and did not cost a lot.

We were ready to build our second dream house, but in spite of all our savings, we still were not able to buy the land we wanted. Therefore, in the beginning of 1978 we decided to build our own house in the big, three-acre backyard of the house we had recently purchased. Saleem took a month's leave from his work in February and very anxiously started construction of the new house. In all his actions he seemed, for some unexplained reason, to be in a hurry to finish the house as quickly as possible. He traveled to nearby towns to buy the best materials he could find. If the bricks, cement, gravel, or wood did not meet his standards, he didn't buy it.

In no time the two-story house stood close to completion. The concrete roof with its metal shingles was finished. The plumbing in the two bathrooms was near completion. The kitchen cabinets had been installed. The woodwork was all completed. The only thing the house needed was paint on the walls and glass in the windows.

We planned to move in by early May. We all were excited. We had each selected the paint color for our bedrooms. Every day after work Saleem and I went to our new house to observe anxiously the day's progress as Saleem gave the masons, carpenters, and plumbers instructions for the next day.

Just when our dreams were about to be realized came that monstrous day in my life – the savage coup of April 27, 1978, that not only destroyed my dreams but in its flames burned the dreams of fifteen million innocent Afghan men and women throughout the country.

The Search

A DIARY

I arrived home from work at five in the afternoon and saw Saleem with his friend Mudere Sahib in the living room. He seemed tired to the point of exhaustion. He had wrapped himself in a brown warm chappan (a special gown), which he had recently bought. I stopped at the door and greeted him and his friend.

"Hi, dear," Saleem replied. "You're a little late today."

"Well, I walked instead of taking the university bus. It feels like spring is just around the corner," I said calmly.

Saleem resumed his conversation with Mudere Sahib. "I paid Mohammad twenty-five thousand afghanis for the bathroom plumbing and fixtures and yet only half the work is completed," he said in an irritated tone.

"Why didn't you use Pakistani-made parts?" Mudere Sahib asked. "They're much cheaper than the German ones."

"No, I want it this way. I want this house to last for many years without trouble." Saleem paused for a moment and then added, "I had enough trouble with the other houses. I never had a decent bathroom, never!"

I smiled at his comment and went to the bedroom to slip into more comfortable clothes. Saleem had fine taste. He bought few but high-quality things. The housekeeper, Rahim, called, "Madam, the tea is ready."

"Could you wait a minute? I'd like to make some *bolanies*," I said. I prepared several *bolanies* – fried tortilla-like flat breads stuffed with hamburger meat, green onions, cilantro, and spices. Rahim took them with the tea into the living room. Saleem loved *bolanies*, especially when they were hot. I heard him laugh loudly and tell his friend, "Mudere Sahib, my wife never cooks so nicely for me. She has made these because of you!"

I joined them and poured myself a cup of tea. Saleem looked rather nervous and depressed, which was unusual for him. Normally whenever he was home the house was full of joy and laughter. I thought he must have had a rough day today. Again the conversation turned to the new house. Saleem mentioned that he would separate the old house from the new one with a wooden wall constructed from the excess wood that was covered with concrete. It had been used for pouring the concrete and was piled high in the backyard. "Such a wall will look so ugly!" I exclaimed.

"Honey, I cannot make it right now from brick. Later, if you like, you can make it yourself," he answered. His tone and words were sharp, but I kept quiet even though I didn't like his response.

Mudere Sahib left after an hour. I called my children in and started to help them with their homework. Saleem sat very quietly and watched us for quite some time, then without a word he went to the bedroom and started writing up the day's expenses for the contracts with the masons, plumbers, and carpenters. He always kept a good record of his financial transactions, and he always said that in case he weren't around I should know where to look for the important documents.

In half an hour or so I heard the clicking of his briefcase being closed and I called from the living room, "Why don't you come here and help your children with their studies? It looks like they are only mine!"

Saleem laughed loudly and exclaimed, "Do you want me to sign a paper saying that they are all yours?" A few minutes later he called out from the bedroom, "Honey, come here. Don't take this world so hard!"

I was almost finished with the children when Rahim came in and announced that dinner was ready. We all went to the dining table but Saleem wasn't there. I found him sound asleep in the bedroom, which was really unusual. Since I had seen him so tired this evening, however, I thought he needed some rest, so we ate alone.

After dinner Omar, Ali, and Sahar went to their bedrooms and I checked the stove, windows, and doors, making sure everything was in order, before I went to bed. Saleem was sleeping heavily. I began reading a book while listening to the evening news. At a few minutes past eight the announcer said something that made me sit up straight and put the book down: several Communist leaders, including Babrak Karmal and Noor Mohammad Taraki, had been arrested following an antigovernment demonstration. I knew that such demonstrations had been taking place during the last few days following the assassination of a senior official of the Communist party, whose murderer was yet unknown.

On hearing the news, I jumped up and shook Saleem by the shoulder and said, "Wake up! Listen to the news!" Saleem raised his head, listened to the radio for a moment, said sleepily, "Who cares!" and went back to sleep.

When the regular program came back on, I turned off the radio and the lights. Drowsiness soon carried my memories back to a nightmare I'd had a couple of nights before. I had dreamed that I came home from work and when I opened the door, I found that everything in the house was gone. The place was empty. In great shock I ran to our bedroom and found that everything had vanished except the empty bed frame. A few scraps of paper blew here and there across the hard cement floor in the strong wind that came through the open windows. The sound of the wind and the rustling papers was eerily unnerving, as if spirits of the dead were dancing and whistling in a graveyard. A deep, cold chill ran through me. I tried to scream and shout but I couldn't make a sound; nobody could hear me. With legs weak and shaking I opened the door to the living room. It too was deserted. The whole house appeared to be haunted. Not a single living soul was present, only the whistling of the wind and the songs of the dead. With all the strength left in me I ran through the yard toward the open door in the wall, but before I could reach it, it slammed shut. I struggled to turn the latch and when it finally opened I ran into the street, where a man was passing on a bicycle. In spite of my screams he didn't even look at me; it was as if I weren't there at all, or I was an invisible visitor from another world.

Remembering the nightmare, I turned and put my arms around Saleem and thanked God for his presence. Saleem always gave me confidence. He made me feel bold and brave. He was always on my side when I needed him. He was like that tall, proud mountain – whenever I leaned on him, he supported me. Above all, he believed in me, and that made a whole lot of difference. With these warm feelings I soon fell asleep.

THURSDAY, APRIL 27, 1978 (SAUR 7, 1357)
Right after we dressed for work, Saleem went to the yard to give the day's instructions to the workers. The mason was almost finished with the stucco on the exterior of the house. Saleem said he would be back in two hours in case he was needed.

At the breakfast table, all Saleem's exhaustion from the previous night was gone. He looked at the fresh boiled eggs, the result of my troublesome project when I'd decided to raise nine hundred chickens in the big backyard. Since fall most of them had died. The few that were left had recently begun to lay eggs. Saleem said, "It's so nice to have fresh eggs in the morning."

He ate breakfast hurriedly. "What was the news you woke me up to hear last night?" he asked.

I explained, adding, "Many people can be easily fooled by the propaganda of 'Food, Shelter, and Clothing' " – that was the Communists' old slogan.

Saleem smiled and left the table, saying he would see me in the after-

66

noon. He hurried out the front door as I watched from the dining room window. He turned back, looked at me for a few seconds, threw a kiss, and left.

My children were still in bed because they had the afternoon school shift that started at twelve-thirty. I got ready and left the house for school. On Thursdays this semester I had only two hours of class. In Afghanistan, offices closed at one on Thursdays – our weekends consisted of a half day Thursday and all of Friday; the week began on Saturday.

At work, for some reason I wanted to talk to my husband, but I didn't call him because I didn't have anything important to say. Noon came and I left my office to catch the university bus for home. While waiting for the bus, I saw my colleague Sooma. He looked very strange. His head seemed longer than usual, his eyes wide and unblinking, with his glasses way down on the tip of his nose. He walked very strangely, as if he were rolling on a wheel. His appearance made me laugh and I turned to a friend and said, "Look at Sooma; he looks very funny today!" We both laughed. Then the bus arrived and I headed for home.

Rahim had almost finished cleaning the house and had taken the children to school. A large pot of shorba (soup) was ready. Next to it sat the gallon-size teakettle, which was also boiling. This food was for the fourteen workers. I poured the soup into bowls and Rahim placed it, along with nans, flat breads, on the front porch. Normally on the weekend Saleem ate with the workers. He always took pleasure in feeding them although they were supposed to provide their own lunch. He thought the workers' pay set by the government was hardly enough to meet their basic needs. Providing food every day for that many people was not an easy job, but we both enjoyed doing it. Saleem always said, "With all the blessings God has granted us, we should help the needy ones."

Saleem was late today. I told Rahim to tell the workers to go ahead and start their lunch. Since the soup was gone, I cooked hamburgers for Saleem and me and put them in the oven to stay warm. I waited and waited but Saleem did not come. His absence made me a little upset because I thought he could at least have called me. I finally ate lunch without him and went into the next room and picked up a newspaper. The quiet of a Thursday afternoon in the warm spring sun was pleasant.

Rahim had just brought me a cup of tea when the doorbell rang. There stood my brother-in-law Yonus, his face pale and full of fear. He rushed in, stuttering, "Wh . . . wh . . . where is my brother?"

"I don't know. I'm waiting for him but he hasn't come yet," I replied calmly.

"Did you hear the noise coming from downtown?"

"What kind of noise?" I asked anxiously.

"Bombs! Bombs are exploding all over town. It's just like hell out there!" he screamed.

I couldn't believe what he had said. I jumped from my chair and ran to the new house and climbed to the second floor. It was true; bombs could be heard exploding all over town. Yonus explained that the palace (Arg) was under attack and businesses were closing. A mob was running up and down the streets, not knowing what to do.

At about four in the afternoon I went to pick my sons up from their school, which was about two miles away. On the way several MIG jets appeared in the sky, climbing steeply and then suddenly diving sharply to disappear behind Asmai Mountain, where the palace was. A few minutes later, explosions! People stood outside their houses watching the MIGs maneuver. Some were trying to get news from the small radios they had with them. Kabul Radio was off the air, which was highly unusual.

Finally, trembling with fear, I made it to the school only to learn that the children had been released an hour before without the parents being notified. On my way back I stopped at Mudere Sahib's house to see if my sons were there. His was the closest house they knew they could go to in an emergency. Mudere Sahib was home but did not know what was going on. His wife tried to bring me a cup of tea. I was too worried about my sons to linger, and felt unwell, so I left in a hurry with Mudere Sahib as an escort back to my house. I was immensely relieved to see Omar and Ali at the door, watching the planes.

About an hour later a short man in a green Volkswagen came to the door and asked my sons, who were still watching the planes, if their father was home. When he learned that Saleem wasn't home, he said, "Never mind, I will find him in his office." His tone and his actions made me very suspicious. I ran to the front door to talk to him, but he was gone.

All the phones in the city were down. I waited another hour and still Saleem did not show up. Before nightfall I tried to go to my mother's and my mother-in-law's houses. They both lived on the other side of Asmai Mountain very close to where the bombs had fallen. I wanted to know if they were safe. I left the house but found that transportation had stopped. There were no buses, no communication; no contact whatsoever was possible. Kabul was on fire and dying in these early evening hours! At first I thought to take our car but I was not sure I could drive in my present nervous state, so I asked Mudere Sahib to go with me to my in-laws' by taxi.

Night was very close. It was getting darker and darker when Mudere Sahib and I headed toward the main road to get a cab. For a long time no cabs passed but finally one came. I almost ran into the middle of the street and it stopped suddenly. The driver was not willing to take us anywhere, even if I paid him five hundred afghanis (the normal charge would have been about twenty-five). A second cab came by after twenty minutes and the driver said, "There are many dead and wounded in town. I have just taken three injured people to the hospital and one died in my car." He pointed to the back seat: "Look, it's all full of blood."

I looked. Blood covered the floor and seats of the car. There was almost no place to sit because it was soaked with blood. The driver looked at me and advised, "If your children are here, go to them and stay there because the roads are very dangerous. Most are closed." Then he added, "Every hundred yards or so, civilian cars are stopped and checked by the army. If the soldiers need a car, they take it and leave the passengers in the street. If you still insist on going there, I will take you. But I won't bring you back."

Night had fallen. I returned home unwillingly and Mudere Sahib left. Machine guns and bombs could be heard from almost every direction. In fact, they were getting closer and closer to us. A few shots were heard from right outside our house. Planes – low-flying helicopters and the Soviet MIGs – filled the sky. I felt totally isolated from the rest of the world, alone with three young children and Rahim. I turned on the radio and tried to listen to shortwave for information, but there wasn't much.

In helpless desperation I sent my son Ali across the wall that separated our yard from our neighbors' and had him tell them that Saleem had not returned and we were alone. I always counted on these good neighbors; whenever we needed something they were there for us. Moments later they and their many guests came to our home to keep us company. We talked of the situation. Everybody speculated on it or repeated the rumors they had heard that day.

Kabul Radio began to air again at this time, playing the national anthem without any announcement. It continued for an hour or more. People knew from past experience that it signaled something very serious. We had heard the anthem when President Daoud seized the government from King Zahir Shah several years before. Sometime between seven and eight in the evening the music stopped. There was an announcement, which I thought had been put together hurriedly, that Daoud had been overthrown and the "enemies of the People" had been killed: "For the first time in the history of Afghanistan an end has been put to the Sultanate of Mohammadzai" (this referred to King Zahir Shah and his family). "All power of the state has passed into the hands of the Military Revolutionary Council."

The music resumed without further comment. We were all stunned. My God, I began to worry more and more until my knees gave way and wouldn't support me any longer. I sat quietly in a chair trying to hold myself together. I tried to hide my fears from the house full of guests, as

I did not know most of them. Rahim broke the silence by bringing in tea and filling the guests' teacups.

My intuition told me that something was very wrong where Saleem worked. I had heard of almost all these pro-Russian leaders from my friends and students at the university and knew their outrageous ideas. A deadly quiet still shadowed the room. Perhaps the guests wanted to digest the words they had heard on the radio. The tea was sipped in a speechless atmosphere.

Our neighbors insisted that we join them for supper in their home. They may have felt we shouldn't be left alone, especially since the explosions had increased considerably after dark and shook the buildings vigorously. I didn't want to leave the house because I was not feeling well, but I relented to their friendly offer. In spite of the curfew that had been imposed a long time before, we all, including my children, used the street door to go to their house rather than climbing the high wall that separated our properties.

After dinner we listened to BBC radio news. They spoke of a coup in Kabul but did not give details. At ten o'clock my children and I returned home. "Don't worry; we'll watch your house all night," my neighbors said.

The shooting and explosions echoed loudly through our quiet house. The children were terrified. I remembered my father's words from many years before: "When everything fails, sit down and think. Then make the best of what you have at hand." God rest his soul in peace; his advice really worked.

The first thing I did was to assume that all our relatives were safe and sound in their homes. Next I had to calm down my children. With all the courage I could muster, I began to smile and tell them that everything would be all right. Then I brought out a deck of playing cards and asked both of my sons to play with me while Sahar kept score. I wanted to restore normalcy. We played until their bedtime, then I sent them to bed and told them that when they got up in the morning their dad would be home. We would all laugh about the events of tonight and have a good breakfast. Although terrified and deeply worried, I controlled my actions nicely and sat with the children until they were all fast asleep in Omar's room.

Although Rahim normally slept in his own room, separate from the main house in the far corner of the front yard, I had him bring his bed in and spread it on the hallway floor. In no time he went to sleep. I decided to stay in the children's room all night. Should something happen, we would all be together.

As I sat quietly in a corner listening to the shelling, my thoughts began to wander. I had heard many stories about soldiers killing or raping families and looting houses in the absence of the male head of the family. Rahim was a handicapped draftee who was not able to undergo strenuous military training and had been assigned to help us at home. I was afraid of him, although he was a very pleasant man. He had been with us for only the past three months and I did not know him very well. So, along with all my other worries, I felt I had to watch him too.

Without awakening Rahim, I tiptoed around his bed and entered the master bedroom to get the pistol that we had bought years before in West Germany. I pulled the bullets from a bag with trembling hands, put them into the chamber, and pulled the trigger. I did not dare release the safety catch. Never before in my life had I touched a gun. In fact, I was scared of them and never thought that one day I might be forced to use one. When Saleem cleaned the pistol he tried to show me how it worked but I always avoided it. Tonight I was determined to use it if necessary, even though the very thought of it made me feel sick. I tiptoed out of the room and passed Rahim's bed carefully. In the darkness my numb toes caught in his blankets and I fell, hitting my head noisily on the wall. I had almost fallen on Rahim. Unbelievably, he did not wake up – or if he did, he pretended not to.

As the darkness of night deepened, the bombing and machine gun fire grew louder. The tanks not far from our house thundered at a constant pace. I thought all the buildings in the vicinity must have been flattened by this time. Huge dark clouds of smoke filled the sky. Every once in a while the moon came out and with each illumination of the terrain the bombing increased.

Unable to sleep, I checked frequently on Rahim. With the pistol in my hand I went out into the yard periodically and scanned the top of the wall in case somebody was crossing over it. I was terrified of robbers and reasoned that they might take advantage of a night like this when there was no law. Once or twice I laughed at my fears and thought that when I told Saleem in the morning he would laugh at the way I had acted tonight. When the noise woke the children, I reassured them that everything would be all right in the morning.

Throughout the night I worried agonizingly about Saleem, and prayed for him and for my relatives and friends too. Scenes from the past ran and danced through my mind like a slide show. I saw my father, who had died many years before; my school friends; the funny and crazy things I had done; my students that I loved so much. As I recalled my grandmother-in-law's old saying – "When you die, your whole life passes in front of your eyes" – a cold chill ran down my spine. I thought I was close to dying and might never see the morning sunshine again. I prayed again; that was all I could do.

Whatever Saleem was doing, I hoped he was not involved in ordering these bombings and the killing of innocent people. I cried for him and prayed in a loud voice, in case God had not heard me. Then I took solace from the idea that since Saleem had not harmed a single soul in his life, nobody could raise a hand to him; God would save him. My tears poured down. Even when my face was still and calm, they fell one after the other. I cried out, "O God, you know I cannot reach him. I also do not know what the hell is going on here. Please . . . please, God, help him. I know he is somewhere out there in the middle of all these fires. God, do not let him kill anybody; just help him!" I even remember asking the souls of my father and my father-in-law to help Saleem.

There was no end to my prayers. After all, God was the only one I could reach.

During my last check of the yard I noticed that the Asmai mountaintops were becoming visible in the early dawn. The mullah's voice, weak and tremulous, came from the loudspeakers of the nearby mosque: "Allah-u-akbar" – God is great – "Allah-u-akbar . . ." It was hardly audible, and with the explosions that followed nearby, I ran inside the house and did not hear the rest. He had probably left the *azan* (prayers) half done.

FRIDAY, APRIL 28, 1978 (SAUR 8, 1357)

The sun was barely up when, exhausted, I fell asleep. I got up around ten in the morning, aroused by the roar of huge planes bombing the Rishkhor Army Qishla (brigade) at Darul Aman, which was a couple of miles west of our house. I assumed that the new regime had lots of trouble with the soldiers who had not accepted the new government. Large planes full of rockets were heading toward the base, releasing their load in the sky above our house. My children were out on the front deck watching the low-flying planes. When I looked carefully, I saw that first there was a shock in the plane itself, then the two released rockets would head toward the military base with a whistling sound. When they hit, columns of fire and smoke would rise high in the air.

My neighbor raised his head over the wall between our yards and asked if I had slept last night. My swollen, red eyes probably gave him the answer. Soon his servant came out with a tray of hot fresh-baked cookies and a kettle of hot milk for our breakfast, which he handed to one of my sons over the wall. I was deeply impressed by their thoughtfulness and felt assured that if anything happened I could trust them.

The roads remained closed and nobody was on the streets. No outside communication was possible, except for the frequent radio announcement that the new government was in complete control and the enemies of Khalq had been destroyed. But it was not explained why the bombing continued all over the city if the country was indeed totally under control. Finally there was an elaboration: "For the first time in the history of Afghanistan the last remnants of monarchy, tyranny, despotism, and the power of the dynasty of the tyrant Nadir Khan has ended and all powers of the state are in the hands of the people of Afghanistan. The power of state rests fully with the Revolutionary Council of the armed forces. Dear compatriots: Your popular state, which is in the hands of the Council of the Revolution, informs you that every antirevolutionary element who would venture to defy the instructions of the Revolution shall be submitted immediately to the revolutionary military centers."

My brother Jaan walked over to see how the family was holding up and a few minutes later my brother-in-law Khalid arrived. I told them that Saleem had not returned. Khalid said that Yosuf and his two cousins, who were also in the armed forces, had not come home since yesterday.

It was now nearly five o'clock and Khalid thought we might be able to drive on side streets, so I asked Jaan to drive me to the two military bases where Saleem and Yosuf were stationed. We could not get very far, though, because all the roads were barricaded. At almost every intersection cars were being stopped and carefully checked. Large convoys slowed the traffic to a crawl. After several attempts we arrived at the road that led to the Qargha Military Base, where Yosuf worked. An ill-mannered army captain stopped the car and asked who we were looking for. Before we could answer, he added, "Are they trained in Russia?" Nodding his head vigorously: "Well, if they were, they are certainly safe and will come home as soon as conditions return to normal."

My mouth dried to the point that my tongue could not moisten my lips. I felt nauseated and a severe pain convulsed my stomach. This was not good news. My husband was trained in the United States, not in Russia. It was so unfair to judge people by the country they were trained in! Afghanistan was a nonaligned country and sent students all over the world.

Anyway, we were not allowed to contact them or get close to their bases. It was getting late in the afternoon and all our efforts had failed, so we returned home. Jaan and Khalid left before dark. I knew there was another long night ahead of me.

Curfew began, and along with it the gunfire intensified. The evening radio announced that everything was under control and all employees must report to their offices early Saturday morning, including ministers and cabinet members of the old regime.

SATURDAY, APRIL 29, 1978 (SAUR 9, 1357)

At about eight the next morning the university bus arrived, five minutes later than usual. I told Rahim not to send the boys to school that day, and Omar and Ali both happily accepted my decision.

As I entered the school, the hall looked normal, except that the two big portraits of President Daoud which hung there had apparently been stoned. The glass and frames were broken. Several of my colleagues were standing around happy and smiling because Daoud's government had been overthrown. A large number of others, however, were very skeptical. I learned that most of their friends and relatives who were in the army or the air force had not returned home, and this news gave me the comfort that I needed to get through the day.

Like some of my colleagues, I was happy initially because of the change in government. I hoped that the new regime might be able to serve better our nation which had had so many setbacks in the past. A government based on the power of people who were selected from various sectors of society and had experienced lots of difficulties in life would understand the nation better and would work harder in its behalf.

At the ten o'clock tea break the custodian, Ahmad, brought a pot of tea to my office as usual and I sent him to buy cookies to serve to the four other faculty members with me at that time. He returned in a few minutes with the cookies and poured tea for everyone. We chatted happily for a few moments. I'd hardly had my first sip when Mariam, my brother-in-law Yosuf's wife, who also worked in the Faculty of Science, entered the room. Her expression told me something was very wrong. I invited her in, but when she insisted on seeing me in private, I apologized to my friends and left the room, filled with anxiety. Mariam said, "Yonus is standing outside. He has some bad news from a friend named Akbar who was on a mission Thursday night at the air force base where Saleem was."

She tried hard to make things easy for me but I was in no mood for her attempts at soothing sentences. "Okay, okay. Please, cut it short! Then what had happened?" I asked, suddenly angry.

"Akbar saw several armed soldiers forcing Saleem into a tank. Saleem was resisting. All of his insignia had been removed."

"What? What did you say?" I cried abruptly.

Mariam caught her breath, then continued, "Akbar also mentioned that after they finally forced Saleem into the tank, he looked at Akbar and gave him a sad smile." She paused for a moment. "Akbar asked us to get help for Saleem as soon as possible. There is no law. It's a hell out there!"

For some time I simply could not comprehend what Mariam was telling me. My heart pounded until I thought it would burst. As the hall began to spin, I lost all track of time and place. I asked Mariam what to do.

I entered my office and told my friends that I had to leave. They knew from my expression that I had received some very bad news and they asked if I needed any help. But I shook my head no and left the university in a hurry to meet Yonus, who was waiting by the outside door. He stood there with his familiar bicycle, his eyes full of tears. He repeated the story that Mariam had told me. It was as if I were deaf; I could not hear Yonus's voice. I knew that we had to rush to help Saleem, but I didn't know how. My only hope was to get advice from someone who had served in the army, who had more experience and knowledge. Uncle Jawad immediately came to mind.

I stopped a taxi and Mariam and I jumped in as Yonus forced his bike into the trunk. Then we all drove to Uncle Jawad's house. Uncle Jawad had always been a good man, experienced and full of advice. Saleem loved him very much. Whenever Uncle needed help, Saleem always assisted him with great joy and respect. He was a retired army officer and lived by himself on a farm outside the city. I was counting on him a great deal.

As soon as we entered Uncle Jawad's house, his face turned dark with anger and fear. It seemed that Yonus had already contacted him and I didn't know it. Jawad turned his face toward Yonus, trying to keep me from seeing it, and asked, "Why did you bring her here? What can I do?" Although I was standing in the far corner of the room, I heard what he said and I felt insulted and very disappointed. Then he came to me and, taking my arm, said, "Let's go out there; it's safer."

I was stunned. Things were happening too fast and unpredictably; my brain was not able to grasp it all. We stood under a cherry tree in blossom and Uncle said he was unable to help me because he didn't know any of the people in the new regime. He added that I should know them better than he because I worked at the university.

In a broken voice I asked him, "Could you show me a way to reach Saleem? Or do you suggest that I should see somebody in the higher ranks? If so, who?"

Uncle Jawad responded without hesitation, "I'm sorry; I don't know what to say."

Wordlessly I walked off and headed for home. I was in such a state of shock and I didn't know what Yonus and Mariam did, whether they left with me or not. I don't know how or when I arrived at home. My body was numb, without any awareness of passing time. I was like a piece of paper floating and drifting in the passing winds.

I came out of this state when I reached my bed and started crying. I cried from being so helpless. I remember jumping out of bed several times, putting on my shoes, and then slipping back into bed thinking that the plan I had just conceived wouldn't work. Then I would start all over again, trying to think of something else to do. Finally after some time I jumped out of bed and got the car out of garage. I told Rahim, "I'll be back soon. Give the children their dinner." Rahim was very surprised by the way I was acting but I had nothing to say. I pressed the accelerator and told him to lock the garage door.

I headed out for Saleem's base, which was at the far end of the city. The roads were still blocked and heavily guarded. It was impossible to get through on the Puli-Baghi Umomi Road, so I made a U-turn and tried the other road, which came from the Shahr-i-Naw area and ran toward the presidential palace, the Arg. In front of the main entrance of the palace stood several tanks, completely destroyed. This main road leading to the palace was full of deep potholes made by exploded shells. The windows of the Kabul Hotel, the Khyber Restaurant, and the Ministry of Communications were entirely blown out and half of the ministry building was gone. The road was blocked with piles of bricks and concrete. Half a block down the street, the Ariana Tourism Information Center, next to the Kabul Hotel, was also badly damaged. The iron frames of its windows were bare and covered with soot, a reminder of the rocket attacks of the previous night. It was impossible to cross this road, so I circled the area and headed for the Mohammed Jan Khan Road, several blocks farther on, and once again for the air force base, praying that this road would be open.

I was not myself at all. I was aware that what was happening was real, but real only in the way one reads a novel. I was stopped many times by soldiers who inspected the inside and the trunk of my car. Somehow, through some small streets that I had never seen before, I came to the Bibi Mahro Road, which ran past the American embassy and the Kabul Radio-Television station. This road led to my destination, the Khoja Rawash Air Force Base, as well as to the Kabul airport. It was heavily guarded with tanks. All army personnel were armed and ready for action, and among the tanks were a few civilians equipped with machine guns. No matter how many roads I tried that day, I always encountered soldiers who blocked the main road leading to the base. I was not concerned with my own safety; my only goal was to reach Saleem's office.

After three hours of driving in circles it seemed hopeless. I was getting nowhere, so I headed back home before curfew. Home at last. Rahim ran and opened the garage door. Oh God, mentally and physically I was prostrate. Rahim said that we had many guests and he had served them tea. I nodded and asked if he could make some fresh tea for me as well.

I stood silently by the garage door a few minutes to catch my breath and calm down before facing my relatives. I wasn't expecting them or ready to meet with them. Nor did I know how they had been informed – perhaps Yonus and Mariam had told them. When I stepped inside, practically everybody was there waiting for me. My sisters, brothers, in-laws, and their families entirely filled the two large rooms. My daughter, Sahar, was playing outside happily, unaware of what was going on. Omar and Ali were among the guests, knowing that something was very wrong. I watched all three of them quietly for a few moments. I prayed to God to grant me the strength I needed so desperately at that very moment.

As soon as I entered the room all conversation stopped. Everyone's eyes were fixed on me. I almost broke into tears, but I pulled myself together and told them with a sad smile that it was too early to come to any conclusions. I added that I simply didn't know much at the moment. I went around the room and greeted each one of them individually. I knew that if I showed the slightest trace of the turmoil inside me, everybody would break out crying, especially my mother and my mother-in-law, whose wailing would be audible miles away. What the outcome would be and how it would affect my children I didn't know, but certainly it would hurt them very badly. So, for their sake, I attempted to be strong as a rock. My actions calmed everyone. I was scared to death, though, wondering how much longer my contrived confidence could possibly last.

Rahim brought my tea. After a short while most of the guests left except for my closest relatives. They thought I should not be left alone. Night came and the curfew began. We all sat quietly. There seemed to be nothing to talk about. Everybody gazed at the TV or listened to the radio. I didn't know what was going on in the kitchen, but Rahim was there doing his best. I did not feel hungry, even though I had not eaten since breakfast. At dinner I reluctantly joined the guests. I couldn't swallow a single morsel of food; my throat felt swollen shut. I couldn't stop thinking about Saleem. It seemed that the parts of my body were separate – my hands, my lips, my ears, my legs, my eyes simply would not function together. I felt myself drowning deeper and deeper in a vast ocean of hopelessness.

An hour after dinner I excused myself and went to bed. Before I left the room, I was very careful not to spoil the evening by any foolish actions. I forced myself to act normal. I kissed my children good night as usual and told Rahim to arrange for everybody's bed. The guests slept all over the house, on the floor, on benches, or any other place they found to be comfortable.

As I lay down, I felt that there were thousands of miles between my husband and me. What a drastic change! Just three short nights ago he was right beside me; now I could not reach him. It made me even more angry and depressed. I wanted to sleep but couldn't. I lay staring at the ceiling for hour after hour. It was one of the longest and most difficult nights of my life.

Hours passed in the darkness. Whenever I heard the roar of a jeep, I would sit up, hoping it was Saleem's car returning home. As soon as the car passed, my hopes died. More than a hundred cars passed and I lost count. Every time my reactions were the same: hope, prayers, and happiness mounted at the rumble of the approaching car, then misery returned as the noise faded away. I don't know how long I lay there languishing in this condition. I don't know whether I slept or not. Around four in the morning I jumped out of my bed as if it were on fire. In this cool spring morning I was hot and perspiring; my clothes were soaked. I needed some fresh air, so I carefully tiptoed through the two long hallways and out onto the front terrace. I begged God to help Saleem wherever he might be. I prayed, "O God! I can't lose him. Please, God, give me a chance to tell him how much I love him."

Somehow the cool, fresh air made me feel better. I returned to my room and slept the rest of the night.

SUNDAY, APRIL 30, 1978 (SAUR 10, 1357)

As I opened my eyes, my troubles came crashing in on me. Today I did not want to wake up. I wished to remain asleep all my life if Saleem did not return home. I remembered a song I had heard years before in America: "Make the world go away."

I stayed in bed for some time, turning from side to side, planning what to do and where to look for Saleem, thinking what strategies I should employ and where to begin. I had a class to teach; yesterday they had announced that all employees should be at work. We were afraid to miss work. As I washed my face, I looked into the mirror and saw that my eyes were red and swollen, so I put on sunglasses.

I left for the university without breakfast. Two friends from yesterday's tea break were waiting at the front stairway and asked if there was anything they could do for me. Their offer seemed completely sincere. I thought to myself, however, that there was nothing they could do, so, feeling very despondent, I smiled, thanked them, and assured them that if I needed anything, I would let them know. We walked to the main office where the daily attendance book was kept. Everyone had to sign the book in the morning. For the last two days all the employees had signed the book as early as possible. I believed the government wanted to make sure that none of the personnel were involved in antigovernment actions, at least during work hours. There was still oppositions to the new regime. Gunfire could still be heard all day long and it increased at night.

During the morning I controlled myself quite well and tried to act as normal as possible, but around noon I decided to visit two of my colleagues, Sooma and Hashimi, who were assigned to the Central Bureau Committee as members of the Politburo in the new regime. I knew them very well since we had worked together in the same department for more than ten years. Efforts to locate them were useless, however, so in the evening my brother Jaan and I headed for the part of the city where they lived. I didn't know their exact addresses and Jaan and I walked up and down the roads for hours before finally finding Sooma's residence, only to learn that he was not there.

My nightmare was becoming a reality. The dream that woke me shivering in the middle of the night a few nights ago now totally surrounded me. My present situation was exactly the same: if I shout, nobody will hear; if I scream, no one will help. Out of great desperation, I thought of Uncle Jawad again. Trying to ignore his actions of two days ago, I decided to see him one more time, the next morning before classes.

MONDAY, MAY I, 1978 (SAUR II, 1357)

Praying to God that he would send me in the right direction this time, I entered Uncle Jawad's house. He was taking a nap in the early-morning sun on a bench in his backyard. The weather was still cool. The spring sun, mixed with the fragrance of the April blossoms of the few cherry trees in his backyard felt soothing to my nerves. As I walked toward him I said, "Salaam!"

He answered my greeting in a low voice, then said nothing for several long minutes, pretending to read the morning newspaper, which I thought was an insultingly rude gesture. I sat quietly for a few minutes, feeling deeply offended and cursing myself for not having known better than to come here. Without a word I stood up and started to leave. Only then did he say, "How are the boys?"

"All right, doing okay."

"I don't know what to tell you. Please try to use the back door after this; I don't want anyone to see you coming here." As he pointed toward the door onto the back alley, I left, disappointed and very hurt. I was feeling very sorry for us. My husband and I had always assumed that we had some really good friends who would help us at any time. But now times had changed. People were running from me as if I were a symbol of death. How badly I wished Saleem were here. I wanted him to see Uncle Jawad's behavior – the uncle he always counted on.

TUESDAY, MAY 2, 1978 (SAUR 12, 1357)

On the fifth day of what was called the bloody April coup, after all my efforts to find Saleem had failed, my sister Mizhgan came and suggested that we should go and ask help from Mahbooba, Babrak Karmal's wife. Mizhgan knew Mahbooba from her school days. The Karmals lived in the Sara-i-Ghazni neighborhood just a couple of blocks from our house. Babrak Karmal was second in command in the Revolutionary Council of the People's Democratic Party of Afghanistan, which was now in power. When we got to his house, we saw a huge crowd standing in front of it. Several military jeeps, a tank, and half a dozen military men, all equipped with weapons, were guarding the small, dilapidated garage door.

My sister and I, after being searched for weapons in the front yard, entered the hall. All the rooms that opened off the hall were full of visitors. When Mahbooba saw us, she came forward, greeted us warmly, and led us into the main living room. My sister whispered, "She hasn't changed a bit."

Everyone in the room seemed happy and was talking of the day's events. A few minutes later when there was a lull in the conversation, one of Karmal's cousins, very proud of the Communist coup and of being a relative of Babrak's, asked my sister loudly and sarcastically, "Are you still working at the American embassy, or do you want to work with us now?" My sister replied, "Yes, I am still working for the CIA – I think that is what you are trying to say. And, for your information, I do not have any intention of changing my job at the present time!"

Mahbooba and all the guests laughed. Babrak's cousin remained silent after that. When we had drunk a cup of tea and were ready to leave, Mahbooba came with us into the hall, where Mizhgan told her of my husband's disappearance. She took Saleem's name and address and promised to ask around and find out about my husband as soon as possible. We all agreed that it would probably take her two to three days to inquire into the matter and Mahbooba told Mizhgan to see her on May 6 late in the afternoon.

WEDNESDAY, MAY 3, 1978 (SAUR 13, 1357)

Jaan and I again went to Sooma's house but again he was not home. Jaan entered the men's parlor and I went to the room where Sooma's wife was. She was breastfeeding her child. She was one of those housewives whom I always admired because of their hospitality and simple direct-ness. As she listened to my story she tried to cheer me up and said, "I don't know why a father" – she meant my husband – "should be kept away from his children."

I don't know whether she was educated or not. The way she dressed and talked convinced me that she didn't know much about what was happening around her. A young girl brought us a tray of cups and some tea, but I wasn't in the mood to drink tea or to stay longer, so I excused myself and said I would be back in an hour. As I walked through the front yard I noticed that men were going in and out of another room. I saw a few familiar faces but most I didn't recognize. A big white cloth, probably six by fifteen feet, was spread on the floor and a huge crowd of male guests were sitting around it eating from many large platters full of pilau, our special rice and meat dish.

Jaan and I passed half an hour driving up and down the streets and I returned to Sooma's house. He was home this time. When he heard my story he replied that many people had been killed at that air base and he assumed that Saleem was one of them. His words hit my brain like a hammer. I nearly broke into tears but I controlled myself and asked him to give me the truth, hard facts, not his assumptions. Sooma looked at me sharply and with surprise, probably expecting more respect due to his new status as a leader in the triumphant party. I was very tired of the whole situation and could not have cared less about showing respect.

During the few moments of his silence I said again in a tone more like an order than a request, "Sooma, what you say is all guesswork. I want to know exactly what did happen in that specific area of the Khoja Rawash Air Force Base where Saleem worked."

Sooma promised that he would ask his friends who had been there. And he would give me the facts if I'd meet him around ten in the morning in his office. Sooma, besides being a member of the Central Committee, had also been appointed minister of higher education. Leaving him, I walked past his numerous bodyguards, who were standing in the yard heavily armed, and returned home, empty-handed as usual. I was very depressed by Sooma's comments but still hoped for the best. Perhaps I would hear something good tomorrow.

A couple of nights before, Noor Mohammad Taraki had been named president and prime minister of the nation and chairman of the Central Committee of the People's Democratic Party in the new regime. In his first public address he promised that he would follow a policy of "active positive neutrality" and free government. Reminding myself of his promise, I thought, "If all this is true, then nothing will happen to Saleem."

THURSDAY, MAY 4, 1978 (SAUR 14, 1357)

When I arrived at the university the next morning, I noticed that the students were standing around outside. Classes had been dismissed and everyone was ordered to go to the lawn in front of the central administration building, where Sooma would address them before assuming his position as minister of higher education. Sooma arrived at about nine-thirty, dressed in a very odd-looking light blue suit that did not fit him properly and had probably been bought at a thrift shop. He was surrounded by a large group of chapaloossan (flatterers) who escorted him, almost carrying him on their arms, to a dais that was decorated much like a stage and had a small podium and a microphone. He looked worried and distracted. Ten minutes passed but still he did not begin. Soon a few people around him began to whisper. The whispering continued for some time; then I heard a friend's voice shouting and laughing out loud, "Look there! See what's happening!" He pointed to the dais.

The people around the dais scurried this way and that, apparently not knowing what to do. Then, with no announcement whatsoever, Sooma was led away by the same charlatans who had brought him in, and in the same way. The crowd stared at them intently, not knowing what was going on.

I knew Sooma very well; after all, we had worked in the same department since 1967. He was a hard-working person who always complained of poverty, although his paychecks were bigger than mine because he had worked a few years more than I had. I never found any grounds for his complaint, but I knew it was a policy of the Communists to impress others by pretending to be poor. Now, watching those flatterers who swarmed around Sooma in a wave of enthusiasm, I impatiently shouted, "For heaven's sake, let him walk! He is used to walking for miles!" The people around me laughed.

The crowd was all as confused as I was by these strange goings-on. Finally we all laughed, but we knew that something was definitely wrong. Rumors came back very quickly that someone had threatened to kill Sooma, so his speech had been canceled.

At ten-thirty I headed for Sooma's new office, which had once been the university rector's. A crowd of people had lined up outside waiting to congratulate him on his new position. I paid no attention to the line but went directly into the outer office. Some fifteen or twenty army officers, each heavily armed, blocked the entrance to Sooma's private office. One of them came forward to see what I wanted, and I asked him to tell Sooma that I was here to see him. He returned quickly with a message from Sooma saying that my husband had been with Rasouli (the recently executed minister of defense). They were both killed at the same site.

Involuntarily I cried out, "That's a lie – a big stupid total lie!" I knew that Saleem couldn't have been with Rasouli because they worked in different areas, something Sooma did not know. My words resounded through the small room. There was a sudden silence; people stopped talking. "Go and tell Sooma that I want to see him personally," I demanded. "Right now!" The officer went back into Sooma's office. I don't know what he said, but this time Sooma told him to let me in.

As I started toward Sooma's room, an army colonel stopped me and asked if I had any weapons on me. He actually searched my clothing and then tried to open my purse, which was still hanging from my shoulder. His act humiliated and sickened me. I removed the purse from my shoulder and threw it on a table in a far corner. It struck the corner of a secretary's desk with a thud, making her scream as papers and pens scattered in every direction. I had never been searched in my own country before; no one could doubt my family's allegiance to our country! Entering Sooma's office, I turned and said, "Damn it! If I want to kill Sooma I will find a better place than this. No, not in front of you!" "In fact," I added, "I should have killed him ten years ago!"

I was not the least afraid of the consequences. I walked straight to Sooma's desk. It was exceptionally shiny today, so shiny it reflected his image. The reflection looked so real that it seemed Sooma had been born with two heads. Sooma's office was full of visitors, most of whom I knew. They sat in a large circle against the walls. Ignoring the crowd, I approached Sooma and sat down in the empty chair opposite him. A silence fell over the room because most of the people knew me and had probably heard about my problems. Without my saying a word, Sooma changed his story: "I am very sorry that your husband was shot in the back as he was running out of his office during the attack on Khoja Rawash."

I looked straight into Sooma's eyes for a few moments while the room remained hushed and everyone strained to hear our conversation. In a low, sad, but strong voice I said, shaking my head in sorrow, "Sooma, I can accept the facts of life and death. If this is truly the case, I want my husband's body now."

Sooma looked surprised and started stammering. He was probably waiting to see me cry but there was not a single tear in my eyes. I was hard as a rock. His voice was heard saying, "Well . . . well, that I do not know. Let me talk to Abdul Qadir [the head of the Military Revolutionary Council]."

I stood up, strong and determined, and shook hands with him. With all the strength I could muster I told him, "Sooma, I want to be the first to congratulate you. I am very sorry that my husband is not here today with me. I am sure that if he were, he would do the same thing. He too came from a very poor but proud family – came a long way – and would certainly have been very happy to see any regime that would promise a brighter future for his countrymen." Sooma did not say a word. I closed my eyes for a moment, paused briefly, and continued, "I am sorry that I am doing this all by myself now."

My sadness, determination, and calm voice shook Sooma a great deal. He rose to his feet. With him, everyone else in the room stood as I left. Sooma even escorted me to the door with great respect, a very unusual gesture for one in his position. The officer I had yelled at was astonished to see Sooma with me at the door and the crowd standing. He quickly pulled himself together and opened the door for me, then brought me the purse I had thrown on the table a few minutes earlier.

As I passed the crowd outside the office, those who knew me asked what had happened. I couldn't answer them, my throat was so dry. But my face told them that the news was bad. One of my close friends left the line and grabbed my arm as I tried to get away from there. He followed me until we reached a bench outside on the lawn. Tears began to flow; I still could not talk.

As I gradually calmed down, I told him of the two different versions of Saleem's disappearance. My friend observed that Rasouli had been killed miles from the air force base where Saleem worked. It was obvious that Sooma didn't know the facts. My friend doubted that he'd had a chance to ask anyone about my husband at this time when nobody knew what was going on.

As we sat there on the bench Mariam came by. I told her what Sooma had told me. She suggested that we go and see Abdul Qadir; he might be able to tell us the truth. After all, he was supposed to have been involved with all the happenings at Khoja Rawash Air Force Base. Now, like Sooma, he was a member of the Central Committee. Mariam knew Qadir's home address. Without much thought, and in desperation, I agreed to go to his house. But Qadir was not home. His doors were locked; his house looked deserted and empty; there were no armed guards in sight.

I called Yosuf at his office and told him what I had heard from Sooma. He said he would go immediately and ask someone he knew who might know the facts. In the meantime I was to wait for him at his house. By now I needed time to think, and I did not want to go home in my present condition and face my children, who were waiting impatiently for news of their father. I didn't have any answers and didn't know what to tell them. All I knew were bits and pieces of contradictory stories, all of which were probably wrong. I'd have preferred the truth, no matter how bad it was. My present situation was worse than physical torture. So I went to Yosuf's house and waited for him.

Yosuf returned after some time. Choking back his tears, he told me that Saleem had been killed. I was horrified. My head felt like it would explode from the pressure. Everyone in the room was crying except Jaan and me. Mariam brought me something to drink but I wasn't thirsty. I had eaten nothing since morning and my stomach was in pain. I felt like throwing up. My throat constricted until I thought I would choke. My world was dead. My hopes were gone. I felt as if I were burning in a fire.

It was getting late and my children were waiting for me. I asked Jaan to drive me home. On the way, he kept trying to sort things out for me. He cautioned me not to judge on mere rumors, noting that both of Sooma's stories had been unrealistic, and said we ought to wait for an official proclamation. Nevertheless, I had lost hope even though I could not accept the fact that Saleem was dead. I thought again and again,

"Why, why him? He did nothing wrong. He was not in any political group. He was completely innocent. He never hurt anyone. Why him?"

Wiping away my tears, I went into the house and saw that the children were playing in the backyard. Mother, who was waiting with others in the living room, could tell everything by merely looking at me. Unable to face them, I fled to the bedroom. I heard Jaan giving the others an explanation. Entering our bedroom was one of the hardest moments of my life. I was very scared to enter our bedroom that day. Every corner of our room carried his memories. His clothing – the new air force uniforms and his more than half a dozen shiny shoes, ready to wear – were all staring at me from the half-opened closet door. I remembered how many times I had complained to Saleem that his air force uniforms with all their insignia and medals were snagging my clothes! Today those clothes were mocking me, as if telling me, "Have it your way now!" His Holy Koran, wrapped in expensive material, still lay on the *jaa-e-namazz* (prayer rug).

As my world spun around me, I sat on the corner of our bed, hiding my eyes from the things that were dancing in front of me. I don't know how long I sat there before I heard Jaan calling me. Word had spread fast and many relatives had come to offer their sympathy. It was nice of them, but I honestly wanted some time to collect my thoughts and decide what and how to tell my children. I washed my face with cold water and went into the living room, which was full of guests. After greeting all of them, I sat with my head bowed, just nodding at the words they were saying to assuage my grief, words I was not really hearing at all.

At one point my husband's cousin came in and told me that under the martial law then in effect we were not allowed to have a large crowd gathered at our house and we must tell the guests to leave. I said, "How can I tell them to leave? No, I can't. And I don't care anymore what the government thinks!" Yosuf heard my angry voice and came to my rescue. He asked the guests politely to go home. Unfortunately, however, he failed to explain to them why, and some were very offended.

Now that only my closest friends and relatives were left, I gave my brother some money to buy sugar, oil, cream of wheat, and fresh-baked nan, the ingredients for *halwa*, the special dish for such an occasion. The survivors must feed the poor and pray to God to give his *sawab* (blessing) to the deceased one. Indeed, all my actions were based on the fact that I had accepted Sooma's words.

I cooked the sweet dish myself, in spite of offers of help from others. But I didn't dare to taste it while it was cooking; I simply couldn't. My tears poured down even as I tried to hide them from others. I thought I should be strong and calm for my children and for the sake of my poor mother-in-law, whose hands were trembling today more than ever before.

My children came in and began to eat, not knowing what was going on. I was not sure whether to tell them about their father or to wait as my brother had suggested. Some more friends and a few relatives, including Uncle Jawad and our friend Mudere Sahib, arrived. I was very surprised to see Uncle Jawad at my house after what he had said to me; I think he could not deny his relationship to my husband and I was sure he loved him. The living room was again almost full, and Rahim, along with Rahmat, our gardener, whom I had asked to help Rahim that day, was busy serving refreshments to everyone.

Faces were long and sad. I was at a loss myself, so I sat among the guests very quietly, buried in my thoughts. I still heard my brother and my brother-in-law repeating Sooma's words in whispers as some of the visitors nodded their heads and looked at me with a pitying expression. I had always hated being the object of pity. I didn't want them to feel sorry for me; my sorrow was only for Saleem. The children had by this time sensed that something was very wrong and were asking my brother to tell them what was happening. But they were not told. There was no reason to upset them without confirmation of Saleem's death.

Around six o'clock, when the evening star, which is famous as the "shepherd's star," was blinking in the western sky, my brother called me into the hall to ask if I would talk to a stranger who had come to see me. I excused myself from the guests and noticed a short man with black hair, a bit on the heavy side and probably in his late thirties. He introduced himself as Colonel Hameed and, taking my hand, held it firmly. I looked into his eyes and asked him indifferently, "What can I do for you?"

Colonel Hameed burst out, "I have come here to tell you that Saleem is alive and very well, and is breathing this fresh air just as you are."

I looked at Jaan. He shrugged his shoulders. I looked again at Hameed, who caught his breath and continued, "They are keeping him in a tent at the Ministry of Interior until things calm down."

"When will be that?" I asked quickly.

"Possibly in the next two or three days," Hameed replied. He paused for a moment and added, "I saw Saleem last night sitting there and thinking, with his cap on his knees. I put my head in his tent and said as a joke, 'Well, who has brought you here to this chicken house?' Since I know Saleem well, I asked him if he needed any money or anything else, but he said he didn't. He just asked me to tell his family he's okay. That's why I'm here tonight."

I stared at him in disbelief, unable to accept a single word. Especially after the interview with Sooma, acceptance of any other news was impossible. Hameed stayed and talked for almost an hour until most of the guests were gone. He swore by God and all the holy places he knew of that he was telling the truth. When I asked him how he had found my house he answered that Saleem had given him the address. Still, I observed that Hameed for some reason did not want to be seen by the guests and stayed outside in a shadow of the house the whole time. And as soon as Uncle Jawad heard that someone we didn't know was there, he left in a great hurry. When all guests were gone, I took Hameed inside the house where Mother was. He repeated his long story to the rest of my family and seemed unwilling to leave. He was so persuasive that I was finally beginning to believe him.

I looked at my watch; the curfew was close. I wanted to give this good news to my close relatives who had left in great sorrow half an hour earlier. Leaving Hameed with Mother and the others, Jaan and I headed for my in-laws' houses. Since the phones were still out of commission, I had to give the message in person. I went first to Yonus's house. As I entered, I saw him weeping with my husband's picture in front of him. I gave him a hug and told him not to cry: "Saleem is all right after all!" He looked puzzled as Jaan gave him Hameed's news. Happy and laughing, we left his house to see Yosuf, who lived on the opposite side of town.

Jaan drove the car like crazy as we rushed toward the Shahr-i-Naw area. We hadn't laughed in the past week, and now we both laughed uproariously over the recent events like two insane people running away from a mental hospital and making fun of the doctors. When we reached Yosuf's house, we went in and told them of the latest development, then left in a hurry to beat the curfew, which was only twenty minutes away.

Halfway home, twelve minutes before the start of the curfew, we were stopped in front of Kabul municipal detention center by a soldier carrying a Russian rifle. He pointed it at us as he released the safety. His booming voice was easily heard behind the closed windows of the car: "Halt!" He searched the car, then told us to turn it around, pointing to the jail's entrance gate.

"Why?" I asked.

"It's curfew time," he responded firmly.

"There's still ten minutes to go," I insisted.

"No, turn your car around and go inside until the curfew is over in the morning."

This was the last thing I needed to hear. My brother whispered, "If we go in, no one will know we're here; they won't allow us to communicate with anyone outside. And it'll take months to get our case before a judge. There'll be a long waiting line."

I didn't know what to do. The soldier's orders sounded final and he still had his rifle pointed at us. One last time I tried to talk him out of it: "Listen, my children are waiting for me at home. There's still ten minutes left. If you don't believe me, please go and ask someone up there." I pointed toward the gate, where a few other soldiers were standing about, but our captor would not relent.

Jaan again whispered, "I'm not going in there. It'd be signing our death warrant." Then: "When I step on the gas, duck your head under the dashboard!"

The soldier saw our hesitation, pulled up his gun, and made the gesture of shooting if we didn't turn the car around. I felt the cold sensation of imminent death. Suddenly the tall iron-barred gate of the prison swung open for a car to pass through. As another soldier ran to lock it behind the car Jaan shouted loudly, "Captain, please tell your friend that the curfew has not begun yet. And please let us go."

The second man – who was not a captain but apparently was flattered by the title – straightened his necktie and came closer. Looking at his watch in the headlights of our car, he said, "Amin, there's about seven minutes left. Let them go."

His heavenly voice echoed in the night. Jaan stuck his head out the window and called loudly, "God bless you!"

Without delay we drove on home, avoiding the main thoroughfares so we wouldn't be confronted by other soldiers or the tanks that blocked the major routes. Mother and my old uncle were waiting for us at the house. Uncle was actually dancing and laughing in his excitement over Hameed's news. After dinner Mother explained that Hameed left just before our return and would come back in a couple of days to keep us informed about Saleem.

That night I thought I'd been born again. There's nothing to worry about, I told myself, everything will be all right. My tortured mind was finally calm. I went to bed and slept all night, all the next day, and the following night.

During the daytime I heard guests come and go, but no matter how many times my mother-in-law called me to wake up and greet them, I could not do so. I hovered somewhere between the conscious and unconscious worlds. I tried to get up but I couldn't; I tried to move but I simply couldn't. This was the second time in my life that I had slept like this for so many hours without food or drink. The first time was when I finished my graduate degree at Auburn University. I slept for twenty-four hours on a Greyhound bus on my way back to Illinois, where Saleem and my two sons were. An old man sitting next to me wanted to talk. He kept on talking for hours, but my brain was asleep. Although I could hear him clearly, I could not respond at all.

SATURDAY, MAY 6, 1978 (SAUR 16, 1357)

I got up in the morning feeling very hungry. When I stepped on the bathroom scale I saw that I had lost almost fifteen pounds in the past ten days.

Later my mother-in-law said that some of the guests who'd come the day before thought I was rejecting them. They had left upset and told her they wouldn't come anymore. I could only assert that it simply wasn't true. I thought I could not possibly explain to her in terms she would understand the state I'd been in, so I let it pass. And actually, those guests never did show up again.

SATURDAY, MAY 13, 1978 (SAUR 23, 1357)

On this date I sat down and wrote up the past six days' events in my diary as follows:

On May 4 when Colonel Hameed came and told us that Saleem would be released in the next two days, we decided on the basis of his information not to complicate things further: Mahbooba should not look for my husband after all. I strongly believed that if Saleem had survived the first day of the attack on Khoja Rawash, as Hameed had said, then we had nothing to fear should his case be put to trial.

Two days passed but there was no news of Saleem. At every knock on the front door Omar and Ali ran happily to answer it, thinking this might be their father.

Hameed appeared again on May 8 and told us that Saleem would be released the following day at one o'clock. His news caused a lot of excitement around the house; even Rahim began running back and forth loudly singing his local songs from the Mazar-i-Sharif region. He had never sung before.

My joy was not less than that of the others, and I started cleaning house, washing clothes, and making Saleem's favorite dish, storing it in the refrigerator. Then I went to Naqash, a marketplace outside the city where farmers brought their herds of goats, sheep, cows, and even old or injured camels for sale. There I selected two fat-tailed sheep for 4,080 afghanis ($80). I wanted to invite everyone for a celebration when Saleem came home. In fact, I wanted the whole world to share in my joy!

Rahim tied the sheep in a corner of the backyard and gave them fresh grass and water. The rest of the day went by almost unnoticed as we were all happily waiting for tomorrow. Well, tomorrow came. As we anxiously waited nothing whatsoever happened. With every knock at the front door my heart pounded heavily in anticipation. Minutes and hours passed – one o'clock, two o'clock, three o'clock, . . . and finally it was night. As time went by, my hopes turned to fear and I begged God to help us.

By nighttime I hated myself for becoming the object of Hameed's games and sick lies. I was very angry and constantly asked myself, "How dare he lie to us?" and "Why?" Finally I questioned myself, "Who is he, really? This man who came out of nowhere to lurk in the shadows that first night, hiding himself from my guests and bearing news of my husband?"

I calmed down my children and the friends who had heard of Saleem's impending release. They had come early on this day to see Saleem and had not left before curfew. That night I'd wrapped myself in a big shawl and sat down to listen to the seven o'clock news, when Hameed appeared at the door and asked for me. I told Rahim to let him in. Before I could say a single word, he started in: "Today they postponed the release of many people because of a crisis in the eastern part of the country." "Don't worry," he added; "Saleem will be here very soon, right there in that chair" – pointing to an empty chair next to me.

Again, expectation and good thoughts surrounded me. I felt the calm that follows a thunderstorm. I didn't really know why I trusted him again, but he always gave me hope. He left after the curfew had started, when no one was allowed on the streets. Afterwards I thought about him a great deal. I didn't know who he was or what the hell he was doing in my house. What was he gaining from it? Why did he try to keep us hopeful? I couldn't figure out his real purpose or the motivation behind it. Was he sent by the government? I didn't know.

All I remember of the succeeding days is going from place to place, visiting many people in the hope of finding my husband. I traveled many times to the military air base in Bagram in spite of the dangers involved. Rural areas were still not under control; there was still fighting in the countryside. All the major roads were barricaded and armed soldiers checked the cars and searched the occupants' pockets. If they suspected someone, they sent that person to a police detention center without further thought. Bagram Air Force Base was way outside the city of Kabul and was heavily guarded around the clock by military personnel. No matter where I went, I returned home at nights empty-handed and exhausted. My children waited all day with hope, desperate to hear any good news. But as soon as I entered the house, my tired, dejected expression told them the truth immediately. They remained silent, but when they looked at me I could feel their unspoken words. The pressure of it weighed me down. How stupidly I tried to avoid looking at them. Oh God, their dark shining eyes, their unnatural calmness, and above all their unasked questions were killing me!

Mother and the others were also waiting painfully. But they also kept silent, giving me all the time in the world that I might need to tell them of my day's search. But my God, I was utterly helpless to answer their questions. So, we would all sit quietly and sadly around the dinner table with no words to say, no hopes to cling to. Then everybody would go to their bedroom or watch TV.

THURSDAY, MAY 18, 1978 (SAUR 28, 1357)

I did not have much to say today, except that for the past five days all my inquiries and running back and forth were completely fruitless. Hameed came occasionally, but his promises were not coming true. He always showed up unexpectedly at very odd times. Now I believe that he was checking up on us, although I couldn't prove it.

So far I'd heard more than a hundred rumors, good and bad, about Saleem and others who were at Khoja Rawash. I didn't know what to believe anymore. One day my brother Khalil said, "Don't wait for Saleem. A friend of mine who worked at Khoja Rawash says that he and many others were executed the first morning after the coup." When I asked who this friend of his was, Khalil added, "He was among the ones who were supposed to be executed, but he was released at the last minute by the order of a general who was his relative." After Khalil left, I cried for a long time, thinking to myself what a giant step his friend had taken, from execution to freedom! No – his friend might be lying. Without evidence I couldn't believe anyone.

Yosuf came one day and was talking to his mother in the next room. As I entered the room, his words stopped me right at the door: "Saleem and others were all run over by a tank and then buried in a mass grave just behind their offices." Another brother-in-law, Yonus, came the next day and said, "Saleem and all the other officers were handcuffed and then were killed inside a tank." Saleem's nephew Jalil came and told us, "Saleem was escaping toward Paktia [a distant province] and was brought back to Kabul and is now in jail." I knew this last rumor was definitely wrong; Saleem would never run away. He never backed down from unpleasant truths.

One of the officers who had worked in the same place with Saleem told me that when things got bad on the day of the coup, most of the people left their offices with all sorts of excuses. But Saleem, in spite of having planned to attend a friend's funeral, canceled his plans and stayed in the office. Later, when arms were distributed for individual safety, Saleem did not take a gun, saying that he could not use it on his fellow countrymen.

Among all the heart-wrenching rumors I heard at home, at the office, and elsewhere, there were a few encouraging ones. A friend who knew someone working at the main prison, Puli-Charkhi, said that Saleem was in section two, the area where political military prisoners were held. These prisoners did not have permission to contact their families at all. When I asked how he could be sure that the person was my husband, he gave Saleem's description and also described the gold ring I had given Saleem the previous year on his thirty-seventh birthday.

There were other rumors that said that nobody was killed during the coup except for the few people whose names had been announced over the radio. I didn't believe a word of it, though; I knew that these were the rumors of the Marxists to calm the people.

I yearned to hear truth but many people repeated rumors or made up stories, heedless of my feelings. I lived and died over and over again.

SUNDAY, MAY 21, 1978 (SAUR 31, 1357)

During the first week of the new government Taraki was elected president and prime minister of the Revolutionary Council of the Democratic Republic of Afghanistan. Babrak Karmal was elected vice president and deputy premier and Hafizullah Amin was deputy prime minister and minister of foreign affairs. The Revolutionary Council was the core of government power. It was made up of twenty cabinet members, who unanimously agreed that martial law should remain in force throughout the country indefinitely. Although the government always announced that all parts of the country were under their control, there were strong indications that the three-week-old regime had still not quelled all the opposition.

In a news conference Taraki declared that Afghanistan was a nonaligned country and that his government would seek friendship from all nations, including Western countries. All the political speeches began hypocritically with the familiar words "In the name of God Almighty we begin . . ."; "In the name of God Almighty the benevolent and merciful. . . . " Taraki and other members of his government were seen on TV attending mosques – a very wise move, but it did not impress many university people. Those who knew the present leaders of Afghanistan and their ties to the Soviet Union could easily guess that this was not a nonaligned country. I think Taraki and his followers figured that an orthodox Communist regime would not be favored by Afghans, so it was important for the survival of the new government to be very careful. Such precautions did not last very long, however. Soon Taraki was collaborating with the Soviet Union, his closest ally. Decree after decree was approved by the inexperienced Central Committee members, who were still giddy with pride and joy at their easily gained positions. They were in a great hurry to make changes, forgetting the ingrained, time-tested old customs and traditions of the Afghan culture.

Every night I listened to broadcasts from outside the country, switching from the BBC to the Voice of America and to Pakistani and Indian radio stations. With great sadness I realized that the outside world, even the United States, did not react strongly to the coup. From my colleagues' comments at the university I could guess that they also were listening to those stations, but none of us dared to talk about it.

During the previous week, classes at the university and other schools had been called off almost every afternoon. The students were ordered to go to the auditoriums and listen to Marxist speeches in which Taraki was touted as the greatest leader of all time. Generally, several school days were wasted for every new decree. Most of us were tired of all the propaganda but we couldn't say a word. Disobedience to the rules or expression of our opinions had no place in the present regime.

The decrees were touted in other ways as well. Songs were written to emphasize their benefits. One of the polemicist-songwriters was Khan-i-Qara Baghi, said to be Taraki's cousin. Opening his songs with the first decree, he ran through each decree in turn. When a new decree was announced, Khan added a new stanza, so every week his songs grew longer.

Now some imported words and slogans from across the border, such as "comrades" and "Be triumphant!" were heard everywhere. Party members proudly called each other "comrade." Official letters also began with "Comrade," and ended with "Be triumphant" instead of "Sincerely" or "Respectfully" as in the past.

In mid-May a committee was appointed to assess prison conditions. According to Taraki, unjustly accused prisoners had often previously been left to die in dark, dank cells. The central Dehmazang prison and others throughout the country were inspected and their inhumane conditions greatly exaggerated in widespread publicity.

The establishment of a Revolutionary Military Court for civilian and military men who had committed crimes against the Saur Revolution, as the April coup was called, was frightening. Men and women went missing every day. Nobody knew where they were. Three professors disappeared from our school. I didn't dare ask anyone about them and no one said anything about them. We quickly learned to keep our mouths shut. There were only orders from the dean that we must take over their classes.

I saw larger and larger crowds every weekend at the Puli-Charkhi prison. This told me that the new government was enforcing its powers with state terror – by kidnapping and executing indiscriminately anyone who got in its way.

People had been invited the previous week to go and tour the palace, where President Daoud had been killed during the coup. Its doors were open for several days. I didn't go, but my colleagues told me that in the front yard of the palace were spread several carpets stained with the blood of Daoud, who had fought until the last moments of his life without surrendering. It was said that a fine silk carpet that had a large picture of Daoud was spread on the floor and people were asked to walk on it. According to the government's propaganda, Daoud-e-Dewana ("crazy Daoud") had killed all the members of his family, including his three-year-old grandchild, before he shot himself.

People peered inside the palace refrigerators and poked around the royal family's kitchen and several living rooms. I remember the day when one of our teaching assistants was talking to her friend in my office: "My God, there were 220 forks and I don't know how many spoons in the palace!" Knowing that she came from a very well-to-do family, I asked, "How many forks do you have at your home?" She stammered as I added, "Well, I have at least several dozen in my house. Don't you think a royal family should have that many?"

The sad thing was that the government's constant brainwashing propaganda did influence the educated young elites and well-to-do families. It conditioned their thoughts. Our assistant knew very well that having a large supply of silverware in one's kitchen did not impoverish the rest of Afghanistan as the Marxists claimed in those days.

A few days later I heard that the royal family's clothing was being sold on the streets. The second-hand dealers were taking advantage of the situation to advertise "Buy the lingerie of Princess ——. It was bought at the latest fashion shows in Paris!" Or "Here are the pajamas of Prince ——. They'll bring you good luck! Wear them tonight!" People swarmed around the street carts just to see what kind of stuff the sellers were offering. Some laughed, others just shook their heads and left.

The wreckage of the tanks outside the palace contained charred bones, the remains of soldiers who had fought Daoud's forces. One man's heavily smoked intestine hung high in the branches of a tree next to a tank. These soldiers were, of course, considered the heroes of the Saur Revolution. Nadiria High School, which was originally named after the former king Nadir Shah, now became Martyr Omar's High School. Omar must have been one of the burned tank heroes.

Radio announcements claimed that very few had been killed during the first few days of the coup. Rumor, however, had it that during the first twenty-four hours more than four hundred loyal presidential guards were killed at the presidential palace alone.

SATURDAY, JUNE 10, 1978 (JAWZA 20, 1357)

Three new decrees, the first two concerning the selection of Revolutionary Council members and the third one the military court, were repeated hour after hour, day and night, on radio, TV, and even at the school assemblies. But still the new regime refused to release any information as to Saleem's whereabouts. It seemed that he was a forgotten case, as if he had never existed. Most often, when I asked an official about Saleem, he would give me a dirty look, one that made me freeze for a second. I was treated like an antirevolutionary, with no rights at all.

On weekends (Fridays) I unfailingly joined the mass of people taking clean clothes, food, and other supplies to relatives who were thought to be imprisoned at Puli-Charkhi. I always tried to be among the first few in a very long line of people who were waiting there. The line increased throughout the day, and as time went on, it seemed that there was no end to this infinite queue of worried and miserable human beings. When the gate opened at eight in the morning, we each gave our package to the man in charge to be passed along to the intended recipient. Then we waited for a response. For some a note came back from their beloved one, along with dirty clothing to be washed and returned. For others, the package was kept for hours and then was returned with the simple comment "He is not here." I always hoped that someday they would give my package to Saleem.

The first few weeks after the coup, most of the visitors to the prison were from educated, well-to-do families; I could easily tell from the way they talked and dressed. But later all sorts of men and women from every sect and group of society could be seen: rich, poor, educated, nomads, Uzbeks, Hazaras, Kabulis, Kandaharis – almost every ethnic group of the country was represented.

MONDAY, JUNE 12, 1978 (JAWZA 22, 1357)

In Afghanistan, kinship and friendship ties are very strong. You can do more things in a short period of time if you know the right people. Therefore I decided to keep searching for any information I could get from people who knew Saleem or were familiar with the events of the first day of the coup, especially at the Khoja Rawash headquarters.

One day after school I went to the Ministry of Defense to see a friend. He reported that he had seen Saleem a few days earlier when he was brought into the building for questioning. He assured me that Saleem would be released soon, when the military situation was under control. With this news I rushed back home ecstatic. I excitedly gave the news to Mom and others who were waiting, and then called Rahim to get me something to eat, for I had not yet had lunch.

No sooner had I taken the first bite of food than someone knocked at the door. A small boy, one of my nephew Arif's classmates, was there. He told us that Arif had been hurt during a school demonstration against the coup and was in Aliabad Hospital, in the emergency room. My throat constricted; I tried to swallow the piece of bread in my mouth but couldn't. I rushed to the hospital.

There we found that Arif had a serious eye injury and needed major surgery immediately. We took him to Noor Hospital, the best one available. It was situated near the Rishkhor Army Base, which we had watched the huge planes bomb on April 28. There were no panes left in the hospital windows and shards of glass were still scattered about the entry hallway. The backyard walls were pocked with bullet holes.

Surprisingly, Hameed showed up at the hospital soon after to visit Arif. He promised to get a passport and visa for my nephew to go to Pakistan for treatment. I still don't know how in the world Hameed was always informed whenever anything happened to our family!

WEDNESDAY, JUNE 14, 1978 (JAWZA 24, 1357)

Today was Ali's birthday. Although I had decided not to celebrate it this year, my sister Mizhgan insisted on having a party for him. Since I was busy, she made the cake and invited everyone to come to our house at six in the evening.

Early in the morning I got up and went to the university. After school I went to the military hospital, where a relative of mine worked. A couple of days earlier a colleague had told me that Saleem was injured and was in that hospital. With my relative's help I peered into most of the rooms on several floors, but to no avail. Saleem was not there. My relative was afraid to take me to the area that was off limits. Very disappointed, I returned home around five o'clock thinking that Saleem might be in one of those rooms that I couldn't visit.

At home, the birthday table was ready and we waited for the guests to arrive. Time passed – six o'clock, seven o'clock, seven-thirty, almost eight – yet Mother and the others did not show up. Since I was tired and in a bad mood, we went ahead and started without them. Around eight o'clock the door opened and two of my brothers, Mom, and Mizhgan arrived, white bandages on their heads, arms, and legs, and bloodstains on their clothing. I went totally out of my head. I jumped out of my chair, caught Jaan's wrapped hand, and asked, "What happened? Why is this hand shorter than the other?"

"Our taxi had an accident. We went to the hospital, but we're all right now," he replied.

I wouldn't let him go, and tugged at his arm, trying to compare it with the other one. Somehow the injured arm looked shorter than the other one. I was in utter shock.

That night in bed my mind kept chanting a question, "Why us? . . . Why us? What is going on?" Things were happening to my family so fast and unpredictably that I simply could not comprehend them. All night I prayed: "God, no more of it. Please do not test my strength. I am giving in; I cannot endure any more. Please, God, let me stay with my children. I am afraid of ending up in a mental hospital. Please, let me be with my children, and be myself again."

SATURDAY, JUNE 24, 1978 (SARATAN 3, 1357)

All convicted criminals, even murderers, were released in most parts of country, making big news on radio and TV. According to the minister of education, "The doors of the prisons are being closed and the doors of the schools are being opened." Yet, paradoxically, the political kidnappings continued and people still disappeared. The jails were being emptied to make room for the new political prisoners!

People were getting tired of all such propaganda. As I was crossing Puli-Baghi Umomi Road I noticed that someone had written under the government's famous slogan of "Food, Shelter, and Clothing for All," in large letters that could be read from far away, "Address: Puli-Charkhi Prison." Whoever did it took a big risk to write such words on a very busy road.

FRIDAY, DECEMBER 1, 1978 (QAUS 10, 1357)

I do not know how I survived the months between June and December. Nothing is written in my diary. I think those days must have been very unpleasant, because on rough days I didn't have the patience to record the events in my diary.

In October the government replaced the three-colored (green, red, and black) national flag with one of solid red. The day the red flag was hoisted, all offices were closed and people were ordered to take part in the celebration. Thousands of red posters and small banners were distributed, photos of the True Leader, Taraki, outnumbering the sum total of the rest. I remember the TV announcer said, "All the world around me is red. The sky, the earth, the air, the time – everything is red. Come and see how people willingly and wholeheartedly celebrate this momentous event of the century. It is an occasion that history will remember forever!"

We received a directive from the Ministry of Education to revise the high school science books to include the revolutionary government's philosophy. When I read the letter I asked a professor next to me, "What philosophy? Didn't we revise them a couple of years ago?"

"Yes," he replied, "but they say it was done by 'Western agents' who used English sources."

"To me, the anatomy of an earthworm must be the same regardless of the source. I'm out of it!" I said.

"Me too! They don't know what they're doing." We both laughed.

As usual, I went to the Puli-Charkhi prison early one morning, right after the curfew ended at five. I had been doing it every Friday without fail. On this day I didn't have my car. All the private buses were full; people pushed and shoved each other rudely to squeeze aboard, so Jaan and I joined the crowd walking the several-mile-long dirt road to the prison. At Puli-Charkhi the surroundings looked like fair grounds, except there were no vendors of food or trinkets and the crowd was miserable.

Even though it was a very cold day a great number of people had gathered in front of the two gates, waiting for them to open. The wind blew hard and somehow it seemed that by sitting hunched over on the bare, rocky ground we stayed warmer. The scene looked exactly like a huge flock of crows huddled on the vast bare plain.

The gates finally opened with a loud screeching noise at nine and the gateman yelled, "To save time, everyone should write four letters that will be sent to the four cell blocks inside."

My God! I thought. It looked like there was a large city inside those prison walls. From where I stood I peered behind the gateman but I couldn't see anything except a very high wall about half a block away. I didn't have any paper with me, so I borrowed some from a man next to me. I wrote two sentences on each piece of paper: "Dear Saleem, We are all fine. How are you doing? With love." With trembling hands I signed the four sheets of paper and gave them, along with a small package, to the official at the gate. He examined every item in the package very carefully and read the letters, making sure that they contained no forbidden information or words.

We sat there all day but no news came back. By noon I was very cold and hungry. I watched small sparrows flying up and down the high walls, and the more I watched, the more I realized my frailty and powerlessness. God, how much I wanted to know what was going on there, right behind those walls! I wished I were that tiny bird who could fly so freely. I wished I knew how to make an electronic bird that could fly behind the walls to give a message to all those innocent Afghans inside. I didn't care whether I knew them or not; all I wanted was to reach out and touch them and give them hope that one day we would all overcome these miseries.

Lost in my thoughts I sat there for hours waiting for news to come back from the prison. A painful human cry brought me back to this world. I looked around and saw that a young woman, half frozen and probably hungry and exhausted like me, was crying. It was late in the afternoon and she still had not received any news. I wanted to give her my sweater but I was afraid to do so. If the government spies saw me helping her, they would probably question me later, asking what kind of connections I had with her.

Two men nearby were talking softly, but loudly enough for me to hear. One said, "This is not the only prison in Kabul. Many people are locked up in the tunnels under the palace and the Ministry of Defense, and in the basements of other ministries and rented houses as well. The conditions are so bad that it's hard to recognize the prisoners."

The other man nodded and said, "This prison was built recently, but it's no better than any of the others. The lower cells that are underground are so small that a person can hardly sit or lie down. There are no windows, just a small opening that a piece of bread can be thrown through."

I was half dead with fright. It was obvious that the prison was designed to torture people. The construction of Puli-Charkhi was started during Daoud's government and was half completed when Taraki came to power. Ironically, those cells designed by Daoud's government were later used for members of the royal family during the Communist takeover.

I looked at my watch; the day had ended as all the others had: no news from Saleem.

FRIDAY, DECEMBER 22, 1978 (JADI 1, 1357)

Today as I was waiting outside the Puli-Charkhi prison I saw a very poor woman in nomadic dress but without shoes standing in the long line, wailing, near the prison gate. She was crying in a heartbreaking voice, the kind of voice that echoes and penetrates your heart like a sword. She clutched the iron poles of the tall gate and thrust her face against them even though they had to be as frigid as the glaciers of the North Pole on that bitterly cold early morning. Her cries ended in the murmured words of prayer. I thought she must be freezing, she was so lightly clothed. I called her, "Mother . . . mother, why you are crying?"

"They came to my house and took my son away last week."

"Do you know where he is?" I asked sympathetically.

"No, I went to every place that was suggested but couldn't find him." With a heavy sigh she added, "He might be here."

She broke into tears again and sobbed, "Oh God! My . . . my poor son's cap is still hanging on the wall, just above the *tandoore* [clay oven for baking nan]. They didn't even let him wear his cap! He must be very cold!"

Another woman who was waiting, like me, to learn anything she could about her missing relative said loudly to the two officers standing near the gate, "You say only the feudals have been imprisoned." (The government claimed they had punished only the "feudals" and landlords, but the word "feudal" was used indiscriminately in the daily conversations of party members to mean all those they disliked.) "Look at her" – pointing at the poor woman – "is she a feudal too? You, . . . you hypocrite villains and liars of the century!"

Another voice called out, "You stupid Communist slaves and lunatics!"

One officer started to say something but yet another woman from the far end of the line shouted, "You greedy vultures and psychopaths! When are you going to end all your damned lies?"

Soon everyone in the line was heckling and laughing at the officers, neither of whom knew what to do. They looked around frantically as catcalls came from everywhere. One of them pulled at his coat to straighten it, then they both slowly walked away, escaping the onslaught of laughter and curses. All day long I was scared that they might have reported this outburst and the prison officials might take revenge on us, but nothing came of the incident.

FRIDAY, DECEMBER 29, 1978 (JADI 8, 1357)

On this day I took Omar with me to Puli-Charkhi, again hoping to make contact with Saleem. I was always afraid that maybe one day the policy would change and they would allow prisoners to write to their families, and if I didn't go I would miss such a golden opportunity. So not a single Friday passed that I was not standing there, right next to the iron-barred gates, early in the morning.

I handed in the same small plastic bag as usual today. We waited. Omar seemed very upset at seeing the miserable crowd around him. The day passed and the evening shadows spread. Finally an official called our name. Omar ran and retrieved the bag. He thought it must surely contain some news from his father. He dug hurriedly inside but found nothing new. As he returned to the car where I was waiting and watching closely, his tall figure was as bent as a bow, his face was pale, and his eyes blinked rapidly. I knew his inner disappointment and decided that it was too much for a thirteen-year-old; in the future I would come alone.

On our way back home as we left the prison's dirt road and approached the main highway, I stopped the car. A volley of shots could be heard in the distance. To our right was the Puli-Charkhi Army Base, yet another place where prisoners were being held. According to some, this site was used for exterminating innocent citizens – "enemies of the regime." Shots were often heard from there through the dark hours of night. I decided that one day I should check there also.

THURSDAY, JANUARY 11, 1979 (JADI 21, 1357)

After almost nine months without word of Saleem, I tried to pull my act together. The first thing I did was to complete the new house, which took several weeks. As soon as the painting was done, we moved in. Within a month we had rented out the old house we'd been living in.

Jaan and I went to the Puli-Charkhi Army Base. Jaan's close friend Aman worked there. Jaan thought Aman would tell him the truth if he had seen Saleem among the prisoners. I took Saleem's photo.

At the army base Aman came out and we walked a hundred yards away from the main gate so no one could overhear us. I showed Aman the picture but he couldn't remember seeing Saleem. He spoke very softly, almost in a whisper, of the mass killings that occurred inside the base every night. As he stood there on a loose pile of dirt, he said, "Here, underneath our feet, the earth is filled with human flesh and soaked with human blood."

God, just the thought of it made me nauseated. I looked around frantically. I had heard of mass executions, of mass graves, but never thought that I would walk on top of one. I was so sick I couldn't stand there anymore. I ran to the car and as I sat there waiting for my brother, who was still talking with Aman, I told myself, "Okay, I didn't hear anything; it was his imagination. No, there were no such mass graves." I wanted to convince myself, but I failed.

MONDAY, FEBRUARY 5, 1979 (DALV 16, 1357)

I missed my husband more than ever on holidays. Eid came and along with it all my memories. The year before, during Eid, we were all together, very happy and at home; this Eid his place was vacant.

On Eid, friends and relatives of a newly deceased person often visit the family and express their sympathy, but I didn't know what to do this year. I didn't have the courage to accept their sympathy, nor had we received any condolences so far, because there had been no concrete evidence of Saleem's death or any official announcement of it.

March 1979

My sons were at their grandmother's. Sahar and I stayed home. As I sat there, preoccupied by all the memories of past Eids, I felt I couldn't persist in this emotional state and needed some fresh air. So I took my daughter and together we went to the Kabul Zoo, which was situated along the river at the very base of the high mountains. As Sahar busied herself watching the animals, my thoughts went back in time. When I was in my third year of college, I was one of the three students who worked with the team from the University of Bonn to establish the zoo. It was started with a dozen native animals, a couple of wolves, monkeys, parrots, some reptiles, and so forth. We opened it to the public with a minimum entrance fee. The reaction of the crowd was overwhelming; people waited in long lines to see the few animals. The zoo developed in no time. Now we had a large number of native and nonnative species plus a fairly decent animal museum. The zoo still belonged to our university biology department and faculty members took turns serving as director.

As I sat there in the fresh air for hours and watched Sahar running up and down, I wondered, What am I doing here? I was running away from the sympathy of my friends.

MARCH 15, 1979 (HOOT 24, 1357)

I still had not discovered any reliable news about my husband, no matter where I went. I still could not bear to see my children's questioning faces. By trial and error we all learned to keep quiet. We were all afraid of mentioning Saleem's name, not because he had been forgotten, but because the mention of his name brought back all the pain.

MONDAY, MARCH 26, 1979 (HAMAL 6, 1358)

Our New Year came on March 21 and I don't think people celebrated it the way they used to. School started right after the New Year. My daughter told me that a new subject, one hour daily, had been added recently to their curriculum. It was called *itla-at*, or "information" class. During this class the teacher asked the students about their homes, what went on there, what their parents said about the new regime and who visited them. This was a new wrinkle in the spy network that was spreading through the schools.

Rumors were rampant that even children had been disappearing from schools and the streets. The Marxists had supposedly taken them to special "indoctrination schools," but people kept quiet and didn't talk about their missing family members.

Both of my sons were going into the tenth grade, while my daughter was in the fifth. They were growing fast and making new friends. There were times when I felt so uncertain about decisions. I wanted Saleem's opinion when it came to raising my children. One day Ali wanted to go out and play football with his friends but I wouldn't let him. I was scared, I was scared even of my own shadow. I didn't know who I could trust anymore. I was afraid that if I let him go and play, he would not return safely. I didn't know his friends. Times had changed so much that I was afraid I might lose the children exactly the way I had lost my husband – and I wouldn't be able to find them either. When I told Ali no, he cried. His tearful eyes were killing me.

SUNDAY, APRIL 29, 1979 (SAUR 9, 1358)

The first anniversary of the coup was celebrated on April 27. Two days before the celebration, the director of education called me into his office. In a tone more of ordering than of suggesting he told me that it was the responsibility of the teachers to enlighten society through their students. He said, "You should impress upon your students the benefits of the new regime's programs and how its decrees enable us to overcome the misery and injustices of the Naderi dynasty." He gave me a long, tiresome lecture and ended, "There are very few members of the faculty who are not practicing the principles of our revolution!" I didn't say a word. The day after the anniversary I had an early-morning freshman class of more than two hundred students. I knew that a few faculty members were planning to talk in their classes about the revolution's benefits for workers. They wanted me to do the same in my class.

I thought a great deal about the director's order. Finally I decided that even though I didn't have the power to say anything against the regime, I still could not bring myself to say anything good about it either. Yet I knew that if I told my students my true opinion, I would be in big trouble. For the lack of a better plan, I opted to play dumb.

Early on the morning of Saturday, April 28, as I entered the classroom, I felt sure that the students were waiting for me to say something about the anniversary of the revolution. But I had nothing to say. After laying a few papers and my books on the desk at the front of the room, I turned to the blackboard and wrote, "Chapter 3: Coelenterates." I heard slight murmuring sounds behind me. As I turned to face my pupils, I saw that most of them had pulled out their notebooks and, with a smile of satisfaction, had begun to write. Without hesitation I gave the main characteristics of the animals in question. Soon every student was busy writing.

All day long I felt awful. I waited anxiously, knowing that something would happen soon, even though deep down I was happy I had been honest with my students. I felt proud that nobody had been able to force me to lie. I didn't have long to wait before I was summoned to the director's office. I knew by his face that he was agitated. He told me to sit down in the chair nearby but he continued to write something in a folder. Then raised his head and asked, "How did it go?"

"What? I'm sorry, what did you say?" I answered calmly.

"How was your morning class?"

"Oh, my morning class? Fine, as usual!"

"Did you talk about the April Revolution?" he queried impatiently.

"No. In fact, I am a science teacher and I do not like to get involved in politics and government. I'm sorry, but this is the field that I have been trained in. If I explained things beyond my understanding, I'm afraid I would not be analyzing them honestly and properly," I replied.

The director began his diatribe: "You are not attending any of the organizational meetings either!"

This was something I had not even thought of – but I had a good excuse for it. "I know. I have lots of family problems. Being an only parent is very hard," I said with exasperation.

The director clipped his words: "Okay, I will talk to you later. I just wanted to know whether or not your class was full and to ask how it had gone. Thank you very much."

As I walked down the hall, I knew that he would send a report on me to his boss, whoever that was.

Students were forced to attend organizational meetings, which were watched closely by party members. Reports were made daily. Nonparty students and faculty were afraid not to attend such meetings. Yet I had never attended, even though I was reminded on many occasions of my absence. In fact, that day's confrontation with the director was another hint of just how carefully the regime kept records and how much they knew about everyone.

JUNE 1979 (JAWZA 11–SARATAN 9, 1358)

In the preceding months I had been so consumed with searching for Saleem that I'd had little time to think about what was going on in my own house. Even when I was there physically, my mind was far away.

One day as I was listening to the radio at home, I noticed that my daughter, Sahar, was having trouble using her left hand. It seemed to be out of control. She attempted several times to pick up a brush from the floor, but she couldn't do it. Shocked and very frightened, I also observed that she could not control her legs either. I remembered that lately she had been dropping things frequently. I had taken the matter lightly because I had learned in a psychology class many years before that in adolescence children often grow so fast they become awkward. As a result of their changing anatomy, they break or drop things, making their parents think they are careless. Perhaps, subconsciously, I was trying to avoid adding any new problem to my existing troubles. But when I finally realized the truth on this afternoon, I took her to the nearest doctor right away. He examined her, said she might have chronic chorea, and gave her some medicine. As the days passed, Sahar's condition grew worse and worse.

During the following weeks I took Sahar all over town to the best Afghan and foreign doctors available. Nothing seemed to work. Every doctor had a different opinion. Some gave her medicine, others only vitamins, and a few suggested acupuncture. Overmedication made her condition worse and she became extremely weak. I hospitalized her in the Indian Hospital for Children for several weeks, but there was no improvement. Finally one doctor told me that the only place where her ailment could be treated was at the new military hospital, which had the needed facilities.

WEDNESDAY, AUGUST 8, 1979 (ASAD 17, 1358)

Security was very tight all over town. A few days earlier the Bala Hissar barracks were bombed to suppress a revolt there. Large numbers of jets and helicopter gunships circled overhead continuously, day and night. Rumors said that at least two hundred soldiers had been killed that day and several hundred others had disappeared. On Sunday, August 5, Mother and my sisters went to the Mohammed Jan Khan bridge when they heard of the mutiny and watched the air raid from a short distance away. The helicopters released flat, shiny objects that exploded the tanks on the road outside the fort, sending dust and fire high into the sky. Because of the imposition of martial law and the closing of streets, I was not able to take Sahar to the military hospital. How long I would have to wait, I didn't know.

SATURDAY, SEPTEMBER 1, 1979 (SUNBULA 10, 1358)

I took Sahar to the military hospital. An officer at the information desk gave me a couple of forms to fill out. There was a space on one of them asking my husband's place of employment. I purposely left it blank. The officer took the forms and returned a few minutes later to ask where my husband was. I told the truth – that he had been missing since April 27, 1978, and I did not know his whereabouts. The officer wrote down my words and took the form to the back room again. An hour later word came back that I was not permitted to put my child in that hospital. I knew that after the coup our health insurance had been cut off, so I said, "I will pay all the expenses in cash now."

The officer firmly said, "No!"

When I asked why, he replied that there were no beds available. I sat there for a few moments and noticed that right after me, two other civilian patients were admitted. But they would not accept us; we were rejected without any reason or explanation. I went again to the two officers at the front desk and tried to convince them. I begged. I cried. Finally I cursed the whole world. Nothing helped. We were practically thrown out of the hospital.

In my frustration I began to hate myself, my husband, and everybody around me. We had served this country with great pride and honor. Now, in my own country, I was being turned down by the only hospital that could help my sick child!

I drove home full of hurt and anger. In the past year my expenses had been never-ending. I had spent a great deal of money searching all over the country for my husband. In the whole of Afghanistan no major provincial jail was left unchecked. On the strength of rumors that some prisoners had been taken to different districts, I had asked relatives and friends who lived in Kandahar, Ghazni, Logar, Herat, Zabul, and Balkh to see if Saleem had been taken there. The remainder of my budget was nearly exhausted paying for Sahar's medical bills. My full month's income was barely enough for a week's expenses. I'd sold the two pieces of farmland that we owned in a province, and now even that money was all gone. I could see no end to my problems; things seemed to be piling one on top of the other without any ever being solved. I knew neither who to turn to, nor where it all would end.

I had almost given up trying to hold onto my sanity. I changed completely. I could find comfort only in turning to God. I began to spend lots of time visiting shrines and holy places, thinking that there I would find God, and in reality I did feel very close to him there. I fought him, I cursed him, but mostly I begged him. My demands were enormous and many. I thought that God was the only one who did not resist me or fight back. He did not argue. Instead, he listened patiently. Although I did not see him, I always felt his presence.

One day I went to the holy shrine called Shuhada-e-Saleheen, a place I had visited often in the past couple of months. Faithfully, I removed my shoes at the top of the steps and entered the tall, beautiful marble building. Just being there reminded me of the times that Saleem and I had come here together, especially on religious holidays. Saleem had always filled his pockets with coins for the needy. On this day, my heart was full of pain because I was conducting the rituals alone.

I recalled a spring day when we had come early in the morning. It was during the holiday called Eid following our fasting month, Ramadan. At that time we didn't have a car, so we got off the bus and walked the two miles of dirt road to Shuhada-e-Saleheen. The route lay along a vast marshland, and this time of year the water level was high, nearly to the road. The tall, mud-colored walls of Bala Hissar Fort, built on a hillside, were reflected on the water. The weather was fine, the smell of wildflowers and the feel of spring invigorating. My husband said, "Let's run and see who gets to the shrine first."

I agreed. We both started running and in no time I was way ahead of him. Saleem had injured his knee playing football and couldn't run very fast. When I reached the shrine, I sat down on the steps to wait for him. After a few minutes he showed up, his new dark suit covered with dust and his hair rumpled. I couldn't help laughing. Saleem always dressed so nicely, taking extra time for it. Now he looked so funny.

Today as I sat in the shrine, in my mind I pictured Saleem standing in front of me in that dark, dusty suit. He was looking at me, smiling.

I extended my hands to reach him and put my head on his shoulder, to beg him not to leave me alone. But slowly he disappeared into the corner shadows of the room. I shook my head and realized that I was only daydreaming. I dried my tears. Oh, how I missed him that day!

As I sat quietly on the floor, the mujaver began to read loudly from the Koran. His words echoed majestically. In front of me were two tombs, very long, three or four times the height of an average person, and covered with beautiful carved white and black stone. Several men, women, and children walked slowly around the tombs barefooted. Before leaving, all of them kissed the Holy Koran at the edge of the tombs. I noticed that most of them were crying quietly. I felt greatly comforted by my surroundings. Going to shrines and holy places gave me the peace that I so desperately needed. There I knew that the people around me shared some sort of communal pain – that I was not the only one lost in distress. As the Communists tried to conquer my land ideologically and by force, I rebelled. In fact, the more they tried to force on me their atheistic ideas, the more I became a staunch and obdurate Moslem.

I stayed in the shrine for several hours that day, lost in my own world. My tears began to fall uncontrollably; here, at last, I learned that it was all right to cry. Finally I went to the holy book and kissed it. I tried to ask God for something, but I didn't know what to ask for or where to begin. I needed so many things from him that it made me mute. Outside, it was getting dark; it was time to go home. I said my last prayers, "God, you claim that you know everything. Then you must know why I am here." I asked him why these people were suffering. Since I did not get any response, I reached up toward the sky and said loudly, "God, why the hell are you looking at me like this? Are you blind? Can you do something or not?" The mujaver held the holy book tightly to his chest and watched me closely. I threw my hands up in the air and said to God, "Okay, okay! I'm leaving! Is this what you want?"

My voice was loud and belligerent. I saw that everyone in the shrine had stopped what they were doing. A few women and children turned their faces toward the sky where I was pointing, as if they thought I'd seen God's image up there. I certainly was acting insane. I quickly came to my senses and, under the others' dark looks, walked slowly toward the stairs to retrieve my shoes, leaving a few coins in a mujaver's metal bowl.

As I walked down the street I saw that a couple of women in veils and with several children were following me. Since it was getting dark, I walked faster and faster. The women also walked faster. I heard them calling me to stop. Finally I turned and asked, "What do you want?"

"You are God's friend! Please put your hand on my son's head," the first women said.

"What for?" I asked impatiently.

"How could someone talk to God like that? Unless they'd seen him – ," the second woman added.

Gosh! They thought I really had seen God and could heal their pain. The first woman's voice implored again, "Touch my son's forehead." Soon two other children were brought within my reach. It was getting very dark and I was very tired. I saw no place for further discussion – it would be extremely hard to convince them – so I touched the children's heads and left. They thought that I was a saint. I started laughing and laughing, promising myself not to act so strangely anymore.

When everything else failed, I began to change. My plans changed, my attitudes and ideas changed. Previously I had rejected superstitious and unnatural things, and never believed in them in the least. Not only did I not believe, but I relentlessly disputed the dogma of adherents. But now things were different. Every door that I knocked on I found permanently closed. Or if someone appeared, his face was unfamiliar. It seemed that nobody in this world could help me. I faced dead ends. Even my close friends and relatives tried to stay away from me, or at least thought I'd lost my mind. The only ones who supported me were my brother Jaan, my quiet and cooperative children, and a very few others, whose number would not exceed the fingers on my right hand. I lost faith in everybody. Most people were afraid to be seen with me in public because of my husband. Others regarded me with such pity that I hated to face them.

Naheed, my best friend, was always there for me and I was very grateful for this. She came often and took me to shrines. I sat there faithfully for hours and acted the way she told me. I tied threads to the shrine poles. I took cooked food with me and gave it to the beggars. I lit many candles, and I emptied pockets full of coins that I had taken with me.

Naheed also took me to fortunetellers. She believed in them. With no other options, I followed her steps devotedly. One day she took me to the downtown Rice Market to visit a Hindu fortuneteller. We climbed a narrow, crooked, dark stairway in the back of a small shop. The fortuneteller sat behind a very small table, on a mattress. His office was filled with rows of small tin cans neatly arranged on wooden shelves that covered the entire walls. I don't know what was in the cans, but I thought they might contain herbs, spices, seeds, and so forth, because a strong, musty odor filled the room. It was very hard to breathe. Naheed and I sat down on the floor facing the fortuneteller. He started swinging his head back and forth exactly like a pendulum. His lips moved as he murmured words that were hard to hear. Naheed whispered, "Mahgul [a friend] has told me that he is the best in town!" She looked at me and nudged me with her left arm. She expected me to say something, but I kept quiet. I didn't know what to ask for. The fortuneteller was quietly watching us through his half-open eyes, still swinging back and forth. He had apparently noticed our confusion. He took a very deep breath and then expelled it from his lungs by saying, "Ch – u – u – f – f, ch – u – u – f – f" to bless the surroundings.

A narrow stream of air blew past us on the right and the left. Naheed did not like it and cursed him in whispers, which made me laugh. Finally she said to the fortuneteller, "My brother [she meant Saleem] has disappeared from his office. Can you tell us where he is?"

The Hindu picked up an ancient book that seemed to have been in use for at least ten generations. He closed his eyes, said a few words, put his thumbnail inside the book, and opened it to that page. He started reading a few sentences from it. I peeked. It was a work of old folklore poetry. The Hindu's final conclusions were that Saleem did not exist and I should not waste time going from place to place because no one would give me the information I sought. Feeling greatly let down, I searched my pockets and put twenty afghani bills in his lap and we left.

For several weeks I did such odd things as consult fortunetellers, psychics, astrologers, and magicians. I became a notorious customer of them and spent a lot of money and time on them. Finally, however, reality dawned on me as I was coming home from seeing Ibrahim Kandahari, the famous astrologer, having paid him fifty afghanis and spending two hours. In fact, I think it was my third visit to Kandahari. While riding home on the bus I found myself analyzing the past few weeks' activities. I asked myself, "Why can't I open a book and read the words for myself instead of going to a fortuneteller? Why am I paying Kandahari fifty afghanis every time I see him? After all, what can he do for me? Can he change my fate?" My answer was no.

I felt that I'd been failing myself. I said, "Hey, this is not what I should be. I should be strong and face the realities of life. Above all, I've not been behaving in a way that Saleem would like to see if he were here now. I'm not afraid anymore! For my family's sake I will not run away from my problems! I can do it!"

Slowly, one by one, my tears began to drop. Shielding my face from the other passengers, I wiped away my tears as they welled up in the corners of my eyes under the dark glasses. With every passing block I became more determined and stronger than ever. At home I called my children and clutched them all together in my arms: my world and my comfort were here, not in that fortuneteller's or Kandahari's office! My heart filled with an almost suffocating pain. After a few moments I caught my breath, determined to remain under control. The love of my children gave me the strength I needed. My God, I was changed. I kissed them and said, "I love you all." Then, to change the subject, I said, "Let's see, who has finished their schoolwork today!"

The children were surprised by my actions. They brightened up and everyone said they were doing well in their studies. "Okay, very well. I am very proud of you." I hugged them again. After a few moments I added, "Then let's go and eat. I'm very hungry. Ali, could you help Sahar set the table, and the food will be ready in ten minutes."

That night when I went to bed, I looked down at my sick child in my arms and thought of my lost husband and the multitude of problems that I still had to face. I felt very lonely. The only thing that kept me alive and tied to this world was the heavenly sound of my children breathing deeply in their sleep. I had made a vow to my husband that I would stay with him in good times and bad; now it was time to fulfill that promise and keep the family together, a thing that Saleem always wished to do.

After that day, the more I was tortured under various pains, the stronger my faith in God and my family grew. Love – only the love of my family and God – enabled me to overcome my hardships. Every painful event became bearable. The more pain that came my way, the more determined and stronger I became. Under every pressure I was melted and reshaped. In fact, I was melted and reshaped almost every day. The new me after every reformation was stronger than ever before!

WEDNESDAY, SEPTEMBER 5, 1979 (SUNBULA 14, 1358)

For a very brief period Amin, general secretary of the Central Committee, prime minister, and minister of foreign affairs, issued passports to those who wished to go abroad, but few people were informed of this. I don't think the information was released by the news media; otherwise, many would have applied for passports. Anyhow, my sister Mizhgan was told of the decision and went to the Ministry of Foreign Affairs with an application. As she was entering the building, she noticed that four black limousines, each with windows darkened and bearing identical license plates, arrived at the same time and stopped at the main gate. Then each

Saleem and me with Omar, Sahar, and Ali, November 1972, in the first house we owned.

Saleem's parents in Kabul in the 1920s.

Mother with my brothers Jaan and
Khalil in front of our family home in
Kabul, 1959. A couple of Dad's
recently planted willow trees can be
seen next to the wall at the right.

The Noon Cannon on Sherdarwaza
Mountain, facing the western part of
Kabul. The cannon was used to signal
not only the noon hour but also
important holidays such as the two
Eids. Photo © Bill Witt, July 1973.

View of Kabul from the Noon
Cannon ridge of Sherdarwaza
Mountain. Photo by Dr. Joseph Q.
Young, August 1976.

Students from Rabia Balkhi High School. Their black uniforms with white scarves present a striking contrast to the traditional veils. Photo © Bill Witt, July 1975.

This view of me a few months after our marriage was taken in the back yard of Saleem's and my first home, a rented house in Kabul.

Bibi Jan, Saleem's grandma, with Omar, February 1966.

Here I am with Sahar and Ali in 1970 in Kama, a village near Jalalabad. When traveling in the provinces I felt more comfortable wearing the baggy trousers called *tunban*.

The large waterwheel used for irrigating the fields is seen here on the south side of the Kabul University campus. The Faculty of Sciences building and a corner of the Faculty of Pharmacy are apparent, along with Aliabad Mountain, in the background. Photo by Dr. Joseph Q. Young, October 1975.

The Darul Aman Palace. Used by Amin as
his headquarters, it was damaged heavily
when Amin was killed in a bloody
confrontation with Soviet troops in
December 1979. Photo by Dr. Joseph Q.
Young, December 1978.

Ali, Sahar, and Omar playing Afghan musical
instruments, May 1971.

Saleem appears third from right in this 1971
photograph taken at the Air Command Staff
College at Maxwell Air Force Base,
Montgomery, Alabama.

My brother Jaan with Ali, Sahar, and Omar, April 1975.

The famous Blue Mosque in Mazar-i-Sharif, which we visited in 1975 on March 20, the day before the Afghan New Year's Day.

Lunchtime at a roadside stop on our trip to Mazar-i-Sharif, 1975. From right to left are Sahar, Ali, Omar, and Saleem.

Our first house, built in the mountain slope in Karte-Parwan. Kabul University was right on the other side of this mountain.

Architectural drawing of the new house Saleem was building for us in the spring of 1978. I had it completed later and lived in it with my children till we left Afghanistan.

car's door opened and one well-dressed man descended. All four identical men entered the building. Mizhgan said it was hard to tell which one was Amin.

After being searched twice at the gate, she and others were permitted to see Amin one by one. Mizhgan was the fourth person in the line. The first woman, whose husband had disappeared, asked if her husband could be released during the upcoming Moslem holiday. Amin read her application and said, "Your husband has fled to Pakistan. Go and marry someone else." The second application was made by a mother whose son was in America. She requested to be allowed to visit her son. Amin read her papers and said, "Tell your son to come here to see you."

When Mizhgan's turn came, Amin wrote on her application, "If her education is incomplete, she can obtain a student passport." Since my sister had completed her studies in India a couple of years before, Amin's consent did not help her. She obtained a passport from a different ministry and left for India two months later.

THURSDAY, SEPTEMBER 6, 1979 (SUNBULA 15, 1358)

The play "The Farmer's Daughter," written by Taraki and televised for the past few months, day after day, was boring an entire nation. Recently, on his birthday, a photographer had apparently gone to his house in Ghazni, where he was born. His discolored home-made crib, which hung from the walls by ropes, was photographed. As it rocked, the announcer said, "Here is the holy place where the Great Leader spent his early childhood!" The scene was shown on TV on Taraki's birthday while his cabinet members were wishing him, "Long live our Great Leader!" Those same charlatans who wished him happy birthday and long life suffocated him with a pillow not long after. I believe this was Taraki's first and last birthday party. (In Afghanistan birthday celebrations were not common, especially among the older generation.)

When Afghans cannot speak freely, they pass news and criticism along disguised as jokes or funny anecdotes that spread like wildfire. The rumors and stories reflect the unspoken views of a society under stress and censorship. They were called *awaza-e-sari chauk*, "crossroads rumors." It was rumored, for example, that there was dissension between "Student Disciple" Amin and "Great Leader" Taraki. People laughed and said, "Don't underestimate our student's strength!"

SUNDAY, SEPTEMBER 9, 1979 (SUNBULA 18, 1358)

Today Karima, one of our teaching assistants, laughed and said, "*Ostad* [Professor], for some reason we have been told to omit Taraki's name from our speeches!"

I put down the book I was reading and asked with great surprise, "Why? Why is that?"

"I don't know. How could they do that – one day praise him and the next day switch to another one; berate and condemn the first one!" Karima said unhappily.

I kept quiet because I was very suspicious of her. I knew Karima was a member of the PDPA. She had been hired to assist us in our classes although we didn't need additional help. The central office had given her a desk in my office.

MONDAY, SEPTEMBER 17, 1979 (SUNBULA 26, 1358)

Laila, my sister, saw several flower-covered coffins being carried away from the presidential palace, followed by several cars with special license plates. It looked like there had been a fight in the People's House. That night I listened carefully to the news, but there was no mention of any battle or accident in the palace.

Throughout the following nights and days explosions could be heard at intervals of every two to three minutes from the nearby mountains. The government hadn't said a single word so far. It seemed that the war was getting very close to us.

September 1979

THURSDAY, SEPTEMBER 20, 1979 (SUNBULA 29, 1358)

Before entering my office in the morning, as I was walking up the stairway, I found shards of glass covering the steps. I looked around to see where they came from. The big picture of Taraki at the end of the main hall was broken to pieces. I looked at the other end of the hall, where a second picture of Taraki hung. That one was broken too. Several bullets had ripped his eyes and mouth. Part of the paper near his lips was torn. He looked funny, his lips hanging down as if he had an upset stomach and wanted to throw up.

I remembered, exactly seventeen months before, Taraki's pictures had replaced President Daoud's photos in the same manner. The only difference was that Daoud's pictures were stoned, while Taraki's were struck by scores of bullets. The reason? Because so many firearms were now in the hands of inexperienced students who belonged to the Communist parties – many thanks to our so-called friends, the Russians.

I went into the main office to sign the daily attendance book. One of my colleagues, who was also there to sign, looked at Taraki's picture and smiled. He asked me in a whisper what was going on. I told him, "I don't know. But whatever it is, it must be very serious!" Taraki's pictures were gone from the clerks' desks and the office walls too.

SUNDAY, SEPTEMBER 23, 1979 (MEZAN 1, 1358)

Well, it turned out that we had a new president. Amin, the "True Disciple of Taraki," had taken the leadership of the country. Taraki's resignation, according to the news, was due to his incurable health problems. But the coffins leaving the palace, the broken pictures in the hall, and the exclusion of Taraki's name from speeches did not seem like a resignation. I thought that a fierce battle must have taken place at the highest echelon.

The new regime was no different than the previous one. In no time Amin's slogan, "Justice, Security, and Legality," filled the air, replacing Taraki's slogan of "Food, Shelter, and Clothing." With great sorrow I saw

127

that the same charlatans who had admired Taraki now switched their allegiance to the new regime and condemned Taraki while expressing admiration for Amin.

A large meeting was held in the Faculty of Science auditorium. A few professors liked the new government. They praised the promises of the government's slogan as heaven-sent. These professors had done the same during Taraki's time. I thought it a disgrace; where had their pride and dignity gone? How in the world could they face their students with such lies? What would the students learn from them? If these were the top educators of the country, then indeed the future of Afghanistan seemed very grave. I was disgusted and irritated by the speeches and all the clapping. I knew we had to applaud; otherwise we would be reported as antirevolutionists.

Community work was part of the new government's plan. It didn't matter if the job was done at the expense of a day's schoolwork or the loss of a day's pay. Since it was a government of the workers, it was decided that faculty members must help the custodians. Our director of education came to my office and said, "Faculty members are coming this weekend to clean and wash the windows. Would you like to come also?"

I asked, "What is the reason behind it?"

"Well, as you know, we must help the workers."

"We are workers too, right? Will the custodians teach my classes next week?" I asked him calmly.

He got the message. "It's volunteer work only," he replied impatiently.

"Good. Then don't count on me!" As he was leaving the room, I added angrily, "Why in hell are the custodians hired if we are expected to do their work?"

Another plan conceived at the upper levels of government was that all office employees and students should help the masons and carpenters at a widely publicized housing project for low-income families that the government wanted to build on the outskirts of town. This made-in-heaven decision sparked a fierce competition among schools because the principals wanted their school names to be broadcast on the national news.

So today was our turn. With no previous notice, we were all told to go to the project to help the builders. We arrived there at lunch hour. Most of us were not dressed properly for the occasion and didn't know how to use the tools and the carts, or how to carry the bricks and stones or mix the concrete. Confused and annoyed, I watched the chaos as government devotees and puppets ran ahead of everyone else, stepping and jumping like restless goats, trying hard to do their best. They happily carried heavy loads and smiled at the cameras. News reporters were all over the place. The whole scene was being recorded for the evening news.

No sooner had I decided to stay in a far corner, away from anyone's attention, than a former student of mine who worked for the construction company approached the small group I was with. "Professor," he said, "would you like to come to my office and have some raisins and tea? It is not good for you to be standing here."

"Yes, Amir, it would be very nice of you." I turned to my friends and told them, "Let's get out of here! The TV cameras should not focus on us."

We all went inside Amir's office and waited for the others to finish their labors. While we were drinking tea, Amir told us that bringing inexperienced crowds from schools and other ministries had created lots of problems for them. In fact, it had really slowed down their construction work. "Two days ago," he observed, "students from two high schools – the Rabia Balkhi Girls' High School and the Ghazi High School for boys – came. Both schools arrived at the same time. As soon as the students got off the buses, they started throwing rocks at each other and chasing one another up and down around the site. No one could control them. Finally, when they left, there was a big mess for us to clean up." He laughed and added, "They even destroyed some of the already built foundations and walls."

Around four o'clock in the afternoon we returned to the university. On the bus someone said loudly enough for me to hear, "Well, some people enjoyed the tea break!"

A second voice was heard from behind: "Oh, let them alone. After all, how could they pull those heavy carts!" I pretended not to hear them.

SUNDAY, OCTOBER 14, 1979 (MEZAN 22, 1358)

A few days earlier around noon, as I was grading students' lab reports, someone knocked at the door. "Come in," I called out. Our director of education entered and said, "President Amin wants to visit our college teachers today. Would you like to join us?"

It was a very unexpected invitation. I looked at my dusty shoes and the informal everyday clothes I had on and replied, "I'm afraid I'm not dressed properly for the occasion."

He said, "You are just fine. We are all going in our regular clothes. Fancy dress is no longer required as in the past. We are poor workers, *Ostad!*"

Such cheap Marxist talk was heard all over the country. I was used to it. Strange things were happening now. Just before the Communist coup, people were always bragging about their wealth, expensive rugs, and the nice comfortable life they had. After the coup, however, the same people complained of not having even the bare necessities of a decent life. I often wondered where all their wealth had gone and marveled at how fast people change. I remembered the first weeks of Taraki's regime, when the TV showed his house. They focused the camera on torn areas of his living room carpet, ripped bedsheets, broken doorknobs, his *charpoi* – woven wooden bed frame and chaise – from which he gave instructions to his "True Disciple" student. The program was broadcast not once, not twice, but for weeks! Just watching that disgusting program always made me furious. After all, those worn-out carpets and the broken doorknobs were no big surprise to anyone. For days after the TV show, we at work kept hearing jokes about Taraki's house. The worst thing was that we had only one TV channel.

The education director was standing in front of me, waiting for an answer. I quickly collected my thoughts and said, "Well, I had planned something for the rest of the day but I can do it later." I knew it would be unwise to reject his offer. I gathered up the papers in front of me and followed him to the bus that was waiting outside. There were about twenty of us. We headed for the palace, or as it was called lately, the People's House.

We arrived at the palace after half an hour and were searched thoroughly by several guards as we entered the main gate. Then we passed through the front yard, where many chubby, blond, red-cheeked Russian soldiers walked about freely, as if it were their uncle's house. At the entrance to the building we were again searched for weapons, then the guide led us to the second floor. We were met at the top of the stairway by one of Amin's office assistants, whose appearance reminded me at first glance of the legendary "bigfoot." He greeted us and led us to one of the nearby rooms.

Once inside, I looked around carefully. The room was almost empty; there were no pictures on the walls, no expensive furniture. A large dining table stood in the center, set for lunch with dishes of salad and fruits and with soft drinks. There were also individual bowls of yogurt for everyone. It was obvious that from each of these bowls a spoonful of yogurt had been removed. Later a friend explained to me that Amin distrusted his cooks and others around him. After each meal was prepared, someone he did trust tested each dish for poison. My friend added, "No one knows which chair Amin will take at the dinner table; he switches places all the time."

We all sat quietly around the table, some of us still puzzled, and after a few minutes Amin came in, dressed in a dark, well-tailored suit. He looked energetic and much younger than in his pictures on TV and in the newspapers. He sat right next to me at the very end of the table and greeted every one of us graciously. He was full of laughter and jokes. It was hard to believe that this short, stout man right next to me had tortured and assassinated thousands of innocent people in a very short period of time. How could he be so full of mirth and so lacking in traces of guilt? Had he ever paused to assess his daily deeds and the tragedies he had caused for all our families?

After lunch it was time for Amin's speech. He spoke in a very orderly manner and asked us to help him in explaining the purposes of the Saur Revolution to our students. He reiterated his policies, which we had already heard at least a thousand times. He added that he had a plan for the prosperity of the workers of our country, if others would give him the chance to implement it. I didn't understand what he meant by "others" but assumed that it referred to the people around the country who were resisting the revolution in increasing numbers, or perhaps it meant the foreign advisers who surrounded him.

Amin emphasized that his government would pursue a fair policy of "Justice, Security, and Legality" for everyone. He blamed Taraki's government for all the disappearances and mass killings. He added that he would bring drastic changes in the secret police, noting that he had already changed the name of Taraki's secret force, which had acquired a bad reputation among the public, from AKSA to KAM, "The Workers' Intelligence Office." In the future, no one would be imprisoned or executed without a fair trial.

After almost two hours we left the palace. On my way back to school I thought about Amin's speech. He had spoken clearly and well of his plans for the betterment of the country. He could fool others so easily. I found nothing wrong with his policies; I only wished that I could trust him. I knew that he was a con artist, a big liar. There were no signs of justice, security, or legality in the country. Houses were searched, people were disappearing and were interrogated without reason. Many had died of torture during interrogations without the right to defend themselves. All the large government buildings had been turned into jails. Students and faculty members were arrested without any explanation whatsoever. "Crossroads rumors" said that most were executed, although some people said the detainees were sent to Russia to work in labor camps

– in steel mills, soap factories, and other such places – like prisoners of war.

Positions were given to many inexperienced young school dropouts who would never have dreamed of exercising such power or making so much money. Many young people found easy opportunity in joining the party and would do anything to prove their loyalty to it. Thus, most of them spied on friends, colleagues, and neighbors, filing false reports against them for their own aggrandizement. Unfortunately, many honest and hard-working people were killed, disappeared, or were tortured this way. So Amin's claim for "Justice, Security, and Legality" was empty. People were already badly hurt. It was too late – as the famous Afghan saying goes, "putting henna on one's hand after Eid."

TUESDAY, NOVEMBER 13, 1979 (AQRAB 22, 1358)
It seemed that provincial uprisings were increasing significantly. All that was heard over the news was the government's warnings and ultimatums about the consequences of attending large group discussions in the streets and other public places.

There had been many school uprisings in the city, especially in the two nearby girls' schools. Along the streets, in university washrooms, and around many public areas one could easily find antigovernment papers, called *shab nama*, or night letters. I often saw such pamphlets on my way to work but was afraid to go near them – afraid that someone would think I was distributing them.

Government warnings were repeated so often that most Kabul streets in the early afternoon hours looked as empty as a ghost town. We all tried to get home from work as early as we could. No more loud music was heard from restaurants and cafés. There was no more shopping after work. Convoys of tanks, damaged trucks, and tired soldiers that crossed the main roads were no longer a surprise to anyone. They only indicated the nearby battlegrounds.

Amin tried very hard to put down public uprisings quietly. He continuously blamed Taraki for the arrests and mass murders, but nobody was listening to him. People were hurt and far too upset to listen to his sick lies.

FRIDAY, NOVEMBER 16, 1979 (AQRAB 25, 1358)

To allay public anxiety, Amin ordered the announcement of the names of twelve thousand people massacred during Taraki's time. But the "crossroads rumors" were that the lists in fact carried the names of more than thirty-two thousand executed persons.

It was decided that the names would be read just once in the Ministry of Interior at eight in the morning. That day I was among the first to appear. A huge crowd showed up and kept increasing. Armed men were among the crowd everywhere. We waited for two hours. It seemed that time had come to a standstill. Finally several military men came and stood at the top of the steps leading to the main entrance. One of the officers pulled out a thick bunch of papers. My legs began trembling and my heart raced. Blood rushed to my face. Tears and cries mixed with prayers were heard from all sides.

The officer spoke into the microphone for more than half an hour about Amin's policy of "Justice, Security, and Legality," making the already upset crowd more furious. We started protesting. Finally he started reading the names. A dead silence fell over the crowd for a short time till a name was read from the bottom of the first page. Suddenly the wife of the deceased whose name had just been read jumped out of the crowd and ran screaming directly toward the man reading the names. Then a few others followed her. The women began to attack the officers. I couldn't see the whole scene, but I knew that everyone was running. The onrushing crowd pressed me hard against the side of the stairway.

The crowd was quickly dispersed by a counterattack from soldiers who appeared in no time. Somehow I managed to escape and I kept running all the way to the bus stop. The next thing I heard was that they had handcuffed the women who had started the disturbance. For several nights afterward I didn't sleep well. With every sound around the house I jumped, thinking what if they had taken a picture of me in the crowd and the police were coming after me?

Because it was impossible to keep the crowd under control at the reading of the list, Amin ordered a few days later that the names should be sent to various county police stations. A victim's name would be included on the list sent to the police station in the county where he had been born or had obtained his identification card, and relatives could go there and see the list.

For a couple of weeks I couldn't go to the police station to look for my husband's name on the list. I asked my brother-in-law Khalid to do it for me because I didn't know what my reaction would be if I found Saleem's name. (I wish I knew why at such times I always found myself weak in facing the realities of life!)

All that night and for many nights afterward I prayed to God for hours that Saleem's name would not be listed. My husband's last wish came to mind: "Honey, if I die one day, would you come to my grave and pray for me?" Remembering his words made me even more upset. Eighteen months of looking all over the country and still I had not been able to locate him! Numerous times I had thought to myself, Have I looked everyplace? or Maybe I am not looking hard enough, or How stupid of me for not figuring out where Saleem might be! Oh God, my inabilities were driving me crazy!

MONDAY, NOVEMBER 19, 1979 (AQRAB 28, 1358)
Schoolchildren with good handwriting were ordered by the school principals to skip their classes and write large-lettered slogans on paper, cloth, or cardboard. Later these posters were hung on the walls. Unfortunately, Ali had good handwriting and school officials asked him to make some

of the posters, so he missed many classes and his grades were going down. No one at school seemed to care as long as he carried out their orders and wrote the slogans!

Normally after the April coup of 1978, all school posters were written on red or white material. The government avoided using green because it was the Islamic flag's color. But on this day my son reported, "Mom, they told us to replace the red posters with green ones."

"W-h-at?" I asked.

Ali nodded his head and said, "Yes, today all day long I was busy making big signs on green cloth."

In the afternoon my brother-in-law Yonus came. He worked in an office across from Amin's palace and told us that a green flag had been hoisted on the palace tower the day before, for several hours. He asked if I had seen or heard anything about it at the university. I laughed and told him, "Well, some new developments are going on that we don't know, because the school poster colors are also changing!"

Amin's government had ordered that schools be made a place where our young generation could be happy and enjoy themselves. Thus, plays, readings, concerts, and shows were performed by talented schoolchildren and were broadcast on TV, making big headlines. In no time a fierce competition began and schools became playhouses and theaters. Contests among schools spread like an epidemic. No school wanted to lag in this respect. Soon Afghanistan's school priorities changed as preschools, elementary, and high schools along with centers of higher education all became involved in show business rather than education.

Annoyingly loud music was now heard everywhere in our university, too. I heard it when I taught in the classroom, in my office, and whenever I prepared lecture notes. The tables in the conference room, once covered with books and scientific journals, now held drums, guitars, harmonicas, and accordions. For departmental meetings the custodians were asked to remove the musical instruments so we could use the space. One day a professor got so upset by at all the musical instruments on the table that he said to the dean, "I think this college has to decide what it wants – musicians or something else!"

"Well, as people say, talents are blooming. Don't worry," I replied quickly.

We all laughed except the dean, who kept quiet throughout the conversation. The disturbing fact was the continuing competition for best plays and concerts among schools at all levels. There seemed to be no end to it: song after song, all copied from previous singers or from Indian movies – the tunes were the same but the words were replaced by Communist slogans. Endless school hours were devoted to practice. Finally the talented teenagers would come before the cameras and compete on stage in front of large crowds. Families that had been strict in the past now saw their own children dancing quite professionally in front of large crowds and TV audiences. They became very upset and felt ashamed and embarrassed around those who knew them.

MONDAY, NOVEMBER 26, 1979 (QAUS 5, 1358)

A couple of days ago a student named Magid came up to the front of the classroom and asked me in a whisper if we had put out a "condolences announcement" on the radio yesterday. He thought he had heard a name similar to our family's last name. I shook my head and quietly said no. I looked at Magid. He seemed so sincere and apologized. With a calm smile I told him, "Magid, don't be sorry. Not yet. But you may hear one very soon." The boy nodded his head in sorrow and left. I thought he might have heard of my husband's disappearance from someone else.

A government ultimatum had been given to me a long time ago, just a week after the April 1978 coup, through the university's new rector. He had called me into his office and had told me to keep my family's and my mouth shut. He said, "As far as I know, you are fine and I have nothing to say about you. But your brother-in-law Yosuf cannot keep his mouth shut and has spoken against our revolution." "I want you to take this from me as a friend," he continued. "The consequences of such talk will hurt your family very badly." When I got home that day, I told Yosuf to be more careful.

Since then I'd never said a single word to anyone at the office about Saleem's situation, but nevertheless his disappearance was well known throughout the university. I was becoming famous for withstanding all the pressure; people admired my courage and strength. The sincere looks and offers of help from colleagues and students were encouraging and comforting indications that they did not believe the government's lies about having tortured and killed only antinational people and their families.

In Afghanistan the death of a person was usually announced on the radio, right after the news, for several days, by the survivors. In the past, very few condolence announcements were made each day, but by this time the list kept going on and on. The announcer read names for at least half an hour each time. Also, in the past the death of a young person made big news. Now it was very common to hear that young people had died. In spite of all these long lists, I knew there were families who, like us, were not permitted to announce on the radio or to have a condolences gathering at home. The Communist government told some families that they could not have the customary funeral gatherings, and we were one such family. The reason was that the general public must not be informed of their bloody and outrageous crimes.

TUESDAY, NOVEMBER 27, 1979 (QAUS 6, 1358)
Almost two weeks had passed since the release of the names of those executed. I called my brother-in-law and asked if he had looked for Saleem's name on the lists. His answer was no, so I decided to find Jaan in the morning and go with him to read the names. The uncertainty was getting on my nerves and I couldn't work properly.

After my morning class Jaan came to my office. We were determined to find the lists that afternoon, never realizing that we had a long battle ahead of us. From ten till midafternoon we visited many offices in Microrayan, Pashtunistan Watt, Zarnigar Park, the third through eighth county police headquarters, just to find the location of the released lists. By three-thirty we still had not been able to discover it. No one knew where it was. We drove to every site the officials named. They were tossing us from one desk to the next and did not want to direct us to the right place. But it didn't matter anymore; we both were determined to find the lists, wherever they were. Finally a clerk suggested that we go to the Dehmazang police station and check with them. After we spent almost another half hour there, they sent us to the Nau Abad headquarters, which was outside the city limits.

We drove fast and left the city behind us. It was getting dark and chances were that the office would close before we got there. Finally, after asking directions from various people – shopkeepers and the like – we reached a narrow gravel road. We drove along it for some time until we reached a small village called Ayoub Khan Mena which I had not seen before but certainly had heard of.

A big sign printed on a bright red background indicated the police station from a distance. We drove the narrow street between the high walls until we reached a relatively open area surrounded by three or four large fortress-like structures. The grounds were uneven and barren but for a large, lonely mulberry tree that stood gracefully by a tiny stream. A little boy, probably the shepherd, sat in the tree dropping leaves to the ground for several black and white goats to eat.

Jaan pulled up and stopped the car abruptly. A noisy flock of chickens came out of nowhere and ran in all directions, beating their wings as a cloud of dust and feathers surrounded us. I looked around carefully but did not see any police cars or policemen. The offices were probably inside the fort. In the far corner of the front yard a lone man sat quietly behind a school-like desk with a large wrinkled folder spread in front of him. The late afternoon hours, the dark shadows of the tall mud buildings, the calmness of the surroundings gave the man behind the desk the appearance of the angel of death coming from another world.

Here I was and there were those elusive lists. My heart started pounding and my mouth went dry. Painful blisters began to pop out on my lips one by one and I could trace their pathway as they worked their way out laboriously from the deep tissue to the surface. My condition was so bad that I decided to stay in the car. Jaan went to see the list.

I watched him from afar. Every single change in his facial expression had a great impact on me. Jaan talked to the man. The Death Angel nodded and opened the folder. Jaan looked through the pages carefully, running his fingers down the columns he was searching. With every page turned, I thanked God it did not contain Saleem's name. Moments seemed like years. Finally Jaan looked at me, smiled, and moved his hands in a gesture that Saleem's name was not on that list.

Happy, and thankful to God, we returned home almost in the dark, again with the question where I should start tomorrow. If Saleem was not on those lists, then he was alive, but where?

After dinner, when the children had gone to sleep, Jaan and I sat together. We talked and talked till after midnight. We put all the events, rumors, news, and information together, trying to make sense of all the things we had heard so far. First he questioned and I answered; then I questioned and he answered. We corrected each other's details. I think we were both trying subconsciously to look at the bright side. We talked for hours but it seemed that we were moving in circles and not getting anywhere.

Jaan's presence beside me in those difficult moments was very helpful. I knew I had someone who not only supported me but also believed that I was not insane. I also knew that Jaan loved and respected Saleem very much. He would do almost anything for Saleem. And unlike Uncle Jawad and some others, Jaan was not afraid to be seen with me in public.

THURSDAY, NOVEMBER 29, 1979 (QAUS 8, 1358)

The foreign-language classes in all the schools have been changed to Russian. But strangely enough, in spite of all the Russian-language practice in the schools, the evening news on TV was broadcast for the first time during the Communist regime in English, which surprised us at the university.

As Sahar had told me before, the special class called *itla-at*, or "information," still existed in their school curriculum. One day out of curiosity I asked her what she had told them about us so far. Sahar said proudly, "Mom, I am not that dumb. Whatever they ask me, I talk about Kelli, our new dog. That's it!"

I laughed and put my arms around her and said, "Good! You are a very brave and intelligent young lady now."

Teachers have told their students to tear the ex-king's pictures from their textbooks. Sahar didn't want to tear the page, so she blackened it with ink. In such a manner the Marxists were trying to wipe out our history by brainwashing our youngsters.

Sahar still had not recovered from her sickness but nevertheless she did attend school off and on. None of the doctors' medicines helped. She had lost lots of weight and taken tons of pills, mostly vitamins.

The names of streets had been changed at least twice in the past two years. I think that each new president renamed the roads, schools, and other public facilities after his relatives and friends. It was getting very confusing when one gave an address to a cab driver.

A friend told me that he had seen my husband in the basement of the secret police headquarters about a month before, when he was in police custody. So once again, after school, I went to inquire about the matter at several offices, including the Ministry of Interior and the Ministry of Defense. No luck as usual.

SATURDAY, DECEMBER 8, 1979 (QAUS 17, 1358)
On this morning I got up a little late and missed the university van, so I walked to school. On my way I met Sultan, the school storeroom keeper. He stopped his bicycle and asked me about the type of ditto paper that I had ordered months ago for our department. As I was giving

him instructions about the quality required for our use and where to purchase it, I noticed that a black Benz taxi had stopped at the west end of the street, about a hundred yards away. The driver's big, reflecting eyeglasses attracted my attention. A few moments later the cab left while I continued talking to Sultan. Soon another black Benz taxi drove up and parked about fifty yards from us, this time to the east side. Nothing seemed unusual. When Sultan went on his way, I continued walking toward the university. As I passed the parked taxi I looked at the driver and my whole world began to spin. He wore reflecting eyeglasses and had a ferocious face. He was watching me carefully through the side mirror! The idea that he was following me scared me to death even though I didn't have the slightest idea why I was his target. I had heard from colleagues that most of the cab drivers were secret police.

I passed by him without losing control, but I did not want him, whoever he was, to follow me. Something – probably all the detective books I'd read – gave me the idea that he should not know my place of work or my home address, so at the first intersection I did not take the road leading to the university but instead turned toward the bus stop and boarded the first bus that arrived. I didn't even check its route.

From inside the bus, I saw the cab driver still watching me. After riding half an hour or so, I got off at Puli-Baghi Umomi, a very crowded area of town, and ran. I ran into the mall. I turned around and saw the cab driver with his mirror-like eyeglasses. My God, he was following me! Suddenly I turned back toward the door I had entered and, ducking behind a tall man, left the shopping center. I looked back; the cab driver was still milling with the rest of the crowd and looking for me. I jumped into the nearest bus. Its destination was a village outside Kabul called Waisal Abad, but I didn't care. I wanted to get out of there, and fast!

After an hour's ride, I reached Waisal Abad and from there I took a cab, finally arriving at work about noon. For at least a month afterward I took the faculty bus to school and avoided crossing that street again.

SUNDAY, DECEMBER 9, 1979 (QAUS 18, 1358)

Two faculty members disappeared from their offices as if into thin air. Whenever I asked about them no one seemed to know what had happened to them. Nobody knew when the disappearances would stop or who would be next. The disappearance of one simply meant a heavier load for the rest of us in the department. Very quietly we divided their class hours among those of us who were still left.

My God, I was terrified! The good, honest, dedicated people who loved their land and were proud of its progress were disappearing one by one. Those who were gone never returned. I had lost so many good friends, I constantly asked myself, When will it be my turn? or Who is next?

Panic-stricken, I remembered and carefully reviewed events of the past. I had seen the same black taxi in the street across from my house many times before but had never thought much about it. Now I recalled also seeing a light blue car, an Opel, which was always there when I left for school or for home, and which followed just twenty yards behind to my destination. I didn't dare to look inside the cars and always pretended not to notice their presence. Today I was determined to tell my family of the two cars that were following me.

I knew that sooner or later they would take me, so as soon as I got to my office, I pulled out all my current student grade reports and exam papers from various folders, organized them, and placed them on the lefthand corner of my desk. If I was not there one day, others should be able to take over without trouble. God, it was so hard; it felt like I was dying. But did I have any choice? Was there another alternative? No, not at all.

I went to the bank during my two-hour break between classes. I added the name of my fourteen-year-old son, Omar, to all my bank accounts and told one of my close friends who worked there that, in case I was busy and couldn't make it to the bank one day, my son would come. If he needed some cash, please help him and give him the money. Farhad, my friend, looked at me for a few moments while I tried to avoid his sharp, questioning eyes. He sensed my worry and asked, "Are you okay? Is everything all right at home?"

"Yeah, I'm fine at the moment," I replied, still trying to avoid his eyes.

Farhad realized this was not the right place to talk about things, but he promised, "Of course I will help your son, since I know he has your permission to withdraw the money." Although I knew it was illegal for a fourteen-year-old to withdraw money from a bank, I was sure that Farhad would keep his promise.

On my way back to the office I thought of leaving my children, my mother, my sisters and brothers and friends behind. The mere thought of it was painful beyond words. I was acting like a person who had been given only a few more days to live. If only I knew what my mistakes were, where I'd gone wrong, it would not have been so hard to accept the situation.

I thought of the fresh, clean air of Kabul. I looked at the tall, proud, bare mountains. I loved them so much! No, I was not ready to die. I remembered my grandmother-in-law telling that when she was young, all these mountains were covered with vegetation – wildflowers and shrubs. She said, "People went up on the mountains and collected wild leeks and rhubarb."

In the past the barrenness of the mountains had always brought anguish to my heart with the realization that in only a generation or two we had so misused and destroyed our environment. But on this day I thought, rather, that those mountains were not ours anymore; we were considered by the invaders to be strangers in our own homeland (although the Soviet Union had not yet invaded the country directly, their "advisers" had long since assumed many military and police functions).

In the evening, after dinner, I prepared myself to tell my children the facts. I rehearsed the words mentally several times. Then finally I told them: in case one day I did not come home, they should not worry. Nor should they go out and look for me, because I was sure they would not be able to find me. "I want you to know that I love you very much, and as soon I can I will come home."

Both the older children listened carefully, their eyes wide. After a pause I added, "Listen, here are my bank accounts. If you need money, go to the bank and give the passbook to Farhad and he will give you the cash. Okay?"

I also told them when to collect the rent on our properties and who they should contact if they needed help. My neighbors were a big help; they had always encouraged me to be hopeful. So tonight I told my children to get help from them in case of emergency until my mother, who lived away from us, could help them.

Omar felt keenly the responsibility for taking care of Ali and Sahar in my absence. Although young, he always acted like a daddy. I saw the flickers of sadness and tears in his eyes. Ali and Sahar listened to the news silently. They sat quietly for a while, but I think they both forgot it the next day.

Other than that, I kept everything to myself. I even did not tell Jaan or my mother what I'd said to my children. I always thought I should take events as they came, one by one. Whatever tomorrow might bring, I would think about it when the time came.

FRIDAY, DECEMBER 14, 1979 (QAUS 23, 1358)

People were very impatient and uneasy. Most of them, like us, had not found the names of their missing relatives or friends on the lists that the government had released, so government offices were crowded with those seeking information. Rumors were heard everywhere that there were many more dead than the released names suggested. Amin was forced to address the issue on TV again. He said, "Those persons whose names were released are not with us. They may have fled or perished. How can one say they were arrested or executed? It is groundless to say that several thousand were killed." Amin's words were ambiguous and his confusing speech did nothing to calm the public.

The "crossroads rumors" around the city reported that many prisoners had been taken to Russia, where they were being held.

SUNDAY, DECEMBER 16, 1979 (QAUS 25, 1358)

People say, "Take one day at a time." For me, a day at a time became too long. To survive, I had to hang onto minutes rather than days. In fact, I took one minute at a time. To keep my mind off the problems and to do my regular daily work, I lived only from minute to minute.

For example, on my way to the university I always counted the chimneys of the Darul-Malamine and Ibnesena schools, which flanked the road. One, two, three, four . . . no, I counted wrong and I would start all over again; one, two, three, four, five . . . fifteen, sixteen . . . thirty. . . . I had counted them a thousand times during the previous twenty months. If there was nothing else to count, I counted the cement blocks of sidewalk – one, two, three . . . five hundred sixty, five hundred sixty-one, and so on – till I reached my office building. The next day I counted the tall shrubs, then the houses on the mountainside. In fact, I was counting like a robot, almost anything and everything that came in sight. The only satisfaction I derived from counting was that it passed the time and kept my mind off my troubles. No doubt I was getting very close to insanity.

TUESDAY, DECEMBER 18, 1979 (QAUS 27, 1358)

Deep in thought, I walked home around three-thirty in the afternoon. I didn't wait for the university bus. When I crossed the first intersection, I saw a black car with dark windows approach. It drove by me but skidded to a stop about a hundred yards ahead of me, leaving two dark lines on the pavement. Then it backed up toward me. I looked at its license plate. It did not have a number but rather a special emblem. I was terrified and looked around frantically, searching for a familiar face who could tell my family that I had been taken into police custody, but not a single soul was on the street. I thought, They've finally come for me!

A chauffeur in an army uniform stepped out and opened the back door. A tall, well-dressed young man emerged and saluted me. It was one of my former students, by the name of Samae. We shook hands and after greeting each other I laughed and asked, "What are you doing here?"

Samae said, "Professor, I owe a great deal to you. I learned a lot of things from you. Please let me know if I can be of any help to you. You just name it!"

I knew that Samae had been a member of the PDPA during his school years, but I didn't know what he was doing now. It looked like he had lots of authority in the present government. Nevertheless, he seemed not to have changed a bit; he still had the same sense of humor and the same happy young face. After filling him in on Saleem's situation, I said, "No matter how bad the news might be, I think I am ready to hear it. If you can just give me the facts." I knew it would be very difficult for Samae to tell me the minute details, so I added hastily, "I don't want you to tell me everything that has happened to him. All I want to know is whether Saleem is alive or not."

Samae assured me that if I would call him tomorrow at four o'clock, he would give me the correct information. He offered me a ride home, but I told him that my house was fairly close and I preferred to walk. As Samae was leaving, he turned and said, "Professor, I promise to give you the facts."

WEDNESDAY, DECEMBER 19, 1979 (QAUS 28, 1358)
At school I prayed constantly for my husband today. During the afternoon my heart raced and my face was flushed and hot. I had a terrible headache. As four o'clock approached, my anxiety increased. What if Samae told me that my husband was not living? Several times around four o'clock I went to the phone and tried to call Samae, but each time I replaced the receiver as soon as I picked it up, because my heart was beating so fast I couldn't talk. It felt like I had just run miles and miles. I sat another few minutes trying to catch my breath. Again I tried to pick up the phone but I couldn't. It seemed like a bare electric wire: if I

touched it, it would kill me instantly. Defeated at every effort to pick it up, I just sat there and stared at it. This time the phone became smaller and smaller until I could no longer see it. It seemed somehow to be moving away from me, till finally it hid behind the shadows of my mind. And with it, everything else around me became a blur.

This state of affairs continued another thirty minutes. Finally I decided to get it over with, no matter how difficult it was. At four-thirty, with trembling hands, I dialed Samae's number. I mustered all my courage and asked Samae about his inquiries. I heard Samae's voice on the other end of the line: "Professor, I am so glad to tell you that your Saleem is alive and well! If you will come here tomorrow, I will give you further details."

I jumped out of my chair, full of life and joy, the fatigue and weakness I had felt just a few moments ago vanished! I trusted Samae; after all, he was the one who had offered to help and promised to tell me the truth.

Everything seemed beautiful. The dead world around me suddenly danced to life. I noticed the blue Opel still stupidly following me, but I was not afraid of it. Nothing mattered as long as my husband was alive and well. Today I could forgive the whole world for all the pain I had suffered in the last twenty months. I thought to myself, If someone apologized for the suffering we'd been through, I'd say, "No problem; don't be silly! Apology accepted!"

Almost skipping in happiness, I took my usual route home, but this time I was not counting the chimneys or the houses. Once home, I grabbed my children, kissed them, and told them Samae's words. Tonight our house was full of joy and laughter, the way it used to be. The children played and wrestled around, their voices resounding merrily.

THURSDAY, DECEMBER 20, 1979 (QAUS 29, 1358)
I took Ali and my nephew Arif with me to Samae's office. I wanted them to hear the good news for themselves. Two military guards were on duty in front of his office. One of them came forward and I told him that I

had an appointment. We went in. Samae picked up the phone, called the warden of the Puli-Charkhi prison, and ordered him to bring in Saleem's file.

In about five minutes an army captain brought in a folder and laid it on Samae's desk. Samae opened it and looked at it for some time. Then he said that Saleem was in area number two of Puli-Charkhi and would be kept there till the situation around the country calmed down. "Area number two is for high-ranking officers who are not allowed to contact their families," he explained. "That is why whenever you took his clothes to the prison, they were returned to you without further details."

"When do you think the situation will get back to normal and I should expect Saleem's return?" I asked.

Samae replied reassuringly, "Not very long. Possibly another month or two." His words, along with those of the day before, were the best I had heard in a very long time.

When Samae asked if there was anything else he could do, I told him, "My daughter has been sick and I want to get her a complete medical examination in India. I know that passports are not issued at the present except in special circumstances. Can you help me get one?"

"Yes, of course!" He gave me a piece of paper on which to write my application and promised to get the passport authorization from the Ministry of Foreign Affairs.

I wrote on the application that since my child was very sick and I could not find the proper treatment in Afghanistan, I would like to go to India, our friend and ally, for further medical tests. I underlined the words "India, our friend and ally," knowing that if I specified any Western nation or Pakistan, they would not grant the passport. I also mentioned my destination to Samae, for no matter how much he wanted to help me, he was also a good faithful member of his party.

FRIDAY, DECEMBER 21, 1979 (QAUS 30, 1358)
As usual, I went this weekend to Puli-Charkhi prison and came home

with nothing to report. People told me to keep going in case one day they gave permission to the prisoners to write to their families. It would be terrible if I were not there to receive a message.

The same blue car still followed me. At times I thought how stupid they were. Imagine a car driving at the speed of my walking pace, just twenty steps behind me! If I slowed down, it also slowed down, and if I walked fast, it speeded up. I wondered how much time they had for this nonsense.

Amin decided to move out of the Arg – the presidential palace, or, more recently, the People's House – to a new location, the Darul Aman Palace, which was about five kilometers from our house. The prestigious Kabul Museum in Darul Aman was to be transferred to the Arg. No reason was given for this change.

Yesterday a chemistry professor on the university bus said that lately huge caskets, much bigger than normal human size, were constantly being transferred out of the old palace and to the airport, where they were shipped to the Soviet Union. The government claimed that they contained the bodies of Russian officers killed in combat, but the rumor was that each casket held artifacts collected from the recently excavated Aie-Khanum area.

Tonight again as usual gunshots and heavy explosions were heard all over town. The government explained that the blasts were only to acquire building material for several housing projects. The announcer would add, "Our dear Kabul residents must not worry!"

SUNDAY, DECEMBER 23, 1979 (JADI 2, 1358)

Today I visited Samae again and got the passport application. Yes, it was signed. I think Samae had gone out of his way to persuade the minister of foreign affairs to sign my papers.

But I knew that permission for our passport was just the beginning. There was a long procedure to be followed and tons of trouble lay ahead of me. First, I must get the approval of the secret police, or KAM, which would take another couple of months at minimum. Then the papers must pass through the hands of dozens more bureaucrats before I would be able to leave the country. I also knew that somewhere down the line I would need to put some of my property up as collateral to guarantee our return to Afghanistan.

Getting the passport required a huge sum of cash to be paid as bribes to some greedy officials; otherwise a clerk would hold the papers at his desk forever, even though I had the signature of the country's top man. Thus I had to please everyone. Time was critical and I knew I must not waste it. There was no stability in the government; you might go to sleep one night and wake up the next morning to face a new regime.

Where would I get the cash? I must sell my house. No other choice was left. All the property we had was in my husband's name. How could I sell my house without having Saleem's situation officially clarified on paper? I was sure that no one in the entire country would give me such papers during the present conditions. And even if I had such papers, I could not legally sell the house until all my children were over eighteen years of age – in another nine years. "Tough luck!" I thought to myself.

In the evening I talked to Jaan. We decided to wait, first, for the secret police report, because we couldn't do anything if the Workers' Intelligence Office did not approve of it. Chances were that we would not be permitted to leave the country at all, because of Saleem.

I said to Jaan, "All right, after police approval, we will think about the rest. Will I be able to get it?"

Jaan replied, "Don't worry; we'll find a way. We have to handle the obstacles as they come, one by one."

That night the barriers that stood in the way to freedom for my family seemed insurmountable. My plan was to get the medical treatment needed for Sahar in India, then to leave all three children there with my sister Mizhgan. I would return to Afghanistan until Saleem was out of prison. I did not want Saleem to come out of prison and find his family gone. The potential problems this plan held for me did not matter; I must return to Afghanistan.

Gunshots very close, right behind our house, filled the air and interrupted my thoughts. Soon the sky was full of helicopters. Things looked pretty hectic. In the dark I reached for the short-wave radio. Once again, no news.

MONDAY, DECEMBER 24, 1979 (JADI 3, 1358)

In the early hours of dawn I heard the rattle of our large bedroom windows in the wake of aircraft overhead. I could tell that these were huge planes flying at a very low altitude. Plane after plane kept passing over, making it hard to sleep. At one point Omar woke up and asked, "Mom, what's happening?"

"I don't know, son. Try to sleep," I replied.

Morning came and the streets looked normal. No one dared to ask, but unanswered questions were on the mind of everyone I talked to. The news media kept silent as usual.

WEDNESDAY, DECEMBER 26, 1979 (JADI 5, 1358)

During these three days there was not a single moment when you could not see at least half a dozen planes in the sky at any one time. The sky was always full of big cargo planes. Still no one knew what was going on. I tried to listen to foreign radio stations, but they had no information and it was frustrating to realize that the outside world did not know something was going on.

At work some colleagues glanced at each other knowingly and nodded their heads when they looked at the sky full of Russian planes, but as always we kept our mouths shut. Things had changed so much. I dearly missed the good old times, before the bloody coup of April '78, when we sat together at lunchtime and talked with friends so openly. We said what we felt about everything. We criticized the government in power, the presidents, our bosses and their policies. Today people criticized the ones who were either dead or no longer in power. Every move of the fellow in charge of the country was admired. No matter how contemptible, his gestures and actions were considered glorious.

We had lost trust in our good life-long friends; no one was sure who was a friend or a foe. We were all scared. We had learned not to complain or object to our increased loads whenever a faculty member went missing in our department. Sometimes we did not even know the subject matter, but we were expected to teach.

THURSDAY, DECEMBER 27, 1979 (JADI 6, 1358)

On my way home this afternoon I counted twenty-six Russian planes circling the sky at various levels. They seemed to be waiting their turn to land at the Kabul airport. It appeared that even more planes were coming lately.

At home I prepared dinner and Omar helped me set the table. While still at the dinner table, we heard a loud explosion nearby. It came from the Darul Aman Palace, where Amin had moved recently. This single explosion was soon followed by others. Ali laughed and said, "Good! I want more of it. One is not enough to kill those rascals."

Looking out the windows in the direction of the new presidential palace, we could see large, shiny objects the size of basketballs moving through the sky in all directions, probably to light the area. A huge fireworks show was taking place in front of us. We stopped eating and stood at the second-floor windows to watch this new development. My neighbors were out on their roof. Some were scared, others desperate. My son ran to the TV. It was off the air. I tried to listen to Kabul radio. It was dead too, but I purposely left it on. An hour or so later the same familiar music, the national anthem, was heard – the music we always heard when the government changed. I was happy, though I didn't know what was happening. Whatever it was, it meant a change in the government and a fierce struggle for power. It also pointed up the fallacies of Communist governments in Afghanistan.

The sky over the palace was now completely red from the explosions and the large balloon-shaped light bulbs were still flying, turning the area bright. All the phones were down; no communication was possible. Again we were isolated from the rest of the world.

Scores of helicopters flew in at low altitude, some circling back and forth. Once in a while they searched the ground with their large lights. It so frightened me that we turned off all the indoor lights and spent the rest of the night in darkness. The blasts were nerve-racking. They became louder as time went on, and bullets filled the air in front of our house. Sahar was terrified; she cried inconsolably. I put her head on my chest, while listening to the radio, and tried to cover her ears and face with my hands and the blanket. It still did not give her comfort, so I started singing the old songs that she used to sing with her dad. She liked it very much. Slowly her eyes closed and an hour later she was sound asleep.

By midnight the entire city was on fire. Two huge columns of smoke and fire were seen over the president's new palace. Ali turned on the TV again, this time picking up some sounds. Two men were talking. One asked the other what was happening. The second replied, "I don't know. The whole world around me is in chaos." Then they both laughed. The first man said, "Oh brother, it's like a hell here too!" Several explosions were heard and his voice was cut off.

Very late at night a familiar voice was heard, speaking in Persian. The volume was low and irregular; the broadcast certainly was coming from somewhere far away, probably from outside the country. It was Babrak Karmal speaking from exile, promising a new government in Afghanistan. Later I heard that Babrak talked from the Tashkent radio station in the Soviet Union.

Babrak Karmal had been elected vice president and deputy premier of Afghanistan after the coup of April 1978. In July of 1978, according to widespread rumors, the two Communist parties, Khalq and Parcham, broke with each other, so Babrak, along with five associates, was sent out of the country on a diplomatic mission. Three months later, in October of 1978, all six Parcham leaders were accused of looting their embassies and were denounced as traitors. They were ordered to return home but none of them did. Rumor had it that they were supported by the Soviet Union and lived in hiding in Moscow. Of course, the Parchamis inside Afghanistan also suffered from the split and were removed from important jobs. Some lived in hiding; others were imprisoned or killed.

SATURDAY, DECEMBER 29, 1979 (JADI 8,1358)

The skies were still full of jets and helicopters, and shots were heard here and there but their exact location was hard to determine. I went to the university. At an intersection near the university, young students, heavily armed, were standing in big groups watching people go by. Each of them wore a white band on the left arm. I did not understand what it stood for, but possibly it was so that the group's members could be recognized.

Inside my building, I looked at the large photos that always hung in the hallway. The frames still held Amin's likeness. Perhaps the change of the government was unexpected this time. The participants had not had time to break the pictures as they had in the past. Sooner or later, however, someone would break them.

I went to my morning class. The students were calm, except for two, who seemed restless and very talkative. I called on one of them, Mohammed, to be quiet. He did for a short while, then he began to talk to his friend again. Mohammed had been a student of mine for the past two years, a somewhat less than average student. He was always quiet, but today he could not calm down. I tried to ignore him. But I could not. Finally I asked, "Mohammed, what is your problem? Do you have something to tell us?"

He stood at his desk and, like a prerecorded tape, praised the new government, exaggerating every move of Babrak. He talked for quite some time. Then, finally, with a heroic gesture he said, "*Ostad*, we blocked all the main streets from Amin's soldiers last night. We were up all night and captured so many of Amin's terrorists!" He described how many people, the real enemies of Afghanistan, had cried and begged him not to harm their children. He went on and on, mentioning the names of some important people in Amin's regime who had cried.

I knew that during Amin's regime the Parchamis had gone into hiding. Today people like my student Mohammed acted like great heroes. Their power obviously came from all those Russian cargo planes that had dumped their weapons and personnel in this country. Now the misguided young puppets talked so wholeheartedly of their bravery! I could have sworn that Mohammed had slept all night long and did not really know what was going on. Without thinking I said, "Where the hell were you people yesterday that, out of nowhere, you show up today wearing a white armband and become heroes?"

The other students laughed. Mohammed sat down quietly and didn't say another word.

THURSDAY, JANUARY 3, 1980 (JADI 13, 1358)

Babrak Karmal did not appear on television in person to address the people for several days after his speech from the Soviet Union. Later, when he appeared on January 3, he did exactly as the previous leaders had done: he blamed the preceding government for all of Afghanistan's miseries and misfortunes. Babrak Karmal was the third Communist president since the coup of April 1978. Now that he was back in the country, he announced a general amnesty for political prisoners, regardless of their ideas, race, or religious beliefs. I sincerely welcomed the news and thought that at least now someone would tell me where Saleem was.

SUNDAY, JANUARY 6, 1980 (JADI 16, 1358)

This was the day that all prisoners would be released. It was the big day – a big day in my life, and in the life of many others who wanted to know where their missing family members were!

It was a crystal-clear bitterly cold day in Kabul, one of those days when the door handle would firmly stick to your hand as you went to open your car door. Although the rising sun of the early morning shone brightly, to me it seemed as dark as my own shadow. My heart beat rapidly. Excited, frustrated, and exhausted from last night's lack of sleep, I had wakened early in the morning. I had prayed all night long. I remembered the words of the warden of Puli-Charkhi prison when he had told Jaan that Saleem's name was on the list of prisoners to be released today. My heart was as full of hope that Saleem would come home as it had been in the last twenty months of my life.

As soon as I got up I put the teapot on the electric warmer and prepared breakfast for my children, who were still in bed. I had hardly taken the first sip of tea when Jaan showed up at the front door. I hurriedly left with him, leaving the cup half full. With lots of hope and prayers we headed toward the Puli-Charkhi prison, each of us silent, in our own world.

When we got near the downtown area, we saw that even at this early hour, many roads were closed and thousands of people stood along the several miles of thoroughfares leading to the prison grounds. They must have been waiting there since before dawn. Jaan and I couldn't get through the congestion, so we decided to join the crowd and wait at the corner of Mohammed Jan Khan Road. According to information from a passing policeman, the prisoners were supposed to be released at ten in the morning and their buses would pass through this area.

The morning cold was nearly unbearable and made people very restless. A mother held a crying baby in her arms, its face dark red from the cold. She tried to feed him but it was useless; the baby would not quit crying. A little boy of six or so held onto his uncle's left hand firmly while shivering in his thin, baggy clothes. He asked continuously when his father would come. Once in a while he stood on tiptoe to see if his father was there yet, but his short stature did not let him see much. The overwhelming joy of the possibility of seeing his father made things for this little boy seem much easier than they really were.

A couple of women on my left, still in veils, were talking loudly, both eating popcorn to kill the time. The loud crunching and grinding of the hard kernels of corn close to my ears drove me crazy. It seemed like they were shoveling bag after bag of popcorn into their mouths nonstop.

Behind us many people walked up and down the street to keep warm. I watched the crowd carefully. Glimmers of hope and shadows of fear and doubt were evident in almost everybody's eyes. Prayers were heard all around. Some had brought the Holy Koran, at times pressing it to their breasts firmly and kissing it. Some made promises to God that if they found their missing loved ones, they would sacrifice a sheep or a cow at such and such a shrine and feed it to the needy. Some cried, while others laughed nervously.

A well-dressed elderly woman in front of me cried softly, saying something that didn't make sense. The long, narrow streams of tears down her face were nearly frozen and looked like small icicles reflecting the sunlight. She constantly wiped them off but couldn't stop crying. She shivered in spite of her warm clothing and I could hear the chattering of her teeth. I looked at her for a while. Her white hair and wrinkled face told a story of their own. She must have spent years of her life in hardship and patience to raise her son. Now it was time for the son to hold her hand and walk with her through the rest of her life, but that son had disappeared. I don't know how long I stared at her till our eyes met. I nodded my head and winked, trying to comfort her and tell her that she was not alone. She smiled and wiped her face.

Time passed at a crawl; in fact it seemed to come to a standstill. The little hand of my wristwatch hit nine, ten, eleven, eleven-thirty . . . and still nothing changed; we waited impatiently. The crowd became more and more restless. Finally a loud voice was heard from the back: "Here they come!"

The crowd looked in the direction from which the sound came. A car was approaching down the street. We all thought the prisoners had arrived. Suddenly a wall of people moved forward like a tidal wave. We quickly realized that it was only a police car. Just as I was swept up by the surge of the crowd, so we returned to our original places and the excitement was slowly replaced by a silence – the silence that precedes a storm.

By this time I was very cold, shivering uncontrollably even though I had wrapped myself in a heavy coat and a jacket. It seemed that nothing stopped the cold. I went to my car for a while and watched the people from a distance. From my vantage point the scene looked exactly like a breeze passing over a vast wheat field as all the heads turned first in one direction and then slowly turned back. Between twelve and one o'clock the restless crowd moved forward countless times in response to some sound, only to be forced back with blows from policemen on horses. Somehow, watching the crowd made me feel less lonely. Just the thought of how many missing persons there were in the country made me realize that I was not alone in my adversity, for almost none of the bystanders I asked knew where their loved ones were being held.

At about two o'clock someone called out, "The prisoners won't come this way. They will go down Pashtunistan Street!"

Those who heard it began to run to get ahead of the rest and find the best spot on that street. Mothers cursed and yelled at their cold, hungry, crying children to hurry up. Even the vendors who sold snacks from their carts joined in the race. My brother came running up to the car, where I was watching, paralyzed, and shouted, "Let's go!"

I came to myself, my hands numb and my cheeks and nose still burning from the cold. I felt extremely tired. Jaan drove to Pashtunistan Street, where people stood in rows, looking gaunt and despairing. Three things we all shared in common were hope, prayers – and pain. There was so much pain in the air that I felt indifferent to everything in the world, exactly as your body adjusts to a strong odor and you no longer smell it because your receptors have become fatigued. Yes, I was tired of this entire game, a sad and dirty game the Communist governments of Afghanistan were playing with the people.

I went back to the car and repeated all the prayers that Mother had taught me. Too soon they were finished; I knew I still had to wait. I found myself involuntarily counting the chimney tops in sight, then I divided the final number, twenty-five, by five and it came out even. It made me happy. I took it as a good omen because it represented the number of members in my family including Saleem. My husband would surely return today and we would number five again!

I found myself counting cars, women dressed in green, windows, trees – whatever I could see. Then if the sum was divisible by five, it made me happy; if not, I quit that item and started on a new one. Yes, again the pressure had turned me into a computerized counting robot, out of control!

Hours passed; nothing happened. The sun slowly disappeared behind the tall Kabul Hotel and Ministry of Communications buildings. Shadows became longer and longer as did the faces in this tired crowd. The wind started blowing colder and harder than before. My brother still wandered among the crowd, picking up rumors. Finally he came and said we should move closer to Puli-Charkhi; nothing was happening here. After driving for half an hour through narrow side streets because the main thoroughfares were blocked by the crowd, we finally made it to Microrayan Street. Puli-Charkhi prison was still ten kilometers away, but this was as close as we could get that day. I stepped out of the car and was surprised to see many university friends who were also waiting for missing relatives or friends. They had not disclosed their situations because they were afraid to tell others.

Finally, starting about six in the evening, when the sun had completely disappeared behind the mountains, twenty or so buses finally emerged from the direction of Puli-Charkhi, each carrying perhaps half a dozen prisoners. The rest of the passengers were people who had come to meet their missing relatives but had not found them and were heading back to their homes.

We waited till the last bus passed by. It was now close to eight o'clock. A friend who saw me still standing there came forward and told me that each bus was going to a different part of the city. If we had not seen

Saleem yet, chances were that he was sent directly to the bus stop near-est our house. So Jaan and I rushed to meet the bus that was apparently going toward our house. At the bus stop nearest home we waited for some time. No one came. Then we went to the first bus stop in the other direction. We waited and waited, again with no luck.

At nine o'clock I decided to go home. I had not eaten since morning; I did not even notice that I was hungry. My children, who had waited all day long, came running to greet me but fell silent when they found me alone. I did not dare to look into their eyes as I tried to evade their questions. Whenever I tried to speak to them that night, my voice broke and I could not talk about the day.

That night, how foolishly I wanted to believe Babrak's promises. My eyes and ears were fixed on our door, hoping that Saleem would arrive any minute now and thinking that probably I had missed his bus. To avoid my little girl, Sahar's, eyes, I put her head on my chest and hid my head in the shadows. I hid my tears from everybody in the room. I cried in those protecting shadows for a long time, keeping my voice down, trying hard not to make things worse than they already were for my family. Nobody asked for dinner that night; to this day I don't know whether my children ate or not. We all were quiet.

In order to break the silence, I turned on the TV and we all watched. The day's events at the Puli-Charkhi prison were being aired. As a crowd was shown leaving the prison, my eyes searched frantically for anyone resembling Saleem. The announcer said, "These are the innocent people that the bloodthirsty and infamous butcher Amin imprisoned."

When I left the house the next morning, I met a friend at the near-est intersection. He told me about the situation at Puli-Charkhi. His brother had disappeared six months before when he had gone out shop-ping. No one knew what happened to him or where he was. My friend had managed to reach the prison yesterday. Around ten in the morning the guards opened the main door and told those waiting there to enter and welcome their prisoners up close. They had planned by this action to show the public the empty cells, and also to let people know that the government had released all the prisoners, as Babrak had promised.

My friend said, "Puli-Charkhi prison is divided into five sections, built in concentric circles. The innermost circle, impossible to escape from, is for important political prisoners. Most of the prisoners of this circle are from the army and air force. If anyone tried to escape, he would have to pass through all the rest of the circles before he could leave the prison. Each circle has buildings several stories high."

My friend looked around to make sure no one was nearby. Then he continued, "Yesterday, at first they let the crowd see that all of the first-floor rooms were empty. In contrast to what people expected, they were allowed to tour only the first level. The upper floors were off limits and all their windows were covered with papers, but once in a while you could see a hand move behind one of those covered windows. Maybe someone was trying to tell the crowd that there were still many in those upstairs cells who were not being released." He paused and then went on, "After viewing the first-floor rooms, the crowd wanted to see the rest of the prison. The more they insisted, the more armed guards there were to prevent it."

Then my friend looked at his watch and added, "People waited for their prisoners to be released. They waited for several hours and most were disappointed. Finally they went on a rampage when they saw hands and faces behind the papered windows on the upper floors. Suddenly the prison gates were closed and all the visitors were trapped. Fighting broke out between the crowd and the guards, who opened fire. Nobody knows what the casualties were. Finally when the crowd calmed down, the guards opened the door and a news helicopter that was flying low began to shoot pictures of the people, who were very eager to get out of the place."

"So that's what caused all the delays yesterday!" I said, remembering that the TV had not given the details of the incident, but only showed the crowd leaving the prison – the so-called "innocent people that the bloodthirsty and infamous butcher Amin had imprisoned!"

Later we heard that most of the very few prisoners released that day belonged to Babrak's party. Nevertheless, for months thereafter the newspapers were full of headlines such as "Amin a Megalomaniac"; "Iron Gates of Amin's Bastille Open Forever"; "U.S. Sheds Crocodile Tears for Amin"; and "Puli-Charkhi Prison Doors Swung Open to All Political Prisoners."

MONDAY, JANUARY 14, 1980 (JADI 24, 1358)

The government claimed that by January 14 more than six thousand political prisoners had been released throughout the country. Since Saleem had not returned I went to check with Samae. He was out of his office, so I waited for him. When he returned, he told me that because of unrest inside the prison it was decided that prisoners would be released in small groups sometime this week.

"Crossroads rumors" indicated that several thousand prisoners were still being held in Puli-Charkhi. People said that about a thousand of them had raided the prison offices because they had not been released as promised. Many prisoners were tortured and killed after this incident. I could tell that the rumors were correct because no visitors had been allowed near Puli-Charkhi on Friday, the eleventh.

Babrak announced a general condolence ceremony for all those who were killed during the previous twenty-one months. He attended very faithfully the Revolutionary Council's Congregational Mosque to share the families' tragic loss and also to impress the public with his government's virtue.

One day – I think it was sometime during the fourth week of December – out of desperation I decided to go to the American embassy. I wanted to know what kind of help the embassy could provide me if I left the country. I took a cab, but knowing that most of the taxi drivers were government agents, I got out approximately three blocks from my destination. In the embassy I met someone I will call Tom. My meeting with him had been arranged with the help of a friend who worked there.

I described my situation briefly while Tom took down the information on a piece of paper. It seemed that he knew something about what had taken place at the Khoja Rawash Air Force Base on April 27, 1978. My understanding after this meeting was that when I got to India, political asylum would be granted.

Today as I look back upon the things I did in the past, I am amazed at my impulsiveness. Going to the American embassy was one of the craziest things I have ever done. How in the world did I dare to cross that network of Afghan police cameras and their tight circle of spies? What was I going to tell them if they stopped me? The only thing I had in mind was to tell them I was there to see an Afghan friend who worked there. But what if they asked why I couldn't see my friend at home?

FRIDAY, JANUARY 18, 1980 (JADI 28, 1358)

Yesterday I went to see two officers who worked in the Ministry of Defense who were supposed to find me some files on Saleem's case, but both had been arrested by the secret police and I was not able to meet with them. It seemed that despite Babrak's pronouncements and promises, the facts were quite different. People were still being arrested and tortured. Nothing was changed – the same terroristic Communist government, except that now the Soviet-backed Babrak was in command.

I met Amir, one of my students, in front of Puli-Charkhi this morning. Our conversation centered on the Russian cargo planes, and he said, "My father works at the airport. He says that most of these planes hold three tanks complete with ammunition, the personnel to man the tanks, and food supplies for up to three months."

Amir pointed to a huge Russian plane in the sky overhead and added, "As soon as these planes are unloaded, the orders are that the tanks should move out immediately to a concealed place in the hills near the Kabul airport so people won't know just how much artillery is pouring into this country."

Years later, here in the United States, one of our neighbors who worked at the Kabul airport during the Russian invasion of 1979 told me that all the offices around the runways were occupied by Soviet soldiers, who slept there at night. When the office workers arrived in the morning, they would find the trash and other personal items that were left behind. My neighbor also said that all day long, on an average of every three minutes, a large cargo plane landed, its artillery and personnel dispersing into the nearby villages. Her words certainly confirmed what Amir had told me a long time before.

WEDNESDAY, JANUARY 23, 1980 (DALV 3, 1358)

Babrak's government announced the details of the assassination of Taraki by Amin and his gang as follows: "Taraki was suffocated with a pillow. During the last moments of his life, the "Great Leader" asked that his watch, 45,000 afghanis, and some trinkets that he had with him be delivered to his wife."

A few days after the announcement was made, I met a good friend of mine, a chemistry professor at the university. He said, "*Ostad,* I just want to compare the last wishes and concerns of two leaders of neighboring countries at the time of their death."

I smiled and said, "Let's hear what's on your mind today."

"When the shah of Iran was dying, he wished that his body be buried next to that of a soldier who had fought for the liberation of his country. When Taraki was dying, all he had to say was to give his money to his wife!"

Soon after the announcement of the details of Taraki's death, Amin became the focus of many jokes and sardonic comments. He was recognized as the "Faithful Student" who killed his teacher. Mottos such as "Beware of the Faith and Revenge of a Disciple" echoed everywhere.

TUESDAY, FEBRUARY 19, 1980 (DALV 30, 1358)

I wanted to go shopping, but all the major streets were barricaded. It was impossible to go anywhere, and most of the shops were closed anyway.

It seemed that everyone was on strike. The strike had been in effect off and on for quite some time, but it seemed more serious now. All the promises of the new government could not placate the people.

FRIDAY, FEBRUARY 22, 1980 (HOOT 3, 1358)

Tonight, right after dinner, I heard an indistinct but continuous buzzing sound that was unintelligible at first. We all went outside to listen. Gradually as it became louder and clearer I was able to make out the words "Allah-u-akbar" – "God is great." The cry started at the outskirts of the city and soon spread throughout the capital as thousands of people shouted it full-throatedly from their rooftops. The evening breeze carried the sound from the left. It became louder and louder as it approached us, then faded away into the far right end of Kabul.

Soon all our neighbors joined in and it seemed that everybody was chanting, "Allah-u-akbar!" It was thrilling to know that a nation considered uneducated and backward by many in the rest of the world valued human freedom above all else – that it could no longer stand the lies and repressiveness of Communist rule. The action was magnificent because those sound waves carried the defiance, tears, and heartfelt yearnings of the people of Afghanistan: the right to freedom is a God-given gift to all living beings from the day they are born; no one, no one in the world should try to take it away from them!

Ali ran excitedly to the second floor, opened the window, and started shouting with the rest. His breaking adolescent voice made us all laugh. From the second-floor balcony I watched our new tenant in the house next door who belonged to Babrak's party, Parcham. He went into his living room and hastily removed all of Babrak's photos and slogans from the walls.

During the Communist takeover it was common to decorate houses, offices, and university halls with photos and slogans from the regime in power. With great dismay I observed that those spineless jellyfish kept switching the pictures with each new regime.

I remembered that about a year before, one of the teaching assistants, Karima, had brought me a nicely framed photo of Taraki and placed it on my desk when I was out of the office. The next morning when I saw the picture, I asked her, "Well, who put this picture here?"

"Our director of education sent it for our office," Karima replied.

"Then give it back to him and tell him to put it on his desk." I added quickly, "If I ever put a picture here, it will be of my family, no one else!"

Karima laughed and without another word removed Taraki's picture. Later I heard that because I'd refused to put the "Great Leader's" photo in my office, a report had been added to my file that I was opposed to the government.

SATURDAY, FEBRUARY 23, 1980 (HOOT 4, 1358)

Today we were ordered to stay home and all the offices were closed. I got up at nine and heard anti-Communist slogans coming from the street behind us. It looked like a large group of people were approaching. When they got very close to us, the sound of machine guns filled the air, followed by cries of "Allah-u-akbar!" Again shooting was heard and this time it continued for ten minutes or so. The noise of gunfire mingling with the screams of hundreds of people made me sick to my stomach. Mother put her hands to her head and said, "My God! They've killed everyone!" When the bullets stopped . . . no more shouts were heard.

Since the government had announced that everyone must stay inside, I could not buy fresh vegetables from the nearby shop. I went into the kitchen and started to prepare what I could find on hand. At one o'clock in the afternoon, to my great surprise, I heard again the sounds of another large group of protesters coming from the south side of our house, from the Karta-e-Seh area. They may have been heading downtown. I stopped working in the kitchen and listened carefully. I couldn't believe my ears. Yes, it was women and possibly some children shouting, "Death to Communism and all its puppets!" "Death to those who sold out our nation!" I closed my eyes and pictured myself among those brave women who had taken great risk to oppose the regime publicly. I wished I were among them. My thought did not last very long before the second round of gunfire began. I pictured a war zone outside: cries, screaming, shouting . . . and then not a single sound was heard. Everything seemed dead. I sat on the floor. The idea that they had killed all of them was driving me crazy. I couldn't eat anything that day.

We were under a twenty-four-hour curfew. I remembered that the daughter of my best friend, Naheed, was to have been married the day before. I wondered how the marriage ceremony had gone, with all the unrest and the curfew. The nightly news did not surprise me. As I expected, there were no reports of the day's incident. The government was once again playing its "nothing happened" game.

WEDNESDAY, FEBRUARY 27, 1980 (HOOT 8, 1358)

The twenty-four-hour curfew lasted for three days throughout the entire city. It was hard to keep my apprehensive mother, who could not go home, very happy. We cooked meals from whatever I could find in the house. My children were tired of eating only rice and lentils or beans for three days.

After the curfew ended, I went to school and reported to the central office, as we had been told to do. On my way to work I looked around for clues about the shootings around our house. There were no signs of them, except that the edges of the roads were heavily rutted from the passing of tanks.

MONDAY, MARCH 10, 1980 (HOOT 20, 1358)

Yesterday I went to the home of my friend Naheed, whose daughter Ziagul was to have been married on the night of February 22. I asked her, "How did the wedding go? It must have been an awfully hard day for you!"

Naheed laughed and said, "It certainly was. That morning everything was normal. Ziagul and several close relatives went to a hair stylist, but by noon all the city roads were blocked. We didn't know how to get them out of the salon. We called at least a hundred different places, including all the police stations in the area, the mayor, and the minister of the interior. Finally we were permitted to go and get Ziagul and the others who'd gone with her. It was five o'clock in the afternoon when we managed to bring them home. As we crossed the roads, bullets whizzed by in every direction. We were so afraid of being hit."

"Now listen to this!" Naheed continued. "By early morning that day my house was full of relatives and friends who had the day off and had come to help me. By noon, when the shooting started, I was stuck with more than thirty women, all crying and hysterical! With each bullet that passed over our house, someone screamed and the rest cried."

I pictured my friend trapped at home with that miserable crowd around her for three days. I began to chuckle, "I'm sorry, dear. Go on."

She resumed, "All the food that was prepared at the hotel for the two hundred guests was wasted because there was no way to get it to our house." She looked at me closely and added, "Anyway, since we couldn't get the food, I was stuck with thirty-five highly emotional guests who were hungry and also very upset because they couldn't contact their families. When night came we faced another problem. Most were in their fancy party clothes, and finding them nightgowns and a place to sleep was another big headache."

Naheed paused a moment to join in my laughter, then said, "I think that under stress one eats a lot. I cooked and cooked and cooked all day long – and still I couldn't keep them happy."

At this point Naheed went into the kitchen, brought out a cup of tea for me, and went on, "Most of my guests were old. They not only worried about their immediate families, but about their distant cousins, neighbors, and their maids too! As soon as one woman began to cry, then the whole group started shedding tears. This drove me crazy. It went on and on till a bullet came through our window. It passed through the living room and dining room and finally lodged in the wooden frame of the room divider. Luckily, it didn't hit anyone, but it certainly calmed down the chorus of weeping guests, because now they worried about their own safety rather than that of others!"

Although I felt sorry for Naheed, the situation was very funny the way she described it. She explained further, "After that shot, the situation changed. Now the guests avoided walking in front of the windows and gathered in the corners away from the windows." Naheed's house had extremely large windows and it was impossible to move around a room without passing a window. "After that," she added, "we sat on the floor to eat and tried to stay away from the windows for three days."

FRIDAY, MARCH 21, 1980 (HAMAL 1, 1359)

The New Year was not celebrated this year. Most of the restaurants, cinemas, and shopping centers were closed; only a few small candy shops remained open. No fairs, no carts full of candies and colored eggs on the street corners. It seemed the entire city was in deep grief.

Today, after I returned from Puli-Charkhi, tanks carrying Russian soldiers parked in all the intersections. It looked like they were on alert and ready to fire. Kabul residents were resisting the new Communist rulers and the Russians were getting tougher. When would we have peace again? I did not know. Maybe someday, but not during my lifetime.

SUNDAY, APRIL 27, 1980 (SAUR 7, 1359)

High schools, especially the girls' schools, had been on strike for several weeks. It was common for students to congregate outside their classes and the government was getting impatient.

Most of the widely distributed "night letters" tried to enlist the entire city in a boycott. Some of them threatened that people who did not stay home would be shot. Conditions were extremely bad and people didn't know what to do. On one hand the underground letters told them to stay home; on the other hand, the government ordered them to report to work. In either case the penalty might be death, so I chose to report to school.

The city was divided into sectors and government officials searched the houses for weapons. Whenever they found a firearm, the secret police took the owner in for interrogation. Up to now, there had been no regulations concerning the possession of weapons in Afghanistan and most houses kept one or more. The government was well aware of this, but who could argue with those mutton-head puppets?

On this night I hid the German pistol in the attic very close to the metal roof. If they searched my house with metal detectors, the pistol would not be discovered. Although it would not be easily accessible in an emergency, I thought that was the best place around the house to conceal it from the officials.

MONDAY, APRIL 28, 1980 (SAUR 8, 1359)

The country's conditions had become even worse. Several months had passed since I applied for a passport and I still didn't know whether I would be able to make the planned trip to India, because the report from the secret police had not been made yet. With great sorrow I resolved to leave the country – for who knew how long? – the country to which I owed my entire life, the country my husband took such pride in serving, the land we cherished, treasuring its memories deeply, the one we always felt homesick for when we traveled.

This day, on my way home, I reviewed the situation carefully and these were my conclusions: It had been two years since my husband had gone missing, with no word about him or the reason for his disappearance. I didn't know whether he was alive or not. I had a sick child and was not permitted to have her admitted to the only hospital that had proper facilities, even though I was willing to pay the entire cost up front. We had lost not only the benefits of health insurance but also Saleem's social security and the retirement money he had paid into the fund directly out of his paycheck every month.

Many young students had disappeared lately without a trace. The schools were getting dangerous. I could not send my children to school without worrying about them all day long. I'd had them stay home several times during the past two weeks because of student demonstrations and the brutal efforts of the police to repress them. Omar and Ali both complied with my orders but didn't understand my position. They thought I was paranoid.

I did not have security at my job. Any minute, I thought, they would come and arrest me. There were no guarantees of safety for any one of us anymore. In fact, circumstances were forcing me to leave as soon as possible – not for myself but for the safety of my family. It was the hardest decision I ever made in my life. To assuage my agony, I promised that I would return when conditions became right. Surely the Russians would not last very long.

The day I decided to leave, I cried all the way home from the office. A searing pain shot through my heart when I looked at the Aliabad Mountains behind the university. I remembered the times in college when we frolicked and played games among those steep rocks. We even tried one day to climb a large boulder but didn't get very far before one of our classmates got stuck between two rocks. The rest of us tried to rescue her and the whole class missed a lecture. The dean didn't let us make up the test we missed that day; he never understood the pleasure we derived from going up there.

All night long my head was full of unanswered questions. What was I going to do in a foreign country with no money, all by myself with three children? How would I be able to earn money for their food and education? Would I be able to provide the comforts they had here at home? What if my husband was released and I wasn't home? Would he understand? Was I doing the right thing? What about the promise I'd made to him: "In bad times as well as good, in sickness and in health, I will stay by your side until death parts us"?

I had applied for a passport, but then my idea had been to return home after my daughter's medical treatment. Now I must change the plan and I needed more money. I couldn't sell our real estate because of the uncertainty concerning my husband; and even if he were no longer living, it could not be sold till all the children had passed their eighteenth birthday. I dare not sell the household goods because that would attract attention. Even if I did, they would realize only a small fraction of their original price. So I would have to give away everything we had accumulated and saved bit by bit over the years. My heart broke when I remembered that Saleem had sometimes saved money by canceling a movie or a trip in order to have enough to build our house.

Could I keep my plan secret? I certainly could not tell my husband's family that I was leaving. The very few whom I trusted could not keep the news to themselves, especially my mother-in-law, who would begin to cry, and then others would know. Would our departure be too hard on her, especially at this time when my husband was missing too? What would happen to my mother and brothers and sisters? Would the government arrest them because I had left the country? Many close relatives were arrested and questioned if one family member left the country. Yet how could we all leave with our children, twenty-six of us, without being noticed? The more I thought, the more questions appeared in my head which called for answers – answers that I did not have. In fact, everything seemed impossible, out of reach.

Finally, early in the morning, I decided to put all the negative and all the positive points of my plan on the two sides of an imaginary balance. On the left side went all the negatives, such as lack of money, trouble finding a decent job, starting all over again from zero, leaving all my property behind; on the right side were the positive points, such as having a safer life for my sons and not being afraid of losing them, having proper health care and a good education for my children, not having to worry about spies and false reports. I still was not able to decide. In fact, it seemed I might lose a whole lot more than I gained in the deal. The future lay ahead of me as a somber blur.

At last I realized that what I would really gain from leaving would be freedom. The thought of freedom grew larger and larger in my mind until it completely weighed down the right side of that imaginary balance. It would be well worth fighting for. I thought, I can trade everything in the world, all the luxurious and elegant things in my life, in order to earn freedom for my family and for my mother, my brothers and sisters, and their families. The idea of achieving freedom for all of us gave me the peace of heaven.

TUESDAY, APRIL 29, 1980 (SAUR 9, 1359)

The Malalai Girls' High School students were demonstrating, and army tanks and police had blocked the main streets around the school. It was impossible to get to the stores I wanted to go to, so I changed direction and went past the Lycée Aisha-i-Durani, another girls' high school. Students had gathered in front of it and police had surrounded them. As I left the area I heard a few shots, most probably fired into the air to scare the students. The courage of the high school girls like these was admirable. They continued their protests despite the government's harsh actions.

At the university I saw many students gathered outside the engineering building. It had been more than a week since the government had decided to close Kabul University's Faculty of Engineering, which was staffed by American and Afghan professors. They ordered the students to take classes instead at the Institute of Polytechnics, which was staffed by Russian teachers. The students opposed the idea and went on strike, demanding their own professors and refusing to attend class.

I arrived at my office around noon. After leaving my books in the office and signing the attendance book, I decided to go to the cafeteria, which was about a block from the science building. Half a block away from the cafeteria I saw small groups of students running as fast as they could, followed by a crowd coming from the east side of the campus. Everyone was trying to get into the nearest building. A student next to me shouted, "Something's wrong! Run!"

I ran toward the pharmacy building, which was the one closest to us, and tried to get away from the onrushing crowd. I had almost reached the building when a very low-flying helicopter suddenly showed up from behind the nearby buildings. Shots rang out from all directions. I couldn't tell who was firing or from where. My God, the solid masonry pharmacy building shook heavily and I could hear the shattering of glass as windows broke throughout! I couldn't believe what was going on around me. I felt like I was watching a Vietnam war movie. The scene outside was one of chaos: fallen tree limbs; scattered books, shoes, and purses; and a few screaming students who were running hysterically in every direction. The pages of the books littering the ground fluttered aimlessly in the helicopter's strong wake. Dust and gunsmoke filled the air.

On my right a professor had been stopped by an armed student, who was holding a gun to his chest. Like me, the teacher didn't understand what was going on and had simply been running to escape the gunfire. The student's face was pale and his hands shook badly. It seemed that he didn't have experience in using the pistol. He was babbling something like "Why are you here?" I didn't know what to do. Should I tell the student to leave him alone, or should I run? At that moment another student, who was carrying an automatic rifle and had been chasing the frantic students, ran past and shouted, "Asif, let the professor go." It was clear that they were after the students.

All of the events happened so fast that I hardly had time to climb the few steps leading to the building before another helicopter appeared. A volley of gunshots hit the science building. Windows broke, screams were heard, and students fell where they had been caught in the street or on the grounds.

I barely made it to the basement of the pharmacy building, where I hid for some time in a room along with about thirty students. We were all frightened. Each time someone new entered the room we all screamed, thinking that someone with a rifle might have found our hiding place. I could hear the people around me gasping for breath as if they had just run a strenuous race. We couldn't see outside but we could hear the rattle of machine guns and the sound of people running on the floor above us.

After an hour or so I opened a door leading outside. It faced the small restaurant where I usually went for shish kabob. Not a single soul was present on this side of the pharmacy building. Everyone was on the other side, where the main street was. Gunshots could still be heard from the direction of my office.

Scared and shivering, half a dozen students and I passed behind the shops, auto pool, Faculty of Letters, and engineering and agriculture buildings and finally I made my way to the nearest bus stop. Nearby was a small shopping center that served the university students and the little community behind it. Here everybody stood on the street corner and watched the helicopters attacking the university. Still as frightened as ever and panting for breath, I climbed on a bus heading away from the campus. Close to home I saw one of my neighbors. She asked if I knew what was going on at the university, but I was too upset to talk. I cut the conversation short and replied that no, I didn't.

By now jets and helicopter gunships seemed to cover the sky. I called Mother and asked for my brother who was an engineering student at the university. Fortunately, he had stayed home that day. People said that all the telephone wires were tapped, so I didn't explain why I was concerned about him.

Night came and the radio news came on. The announcer reported that the government had captured and imprisoned the foreign agents of the United States, Pakistan, and Egypt – agents who had duped innocent students with their lies and propaganda. And then there was the familiar ultimatum that we heard whenever something went wrong: "Do not gather or stand around in groups. Everyone must report to their offices and their classes on time. Disobedience will not be tolerated."

All night the sound of low-flying planes and helicopters and of gunfire was heard all over town. At two in the morning I was awakened by machine gun fire very close to our house. It continued the rest of the night.

THURSDAY, MAY 1, 1980 (SAUR 11, 1359)

Yesterday, the day after the attack on the university, I went to school as the government ordered. Amazingly, everything seemed to be in its place. So far, the government had succeeded very well in clearing the roads after each incident in which perhaps many were killed. But when I entered the science hall, I could see the signs of the previous day's battle. Windows were shattered and right across from my office, on the second floor, the roof was heavily damaged. Plaster and chunks of cement from the walls covered the stairways. As I walked toward the end of the hall where the new physics building was, it became apparent that all its huge windows opening onto the small central courtyard were shattered. The lab floors were littered with broken equipment; it looked like a tornado had passed through the area. I didn't say a word, nor did I dare question the office clerks, who were watching me carefully – or at least I believed they were.

Once in my office, I asked Karima what had happened on Tuesday. She said, "The engineering students gathered in front of their building as usual. Around noon when I wanted to go out, I'd hardly stepped out of this building when suddenly a helicopter appeared and shot directly into the crowd." After a brief pause she continued, "Everybody started running for shelter. Frightened and wounded students ran into our building while the helicopters kept firing at them. Now, the armed students inside the building didn't know what was happening outside and thought this screaming crowd was attacking them, so they began firing. Some fired at the students; others fired into the air." Karima opened the door and pointed to the numerous bullet holes in the concrete ceiling. "*Ostad*," she resumed, "it was like hell. Everyone was screaming and crying. When people fell to the ground, the rest stepped over them and left them there." She added that she couldn't help anyone; all she could do was enter one of the offices and lock the door.

During lunch hour an emergency meeting was called in all the departments and the chairmen ordered us to be present every day from eight in the morning till four-thirty in the afternoon. No one was to leave early. I thought this was the government's way of checking on us. Our presence in our offices meant that we were not attending the forbidden protest gatherings, which had become more numerous lately.

Since I was the only woman at the meeting, I said it was not possible for me to be present all day long because of the lack of security on campus. I noted that I would attend all my assigned classes and keep my office hours, but other than that, I would work on my own. The chairman, however, remonstrated that it was an order; he had no choice.

"In that case," I said, "fine! I will come. Will you guarantee my safety? If Tuesday's incident is repeated and you see me in the hall and my life is in danger, will you open your office door and help me to get in? No, I don't think you will, nor can I help anyone under the same circumstances." Nobody dared to comment on my words. Finally the chairman reluctantly agreed that my concerns were realistic.

I liked our new chairman. He was a very talented and honest fellow who often advised me to try to keep my mouth shut. That day, after the meeting, he came to my office and said, "I know you don't mean any harm to anyone, but you can never tell who is who there. Please watch your words." He paused at the door for a moment, then turned back and said, "*Ostad*, I am very concerned about you and your family's safety." He knew of Saleem's disappearance and my struggle to locate him.

At home I heard from my neighbors that the police had shot two high school girls. The government did not want to release their bodies to their families. Finally, after calling numerous government officials and police stations, the families obtained the release of the girls' bodies, with firm orders that burial would not be allowed during the daylight hours. The students were buried in the dark after eight at night.

After my neighbor left, I went to the kitchen to prepare something to eat. I couldn't kept my mind off the families who had lost their daughters. Suddenly I heard my daughter scream. I looked in the direction in which she was pointing and there were grape-like clusters of bright objects being released from planes onto the nearby mountainside. These were followed by the sound of a couple of gunshots. I was scared to death, not having seen anything like it before. Rumors had been spreading about the release of poisonous gases in many areas of the country. Our housemaid cried out, "It must be the poison gas!" She hurriedly pulled the children inside the house and closed the windows. We stayed inside for hours. The shock was so great that I couldn't stand up; whenever I tried to, I would fall down.

SUNDAY, MAY 4, 1980 (SAUR 14, 1359)

It turned out that one of those martyred high school girls was a distant relative of ours. News of the government's brutality in respect to the killing of the two girls spread around the country fast. Soon after their death, strong protests against the Communist regime broke out at all the Kabul schools. It seemed that the more the government tried to enforce its ultimatums, the angrier the students became. They refused to attend class and chanted the two martyred girls' names like those of heroes. Government employees, on the other hand, were quiet, knowing that if they protested, they would lose their jobs and be interrogated or killed. Their families would starve.

All the main streets were controlled by the army. The "crossroads rumors" said that the government planned to draft teenage students and, after a few months of training, send them to fight the resistance fighters who controlled the rural areas.

WEDNESDAY, MAY 7, 1980 (SAUR 17, 1359)

Omar and Ali came home early today and said that a committee of military officers and school authorities had come to their classes to select tall students for military training. Many of the students had fled through the windows. My sons were among them.

I was shocked. The schools were now truly unsafe. I knew two professors from our department whose sons had disappeared from school and their parents did not know where they were. Whenever children were taken to military headquarters by force, the parents did not know where they were, nor were the children allowed to communicate with their parents. Today I told my sons to stay home – no more school!

WEDNESDAY, MAY 14, 1980 (SAUR 24, 1359)
The government had increased its house searches, which were carried out mainly after one o'clock in the morning. During the day the roads were guarded by army personnel. Any teenage boy who crossed the area was kidnapped by the soldiers. Parents would wait and wait for their child, who never came home.

The government had ordered that everyone must carry his or her birth certificate or a valid I.D. when outside the home. It created lots of problems for many who didn't have their correct birth date on their I.D.s. Many children who were born at home did not obtain a birth certificate immediately. When they reached the age of six, or at least when their parents thought they did, then a government I.D. was issued.

I was afraid, for both my sons were tall and looked much older than their real age. Today I told them not only to stay out of school but also to stay off the streets. I felt very bad about it – first to deny them school and then to imprison them inside their own house – but I had no other option. Omar was very understanding and cooperative, but it was impossible to keep Ali at home while I was at work. He simply did not believe what I said, and thought his mother was paranoid.

MONDAY, MAY 19, 1980 (SAUR 29, 1359)
A couple days ago, as Ali was passing along the street near our house, he was stopped by an officer who asked to see his I.D. Luckily, Ali had it in his pocket. The officer looked at his papers and said, "This is not correct. You must be older than it says!" Then he went and talked to the other military personnel inside the tank. They all checked the I.D. carefully. Finally one said, "I'm not sure, though. He looks very young."

Ali came home and told me the story. I knew my son very well. If other children had seen the tank from a distance they would have changed their direction. Ali, however, would go straight toward it. In fact, he was very careless and perhaps stupidly brave. On hearing his words, I got upset and said angrily, "Didn't I tell you not to go out on the streets? Listen carefully! Last week Professor Wasae's son disappeared. So far he hasn't found him. Why are you making things more difficult for me? I don't know what to do with you!"

Later on, when I had calmed down, I told him, "Ali, listen to me carefully." He came and sat next to me and I said, "It's more than two years that your dad has been missing. You know I have checked many provinces, near and far, with no luck. I've spent all my spare time waiting outside jails. Every place I went, I waited all day long and no answer came back. You know most of these prisons are way outside the cities, in the desert where there is no water, no food, not the shade of any tree. In spite of all this, I waited for him. The final word I got after spending each long, depressing day was that he was not there. Now, if they take you, where should I look for you? How strong do you think I am? I simply do not have enough energy left in me to start searching all over again."

I asked him once more, "Please stay home. I know it is hard for you to do and very easy for me to say. But could you tell me what else I should do?"

Omar, who wasn't much older than Ali, told me that he would watch Ali and would not let him go out when I wasn't home. After that day both my sons quit school. I knew their absences would not go unnoticed for very long. Government officials would come looking for them and would search the house. I had to find a hiding place for the boys in case the house was unexpectedly searched. I made them a place among the huge grapevines that covered the high fences we had built years before. The wood fence was constructed like a roofed corridor, the flat roof being completely covered with vines. When the grapes were ripe they hung inside the fence and bees and wasps swarmed around them by the thousands. I told Omar that as soon as someone came to search the house, he should climb the fence and conceal himself among the dense vines and leaves. "Make sure to wear a heavy coat to prevent bee stings and don't make any noise even if the bees do sting!"

For months after this my sons stayed at home no matter where I went. Sahar, my daughter, went to school off and on, whenever her health permitted her to. I knew it was very hard on the boys to live this way. I always told them to bear with me; maybe someday I would find a way out of this mess.

TUESDAY, MAY 20, 1980 (SAUR 30, 1359)

After my morning class, we had a meeting at two in the afternoon. As I was collecting material for the meeting, one of my previous *chaprasi* (custodians) came into my office. Behaving in a completely unprecedented manner, he came up to my desk and leaned his head over close to me. Since I was busy writing a committee report, I didn't see him, but I felt his breath on my face and I jumped. I said, "Baba, what is your problem?"

He looked frightened and whispered words that I couldn't understand at first. He spoke into my ear very nervously, glancing frequently at the door as if someone might come in and see him talking to me. "Please," he said, "please, sister, go home; it isn't safe for you here." This was the first time Baba had ever called me "sister," a common term of address in Afghan conversation; normally he called me "professor." His wording caught my full attention; I thought something must have frightened him very badly. I shook my head in surprise and said, "Calm down. What's wrong?"

"Someone has left a bomb in the men's restroom just across the hall. It has two long ears." He held his arms up in the air to suggest antennae. "One of the custodians saw the bomb and then smelled it and fainted," Baba continued. "Now the Parcham students are outside the restroom door and won't let anyone in until help arrives. It may explode anytime. Please, for heaven's sake leave and go home."

I had helped Baba financially in the past. I always gave him money and used clothing, and at times I'd bought him a few grocery items too. I knew that people like him worked hard but were ineligible for any sort of government help. Their pay was so low it hardly met their minimal needs. Baba took a big risk telling me about the bomb and asking me to leave. I don't know why he put his life in jeopardy. The Parcham students were gathered across from my office door and had watched him enter my office. He apparently simply wanted to help me.

I thanked Baba as he left. From the description he had given, I thought it must be a time bomb, but why had someone fainted from its odor? I didn't want others to know that Baba had told me about it, so I forced myself to stay in my office for ten minutes, thinking my desk might blow up in my face at any moment. Finally the ten long minutes passed. Very calmly I took my purse and books and stepped outside. Some twenty Parchami students sat quietly on the floor in front of my office, guarding the restroom door so that no one could enter. To throw them off the track, I stopped and talked to one of my students who was among the Parchamis. Then I slowly walked away down the hall. God knows how badly I wanted to run, but for Baba's sake I walked.

As I entered the meeting room I saw two men in special clothing and masks come and remove the bomb. They took it outside and exploded it an hour later some distance away in the fields. It shook the buildings, but no one said a single word about it in the meeting. It was funny that we all played deaf.

Bomb explosions were not new anymore. They were heard all over the city at times. Bomb threats were common too. On occasion the dean showed up when I was teaching a large freshman class in the school auditorium and ordered everyone to leave the building because someone had phoned and told him that a bomb had been left there.

THURSDAY, MAY 29, 1980 (JAWZA 8, 1359)
"Crossroads rumors" indicated that many students had been arrested or

killed in the high schools. People were saying that at least seven girls had been martyred by police brutality.

We were ordered to take attendance every day, no matter how big the classes were. It was a time-consuming job in the large freshman classes. When I went into my class on this day, I noticed that most of the boys were absent. In answer to my question why they were not there, a girl spoke up, "Professor, they got a full scholarship – to Puli-Charkhi!" The whole class laughed but I kept quiet.

In my second class a student by the name of Karim was absent. The day before, he had come to my office and wanted to take a makeup test. I asked if anyone knew where he was, but no one said a word. After the class a student came and told me in whispers that Karim had been shot the previous night while guarding a building and had died around four in the morning on his way to the university hospital.

When I got back to my office I threw my books on the table and wept for Karim. He was too young to be dead! My memories went to yesterday, when Karim came to my office. In his long black coat and white muffler and proper formal suit he looked so nice. After we set a time for his makeup test, as Karim was walking toward the door, I said, "Karim, you look so sharp in your suit. What's the occasion?"

He turned back and replied, "Thanks, Professor. Today is my engagement party. I'm engaged to a nice girl who's in the third year of medical school." He laughed and added, "Oh, *Ostad*! She's so pretty. I'll bring her here. I want you to meet her." I smiled and wished him good luck as he left.

Since Karim had been guarding one of the important government buildings, he probably belonged to the Parcham party, a fact I hadn't known before. I hated Babrak's regime. I hated their war against the people who opposed the Communist rulers. The toll was heavy, Afghans being killed on both sides. I felt so sad that when my assistant, Karima, entered the office I asked her, "Why can't we stop wars and live in peace?"

I shook my head and continued, "I don't know what is wrong with these people!"

Karima looked at me with surprise and perplexity and kept quiet. I didn't have the energy to explain.

WEDNESDAY, JUNE 11, 1980 (JAWZA 21, 1359)

Today around eleven o'clock in the morning Saleem's niece came to our house. She attended Souria High School and could not find a bus to her home, so she came to us. She said it was the third day in a row that their school water had been poisoned. Several schoolchildren had been hospitalized or had died. Many other schools had similar problems. As usual, no one admitted to these evil deeds.

Rumors abounded that acid was thrown in the faces of people on the streets, especially girls. Many were reported to have been injured and permanently disfigured. So now, walking on the streets of Kabul was becoming very dangerous.

THURSDAY, JUNE 12, 1980 (JAWZA 22, 1359)

Yesterday several hundred students from six different schools were poisoned to death.

Gradually I was preparing to leave the country. First I wanted to paint the house and get it ready for a quick sale. At the moment I didn't know if I would be able to sell it, but I would try anyway.

I had official permission for a passport. The next important step was to get the clearance from the secret police. When I filled out the application for the police, a friend of mine told me to keep quiet about Saleem's disappearance and leave the lines blank. I replied that I better not hide anything. The secret police knew everything about me anyway. I would simply tell the truth. Whatever the government decided, it would be better to know now than to have them arrest me at the airport after I had sold everything. On the police forms I wrote the name and the work place of my husband, adding that he had been taken from his office on April 27, 1978.

TUESDAY, AUGUST 12, 1980 (ASAD 21, 1359)

The report from the secret police was not back yet. I was not sure whether I would be able to leave Afghanistan or not.

Two weeks earlier I had told Mother that I wanted to leave the country before next winter, and possibly for a long period of time until things get better at home. Although she knew that I'd applied for a passport eight months ago, she thought I was not so serious. Mother heard my news at first with great surprise and discomfort. After some thought she indicated that I was doing the right thing and that there was no hope of betterment in the country at the present time.

The situation around us was very discouraging. Here are a few examples. A relative who had returned from Kandahar said that conditions there were terrible. A couple of weeks before, someone had kidnapped their son and demanded a large sum of money. They were forced to pay the ransom to get their son back. After that, they decided to leave the area and come to Kabul. They left everything behind. Because of the lack of security, people had to leave to save their lives.

My sister Sofia, who worked in a foreign embassy, was questioned by the secret police. They asked her about the embassy's visitors and the nature of her employers' phone calls. They also wanted to know where, when, and whom the embassy's personnel had called. Sofia refused to supply this information. Eventually it cost her her job because the police would not give her a work permit unless she signed papers indicating that she would cooperate.

One of our close friends who worked in the military in Paktia province came home very frightened and upset. He said that the Russian advisers and the Afghan officers had ordered them to shoot and kill civilians. He couldn't take it anymore; he ran away and went into hiding. His house was searched several times, but he always managed to escape.

My young brother who was barely eighteen years old and a college student was on the government list of draftees. The government agents came after him several times. We hid him. So he too lived in hiding as a fugitive. He spent nights away from his home, at friends' or relatives' houses.

The fact is that we were not the only ones who lived under such pressure in Afghanistan. Stories told by many friends reflected similar situations that made daily life for everyone very difficult and miserable. Living in such an atmosphere seemed impossible.

Food prices were skyrocketing while the salaries of the few lucky ones who did not lose their jobs remained the same. People were fired without any reason. The only way to keep a job was to become a loyal party member. Jobs were not distributed on the basis of ability, knowledge, or expertise. The main criterion for getting a job was to be a loyal puppet member of the Communist party. Some of the dunderheads who lacked the necessary qualifications for a position did everything to save their job: spied on others and filed hundreds of false reports about good citizens. Such jobs were well paid and encouraged others to join the party.

MONDAY, AUGUST 25, 1980 (SUNBULA 3, 1359)
During the past few days, in my absence, my brothers and sisters and their families held private meetings every night at Mom's house to begin to map out their escape. As a precaution, the children were not allowed to attend these meetings. I knew a little about the gatherings because Jaan always told me about them the following day, but I usually did not join them because they were held late at night when I needed to be home with my youngsters.

TUESDAY, AUGUST 26, 1980 (SUNBULA 4, 1359)
People everywhere blamed Babrak for selling out to the Russians. Animosity toward the Communist regime was expressed on posters all over town. During the three short-lived Communist governments of the past twenty-eight months, huge posters and photographs of the leaders were

hung on walls on our campus. One of these pictures happened to be posted in front of my office. Every day new graffiti were added. Some of the comments that I remember went like this: "You bastard son of a bitch!" "Hypocrite Shah Shoja!" "Death to you, traitor!" "Lying crook!" "History will judge you!" "Agent of the KGB!" The rest of the posters throughout the building had similar comments. The office could not control the situation and kept replacing them with new ones.

Babrak was readily compared to Shah Shoja, a nineteenth-century ruler who was deposed. This historical event was alluded to everywhere on campus. It was described by Eqbal Ahmad and Richard J. Barnet in the April 11, 1988, issue of the *New Yorker* magazine as follows: "A Soviet historian, Naftula Khalfain, recounts the story . . . in his 1981 book *British Plots against Afghanistan.* In October of 1838, he writes, Lord Auckland announced that Britain's candidate to rule Afghanistan, Shah Shoja, would enter the country 'supported against foreign interference and factious opposition by a British army.' A British expeditionary force of more than fifty thousand, grandly named the Army of the Indus, marched into Kalat, a principality that is now part of Pakistan. In order to impress the local ruler, a British official bragged that his army had entered Kabul without firing a shot. The Khan of Kalat was silent. 'You make no answer. You seem lost in the thought,' the official said. 'Yes, I am thinking. You people have entered this country, but how you will get out?'"

Most people thought Babrak worse than Shah Shoja. A professor told me one day, "When Shah Shoja signed the deal with Britain, he cried for twenty-four hours and prayed to God to forgive him for selling his country to foreigners." He added, "Shamefully, Babrak did not shed a tear."

At first the posters were hung fairly low on the walls and students could easily reach them to write on them. But later, as the comments increased, the school authorities had no choice but to hang the posters higher. Since the students couldn't then reach them, they threw paint and ink on them, most often covering the walls as well as the posters. Fountain pen ink sprayed from every direction left a web of tracks across the walls that looked like straight lines composed of many individual dots in a row. Every day Babrak's face was buried deeper and deeper under the stains.

As usual, jokes and stories were passed around the city. This one I heard at school: A street vendor had fresh cucumbers to sell and a customer approached him and asked the price. When the vendor told him the price of the cucumbers, the customer began to bargain, insisting that the price must be reduced. Finally the seller impatiently exploded, "Brother, these are not *khak* [dust] that can be sold so cheaply! For heaven's sake, these are vegetables!" In the Dari language the word *khak* can mean either "dust" or "the land" – that is, the country, Afghanistan.

FRIDAY, AUGUST 29, 1980 (SUNBULA 7, 1359)

Since the previous year, explosions from the mountains surrounding Kabul had frequently been heard throughout the city. Rumors said that they came from nearby provincial villages that were being pounded by government forces. After a long silence on the subject, the news media finally came up with the bright idea of explaining the explosions as follows: "Our dear citizens should be aware that tomorrow the construction companies will blast stone from the mountains around the city for building." Such announcements had been repeated every evening for the past few months in the government's efforts to persuade the public that the explosions didn't mean a thing.

A friend of mine who worked at the Kabul radio station said that one day someone called the office and very politely praised the government for being so thoughtful and attentive in informing the public of the construction companies' daily activities in the nearby mountains. The caller added slyly, "Would you please also inform the citizens that the companies' work has extended to the nighttime hours – so that we can sleep without concern about the source of the explosions at night?"

My daughter Sahar's illness persisted and I kept switching from doctor to doctor. So far I'd spent more than fifty thousand afghanis on her medical treatment without getting anywhere. Just two weeks previously my sister Laila, who was a medical doctor in Herat, had come to Kabul. She looked at Sahar and told me to take her to Dr. Hassan, a neurologist. I did so – reluctantly, because like my father, I had lost faith in all the doctors in Kabul. Dr. Hassan prescribed a generic medicine that cost only seventy afghanis (less than two dollars). Sahar started with a high dose of it at first and then reduced the amount. In one week's time, as soon as the medicine was finished, her involuntary movements of her hand came under control. It was a miracle!

SEPTEMBER 1980 (SUNBULA 10–MEZAN 8, 1359)

Sahar's condition was getting better and better every day, but the medication made her extremely weak. She lost lots of weight, so I took her again to the neurologist. This time he prescribed a course of shots for at least another three weeks. I took Sahar every day to a nurse who lived across the street from our house for her daily injections. One day our conversation turned to the day several months before when the helicopters invaded the university. My neighbor said that on that day many injured students were brought to Aliabad Hospital. Most of them had simple injuries, such as a broken limb or a gunshot wound in the hand or thigh. The next morning when she went to work, she found that most of those students had died the night before. She sadly said, "No one would die overnight from those simple injuries."

Finally, nine months after I had made application for a passport, I called the passport office and learned that the police report was back. The following day I went to the passport office and stood at the end of a long line in the hall of the Ministry of Interior to wait my turn.

At nine in the morning the small window of the police office, facing the hall, opened. When my turn arrived I explained to the plainclothes officer my name and the nature of my application. He went to the end of the room, pulled out a large, heavy blue binder, and found my application. He looked at the secret police report, closed the binder, and said, "Yes, of course . . . of course . . . You can go. I don't see any reason not to."

Then he signed a special form, handed it to me, and told me to complete the rest of the steps. I took the papers but did not move away from the window. I asked him politely, "Sir, what about my husband? What did the report say about Saleem?"

He looked at me with surprise for a moment and opened the big binder again. He read the information silently and answered in a hurry, "Well, he is fine and will come home. And . . . now . . . you can go."

I still didn't move away from my place, but insisted that he let me read it for myself. He refused, closed the binder. He took the binder back to its original place while I still stood in front of the window and gazed at him. How dearly I wanted to know what information those pages held about Saleem. After all, those were the police reports and must be correct.

The policeman came back, sat down again at the window, and shouted, "Next!"

I reluctantly walked away from the window and stood in a corner as the well-dressed gentleman behind me approached the window. He asked for his papers, which were supposed to have been signed weeks before but were not completed yet. The man insisted, "My application has been here for months and I don't know what the reason for the delay is. How long must I wait?"

His words hit the officer like a bullet. He began shouting, loudly enough that everyone in the hall could easily hear him: "Brother, all you can think about is yourself. We all work hard day and night to rebuild our country and you apply for a West German vacation?"

The man said, "Sorry, sir; I didn't mean to upset you. I apologize. The goods I'm exporting are waiting for shipment and the delay is costing me a fortune."

The policeman didn't hear. Still shouting, his face red and with puffy droplets of spit flying out of his mouth, saturating the air around the window, he cried, "Dishonest agents of the CIA – people like you want to leave the country when you're needed here the most!" There was no end to his insulting speech even though the gentleman kept apologizing.

The situation was getting worse and had attracted everybody's attention. All the policemen in the office gathered around the window. I took advantage of the moment. With a great courage very unfamiliar to me, I went from the far door at the right end of the hall and crossed two large rooms until I was inside the office right behind the policemen where no one was permitted to enter. I ignored all the signs on the doors that said, "Authorized Personnel Only Beyond This Point."

I approached the rows of shelves filled with the big blue binders and pulled out the one that had the secret police report on us. I took the binder into the far corner of the room. I even stupidly sat on one of the police desks and opened it. I found the right page and read it. The report was very brief: "Saleem was an antirevolutionary element and was eliminated the first day. We do not have any information on his wife in our records." I crossed the room again and put the binder back in its place. Then I quickly stepped out of the office, recrossing the restricted areas once more. Nobody had even noticed my presence there!

Now whenever I think about that day, I wonder why I didn't leave the binder on the desk after reading the report rather than crossing the entire room again to take it back to its original place. Probably all of those secret police, so well trained in East Germany, would never dream that a person like me would ever do such a crazy thing in their presence.

After I left the police office I went to a corner of the hall and stood near a window, my face bathed in a cold sweat. My hands shook and I could not speak. All the world in front of me became blurred and dark. Everything hid behind the shadowy curtains of my vibrating teardrops. I heard someone say, "You need to sign the forms in this office before you leave." I didn't care anymore. Whoever he was didn't matter. My body felt numb all over and the whole world turned around me in circles. My insides heaved and I began to throw up. The pain in my stomach was excruciating. A couple of men and a woman passed by and noticed my condition. They came forward to help, and I told them I would be all right.

I leaned on a windowsill. I don't know how long I was there, but long enough to feel a little better. I looked at my watch. I had got there before nine in the morning; it was now two-thirty in the afternoon. I went to the nearest bus stop and got on a bus. I felt so miserable that I didn't want my children to see me in my present condition, so I got off at Dehmazang and went into the Kabul Zoo. All the guys at the ticket office knew me, but I wasn't ready or willing to talk to them. Reluctantly I put my hand in my pocket, pulled the money out, and bought a ticket. I didn't wait for the change. My world was dead. I was breathing like a dying person who still hangs on to this world, trying hard to breathe all the last breaths of air that are possible.

I wasn't there to see the animals; I was there to overcome my shock and needed some time and space. I needed a quiet place to think and to be left alone. I'd lost track of time. I needed to pull myself together. I selected a table in a far corner, facing the Chamchamast River and the mountain that the Noon Cannon stood on. The air was fresh; the earth was covered with a green carpet of low plants. The trees had just begun to change color and the rows of poplars already displayed their bright fall colors. Once in a while a cool breeze swept gently across my face from green fields. Nature had always fascinated me. It gave me peace and comfort. I loved the soothing quietness of its fresh, slow breezes. There I always found the beauty and greatness of God. In fact, I saw the presence of God right next to me.

After some time, the busboy brought me a pot of hot tea with a small plate that held a few sugar-coated almonds. He said something, but I didn't answer, nor did I move. He stood there for a few moments and then left without a word from me. I heard his low murmurs as he walked away. He must have thought I was totally deaf or insane.

As I looked at the cannon mountain, my thoughts went back to the years when the cannon was always fired at noon, announcing the beginning of the afternoon hours. Hence, it became famous as the Noon Cannon. I remembered Eid, our religious holiday, and the day I saw Saleem for the first time in my family's house, when he came to visit my father. All the scenes of my past life began to dance in front of me – my marriage days, our overseas trips, the times we spent together and also the times we were apart. I was married for fourteen years, out of which five were spent separately; either Saleem was out of country or I was away for my studies. Today how much I regretted those moments and asked myself why we had spent that time away from each other.

Saleem always told me that he wanted me to be self-reliant, especially for the times he was not around. I remembered the time I was going on a scholarship out of country and he said to me, "Honey, I wish we had a baby girl so whenever you are away she would remind me of you."

Saleem took such good care of our children when I was away. God, how dearly I felt his loss tonight! He was always there for me when I needed him. Just the idea that I would be by myself the rest of my life made me despair. If I knew what we had done wrong, it probably wouldn't have been so hard for me. I knew there had been no trial, that Saleem had never been given a chance to defend himself. This idea hurt.

I began talking to myself loudly: "Murderers, what was your proof? When and where was the court? Who defended us? What about our rights?" It all seemed so hopeless! In a Communist regime you can never find answers to such questions.

I thought about my children. They were waiting for me at home and I didn't know what to tell them now. I had gone through this situation so many times before! And I felt so weak doing it again. God, what should I say to Ali? How should I disclose the facts to Omar? And then, . . . what about Sahar? Tonight I could not find the courage to face my children, so I sat there still and did not move.

Night was close. The streetlights came on one by one. A swirl of cold air and a humming above my head indicated that fast-flying bats were out chasing insects. The groups of women by the river collected their last pieces of laundry, sheets that had been spread over the grass to dry. They folded them carefully, put the huge bundles on their heads, and started for their homes, their small children following behind. A couple of old men spread their prayer rugs by the river, facing west, and began their evening prayers. The busboy approached and saw that the teapot in front of me was still full – that it hadn't been touched at all. He asked if he could remove it. I nodded yes and put two afghanis for him on the table. I looked around and saw that most of the zoo visitors had gone. Here and there an animal's sound broke the silence of this cool autumn night.

My mind wasn't cleared yet but I headed for home, confused and feeling low. I still didn't know why Samae, my student, had lied to me. Why the man who came to my home those first weeks, Colonel Hameed, had lied. And why the friend who gave me the description of Saleem's ring and claimed that he had seen him in Puli-Charkhi had lied – all when the police report indicated that he was shot the first day of the bloody coup.

On my way home I remembered the words of a good colleague, whom I had met one day in September the year before. He had ties with the government's opposition and appeared to be a leader of the group. He told me that Saleem was kept in the Puli-Charkhi prison for a long time after the coup. I trusted my friend. He said, "Professor, I think we made a big mistake. We knew Sooma and Hashimi, Taraki's Central Committee members, very well. We should have reported their activities to the government."

"You think the stupid government didn't know what they were up to?"

"I don't know," he replied.

"How about all the student demands and political activities at the university in the years before the coup? Did Daoud's regime claim they still didn't know what was going on?" I asked him again.

Now I think he was right. We all knew of these two Khalqis, but I honestly never thought that one day they would occupy those important jobs and have a part in the mass killing of innocent people. Terrible news was heard about Hashimi's slaughter of people in Badakhshan. Rumors said that Hashimi tied people to the mouths of canons and gave orders to fire. He also was blamed for throwing hundreds of people out of his helicopter. I never thought that a very quiet and obedient physics teacher, whom I had known for years, could carry out such horrendous deeds against the people of his own province, the province in which he was born and raised and had friends and relatives.

I don't know how I got there, but I found myself at home. My children were waiting for me. Omar especially was very concerned and met me at the door, asking why I hadn't called to let them know I would be late. I hadn't the strength to say a word. Whenever I tried to speak, my voice broke and refused to come out, so I kept quiet and entered my bedroom. I sat there on my bed and supported my head with my hands because it felt big and heavy. Omar, who had probably noticed my swollen eyes, knocked at the door and said, "Mom, can I come in?"

"Yes, come in," I replied.

He came over and put his arms around me and held me. I broke into tears and cried like a baby as he tried to calm me. His warmth and love were what I needed at that time. It took me half an hour to calm down and we neither said a word but held each other quietly. Finally he broke the silence: "Mom, let's go and eat. See, I've also made some nice tea just for you. It was hard keeping it warm for you till now."

We ate dinner and went upstairs to watch TV. As usual, I hid my face in the shadows of the corner bunk bed. Omar, Ali, and Sahar played with each other as I watched from my corner. Omar's tall figure and loving hands, Ali's warmth and kindness, and Sahar's innocence and beautiful eyes – how much they all resembled their father, and reminded me of Saleem. I was still foolishly trying to find excuses for not accepting the police report, because of all the thousands of pieces of bad and good news that I had heard about Saleem, there were facts I still could not understand. I asked myself the questions again and again.

Why had the Communist government, if it had killed my husband the first day of the coup, let us keep Rahim, the soldier who worked at our house? They did not call him back. The government took away everybody else's in-house soldiers, but why not ours? Normally when officers died or were fired, they called back the in-house soldiers forty days afterwards. No one called Rahim back; even six months after the coup he was still with us. After six months, since I had not heard from Saleem, I told Rahim to report to his headquarters. I was afraid the poor guy would be considered absent without leave. Rahim left us with great sorrow.

Again, my mind went to the negative side of the issue: maybe Rahim was left here to spy on us. A week after telling him to report back to headquarters, I called the office to make sure he was doing all right. His headquarters assured me that Rahim had received proper credit for all the months he was with us after the coup and they had been counted toward his service time.

Okay, if Rahim was their spy, then who was Colonel Hameed? Thus far I'd thought he might have been a government agent. Were we such important people that the Communist government had to spy on us? What happened to Colonel Hameed and why did he suddenly disappear? How come Rahim got credit for the last six months he spent with us? Was the government feeling sorry for us? No, Communist governments never feel sorry for anyone.

Another thing that didn't make sense was that two months after the April coup, some of the military officers received promotions and their names were read on the nightly news. My husband's name was included among those of his fellow officers who were promoted. On hearing the announcement, Rahim began to jump up and down in excitement and cried, "Madam, thank God he is alive!" The next day when Rahim went to buy supplies from a shop near our house, the proprietor told him of Saleem's promotion and even congratulated him on the news. Daoud's government had postponed Saleem's promotion the year before, but now this Communist government had promoted him!

All night long, positive and negative events of the past haunted me.

There were no logical answers to the puzzles. I sadly acknowledged to myself that the police report contained the government's only written and concrete words that I had on my husband. Yet, if Saleem was killed the first day of the coup, then why didn't his name appear on the government lists released by Amin? Was the government afraid of us? No, we had neither the power nor the desire to rule Afghanistan. So, who should I listen to? Who was telling the truth?

How badly I needed to know how the last moments of Saleem's life were spent. Was he tortured? Was he killed right away, or was he sent to Russia? I still don't know and probably will never know what happened to him. Do I have to live with such haunting thoughts all my life? What were our sins? At times I think, Is there anyone in this world who can help me overcome my nightmares? What proof do they have to convince me? Could I believe anyone after pursuing so many rumors? Will they tell me the truth this time? No, I do not think so! Almost all the people who were in the office with Saleem are either afraid, transferred, or dead.

After I read the secret police report on my husband, things began to look different. I became more determined to leave my beloved country, Afghanistan, for as long as the Communists were in power. I didn't want to see my children grow up in an environment of suspicion and hatred. As long as the Marxists were in power, we were all considered "antirevolutionary elements," which in their terms meant we opposed "progress" for Afghanistan's people.

So, for the rest of September I started covertly selling the household items one by one. I called the owner of the nearby thrift store, who I believe sensed that I was leaving. As a result, he did not pay even a tenth of the original price of the things I had to sell. Whatever he offered, I accepted with great disappointment.

Among the other items, there were three full closets of my husband's recently made suits. They were all hand-tailored from the best English fabric available in Kabul and had cost four to five thousand afghanis each. The thrift-store man bought all the clothes for a total of twenty-two hundred afghanis (the equivalent of forty-four U.S. dollars). I remembered that once in the past, when I had needed some money, I sold my camera. I hadn't liked the idea of selling it for less than I had paid for it. But now I didn't care; what was important was to get rid of everything as quietly and as quickly as possible and not even think about it.

One day the thrift-store man came and told me, "An officer came and looked around and picked up one of the military caps. He looked inside it and found Saleem's name there. He seemed to know your husband, because he left the shop with tears in his eyes. Afterwards," the store proprietor added, "I removed the names from all of the rest of the clothing."

It was true, I hadn't even checked my husband's pockets to see if they contained anything important. The pain had been too great and I hated the moments when I opened his closets. I always tried to put difficult things behind me, but in the end I failed. People told me to get on with my life, but I couldn't convince myself to do so. Everywhere I went or looked in the house, there were memories . . . all good memories of Saleem.

I needed lots of money for the completion of my passport and also to live in India for an unknown period of time. Such money could not be obtained solely from selling my household goods. The only way to get it was to sell our property, but that would not be easy. I knew I had a struggle ahead, because under the law a woman could sell the property of her husband only if there was legal proof of the husband's death and all the children were of legal age and consented to the sale. (If the children were underage, a legal guardian was selected by the court to take care of the money till the child reached legal age.) Under Islamic law, the widow receives one-eighth of the inheritance.

There were many discrepancies in the interpretation of legal age. One county judge told us that legal age was attained on the eighteenth birthday, while a second county judge in Kabul placed it at the completion of child's nineteenth year. Moreover, the Communist government of Afghanistan stipulated that no one could receive more than 400,000 afghanis ($8,000) at one time. Any additional sums must be kept under the supervision of the government in a bank. Thus, if I sold my house for more than 400,000 afghanis, the government would take the rest of the money even if I stayed in the country! The amount of money that an individual was allowed to take out of the country was far less than the total one could keep in the country: only 10,000 afghanis ($200) per person with a tourist visa, or $600 per person if the passport was issued for medical treatment.

All odds were against me. Jaan and I spent endless hours inside countless government offices trying to obtain the necessary documents about Saleem, but no one would provide them. I had an extremely hard time convincing the bureaucrats that, not very long ago, someone named Saleem had existed. There were times when I felt that either Saleem had vanished into thin air and no one really knew what happened to him, or . . . he never existed and I was merely dreaming!

In addition, my children were not of legal age – Sahar would not reach nineteen for another ten years – and the value of my property was far greater than the amount the government would let us have. I knew that if I put the extra money in the bank, the government would never give it back, so I would have to forget about anything more than 400,000 afghanis, which was hardly enough to live on in India for several months with a sick child.

Meantime, as I wrestled with the problem of how I could take all of my money out of the country, Sahar still needed medical care even though her condition was improving. Our safety was in question. Omar and Ali were getting no education. It had been six months now since I'd pulled my sons out of school and in all that time I had not let them leave the house.

One day I ran into Abdul, an old friend of Saleem's from Jalalabad. He asked about Saleem and I told him briefly of my problems. He said,

"I hate to see the way the government has treated you." After a pause he added, "I think I can help you."

"How? You will have to perform miracles, Abdul!" I laughed.

"Remember, no one will give you any sort of written documents about Saleem, so don't waste your time trying to get such papers. The only choice you have is to increase your children's age temporarily and sell the house." After a pause he continued, "Put in an application stating that you have lost their I.D.s."

"Lost their I.D.s? How?" I asked.

"Well, everyone loses something sometime. Make an excuse, like you lost it in a fire, someone broke into your car, or . . . ," Abdul continued with a dozen excuses.

"Okay, okay, and then?"

"Then I will take it to the right person and get fake I.D.s."

I thought about it for a bit and said, "Wait a minute! Then both my sons would be eligible for military service and couldn't leave the country."

Abdul laughed and explained, "That is why I said a temporary, fake I.D. First, it will not be recorded officially. Second, you won't need the false I.D.s for more than a week."

"I can't do that, Abdul, but thanks all the same," I replied. "No . . . it doesn't seem safe. I don't want to put my sons' lives in jeopardy."

"Those good old days that you are thinking of are gone," Abdul said. "No one goes by the book today. Things are so complicated that you have no choice."

I knew Abdul was going out of his way. There were lots of risks involved for him as well as for us. Still I was reluctant. "Today the law of the jungle governs us!" Abdul hissed. "Sister, I don't want to insult you. The present situation leaves you with no alternative. I owe it to Saleem to help his family."

I said good-bye to Abdul with thanks for his concern and his offer of help, assuring him that I would let him know if I decided to proceed with his plan.

As days went by I became more discouraged. I decided that before at-tempting to sell the house, I should complete the passport; perhaps the money I received from the sale of household goods would cover the costs. Jaan and I both made several attempts to complete the court paperwork in the legal way, but it was not possible.

My experience with the courts and the passport office was new. Sur-prisingly, I found that Abdul was absolutely right. Government agencies were in a big mess. The new Communist rules and decrees, combined with the previous laws (which were not forgotten yet), plus all the new inexperienced and unqualified office personnel had created lots of confusion and irregularities.

The Communist governments had imprisoned, executed, or forced into exile not only our religious scholars, teachers, lawyers, and other in-tellectuals, but also our clerks and bureaucrats, who had been replaced with new, untrained personnel. People assigned to the higher positions were not sure how long their jobs would last; with four governments in two and a half years, no one had job security. Nepotism and favoritism were rampant. Each new government assigned its own party members to positions, not on the basis of their knowledge or expertise, but on the basis of political ties or connections with higher officials. Many wanted to loot the country, because who knew what tomorrow would bring?

Corruption and bribery were common in all government offices, especially in the passport division, which was very crowded at this time. Scores of people wanted to leave the country. Getting a passport was based on one's ability to bribe the hungry vultures, the passport clerks. If you had money, you could pay your way out; otherwise you were stuck forever. Complaining to higher authorities did not work, because it re-quired months to solve any problem. People simply did not have that much time, so they had to obey the greedy officials' rules, which dif-fered widely from one clerk to the next. Because of the chaos, clerks set their own rules and ended up with more authority than the minister of interior himself.

One day in the passport office, when Jaan and I were trying to complete the remaining steps to obtain a passport, lunchtime arrived. One of the county judges who was supposed to sign the papers was in the lunchroom. At ten minutes to one, Jaan went into the lunchroom to see the judge as I waited outside. Twenty minutes later the judge and my brother appeared in the hall, arguing. The judge, who had barely finished his meal, pointed at Jaan with the fork still in his hand and said, "I can't sign the papers! I won't do it!"

Jaan was very agitated. "You'll see! I'll finish this work without your damn signature!"

When Jaan returned to where I was waiting, I asked, "Well, what was all that about?"

Jaan, still upset, replied, "He thinks you should get two separate passports because he says Omar is sixteen and can't be put on your passport."

"Why sixteen? He's only fifteen."

"That stupid man actually counted the day that Omar was born as one year and then figured from there on," Jaan responded angrily. "Since he wasn't convinced by what I said, I told him he needed to brush up on his math and logic before becoming a judge. That's why he got so mad."

I began to laugh. What a strange world it was! When I tried to sell my houses, Omar was underage. When it came to the passport, he was an adult who couldn't share the same passport with me.

I really didn't want to get a separate passport for Omar or to represent his age as a year older than he was. I was afraid of making him closer to the draftee age because then the government would not let him leave the country. Moreover, two passports would cost twice the money, which I simply didn't have.

As we were standing in the courtyard, our friend Fahim came by and asked what we were doing there. Fahim was a family friend and a humorous sort who always had funny stories to tell. Jaan unhappily recounted the situation and Fahim asked, "May I see Omar's I.D.?" I gave it to him. He looked at the red booklet carefully, examined the stamp, and said, "May I take it for a few minutes? Wait. I'll be right back."

Before Jaan could utter a word, Fahim left. After a few minutes he returned, handed me the I.D., and said, "Here! You're all set." Fahim left in a hurry, promising to come to our house that weekend. We didn't know what was going on, but when Jaan opened the small red I.D. booklet he saw that our friend had lowered Omar's age by a year, making him now, by the judge's method of calculation, fifteen.

My brother's eyes widened as he gasped, "Look! That silly man has changed it without telling us!"

I laughed and laughed until my brother joined in too. I hadn't known it was so easy to do such things! At home, however, the more I thought about it, the more frightened I became. What if they discovered that we carried a false I.D.? I decided that I would not go to the passport office with a fake I.D., but Jaan pointed out that the only chance we had was to go ahead and complete the forms.

Time was running very short. We couldn't apply for a new I.D. Jaan was leaving the country soon. He tried his best to complete as much of my passport work as he could before his departure. With no alternative, Jaan took the papers the following day to a different county office, trying to avoid the previous day's angered judge, who knew we had a problem over Omar's age. The second judge signed the papers, so half the passport process was completed. I'd have to finish the rest myself.

One night after Jaan had finished that section of my passport requiring my children's birth dates, I remembered Fahim's "correction" of Omar's age and I jumped out of bed and ran into the next room. I shuffled through the papers to find my sons' I.D.s. I looked at their birth dates. I was shocked; what I was thinking was true! How was it that no one in the court had noticed that according to the documents we now carried, with Omar's age reduced by a year, the difference between his age and Ali's was only four months! The entire deal had gone through unnoticed.

Several weeks later I saw Fahim and told him, "You devil! You nearly got us all killed!"

"What are you talking about?" Fahim asked.

When I told him the result of changing the I.D., he laughed and said, "Since I work there, I know what's going on. There's a continuous underground battle between the two Communist parties. The members of Taraki's and Amin's Khalq party are very upset about their leaders' executions and are trying to cause irregularities in the agencies so Babrak and his Parchamis will be blamed for all the problems that have been created in Afghanistan." After a pause he continued, "The Khalqis are trying to paralyze the Parchamis by helping people leave the country, especially the ones who have education and potential for leadership."

Fahim's comments made a lot of sense. This was exactly what Abdul had tried to tell me. Fahim said very philosophically, with a spark of humor in his eyes, "So, you have all their help and still hesitate to use it! God is arranging things on your side and you don't know it." We both laughed as he turned away to leave.

Not only was it a hassle to complete the rest of the steps in getting the passport, but I still had no buyer for the houses. Besides, I couldn't sell them with Omar's and Ali's present I.D.s. I knew I must get rid of the fake one. The only option was to do exactly what Abdul had told me. I should get rid of the false I.D. and tell the authorities I had lost it. The few prospective homebuyers that came didn't want to pay the price I asked. And although I'd got rid of most of the household goods, some were left. The rooms still seemed full of items.

October was just a few days away. Jaan was very concerned about leaving me with all my problems. I told him, "I'll be all right. You go ahead and leave. I'll join you in India as soon as I finish here." My plan was to leave about the time of the schools' winter vacation, some three months away. If I didn't leave during the winter vacation, people would ask why I was taking my children out of the country when they were supposed to be in school.

In fact, I tried very hard to avoid arousing any suspicions. I worked full school hours, attended all the meetings at school, and never missed a single hour of class time. And I still went to the Puli-Charkhi prison on Fridays. Life had taught me to be very careful and not to make even a tiny mistake that could cost me or my family lots of trouble.

WEDNESDAY, OCTOBER 1, 1980 (MEZAN 9, 1359)

Mother, my two brothers, and all five of my sisters who were still in Afghanistan, along with their families, were leaving tomorrow. After a long search, Laila's husband, Wali, had found a guide who worked with the government and also had ties with people at the border. The guide would help them cross the border. We all knew that this plan had to be kept secret.

My family would get to Kandahar city on their own and stay overnight there. The next day they would start for the border. Crossing the border was not easy; in fact, it was very dangerous. Many stories were told about families that didn't make it. They were turned back by Russian forces and ended up in prison. Some had even lost their lives. Because of the numerous pitfalls involved, the guide told my family that all of them should dress exactly like the tribespeople who lived on the border. He said, "You must avoid being noticed by the Russian soldiers or the Afghan army."

So the bottom line was that my family could not take anything except the tribal clothes they wore, and of course their clothes must be used and old to avoid catching the attention of the soldiers and the road patrol. The night before their departure Mother emphasized once again the importance of not taking anything, telling everybody to be very careful to consider the safety of the group and especially the nine young children who accompanied them. It was very hard on my two young sisters, who always dressed nicely and dearly loved their jewelry and clothes, to give away everything they had.

Finding twenty-one airline tickets, all on one plane, was not very easy either. Yesterday, again with many difficulties, my brother-in-law Wali was finally able to get the tickets for tomorrow at eleven o'clock in the morning. It meant that Mother had to rush to get ready to leave. One day was simply not enough time to sell the house and all its contents, but there was no other option.

After my class today I went to see Mother around eleven in the morning. Everybody had gone to work except my youngest brother and youngest sister. The rest had decided to go to work and to stay in their offices until the last minute to avoid suspicion. As I entered Mother's house I was shocked to see that everything was as usual. All the rooms were full of the normal household goods and nothing had changed a bit. Surprised and a little angry, I said, "Mom, I thought you would have sold at least some of your stuff by now! You know you are leaving tomorrow at eleven."

I looked at her; she was in a state of shock, unable to comprehend that she had to leave everything behind. She was still bound to all those things that had accumulated over the years. After a long pause she said, "Well, I don't know what to do and where to start."

"Mom, you should have called someone to buy the stuff. There's no time left and we have to hurry," I replied quietly. "What are you going to do with all this if your family's life is on the line?" I added, hoping to give her some support.

She nodded but didn't say a word. I looked at her and continued, "Mother, you need Jaan, you need Nasir, you need Laila, Mizhgan, Sophia, and . . . everybody around you to be safe. Don't you, Mom?"

She agreed. "Of course! You are right. Let's call someone."

I asked my brother Nasir to bring someone from the neighborhood thrift shop and in about half an hour the proprietor arrived, accompanied by three other men. Now, that time was a heyday for thrift-shop owners. They were collecting items from people who were fleeing the country for their lives. By 1980 Kabul shops were loaded with second-hand modern and antique merchandise. Until two years before, people had invested in rugs and copper pots, pans, and trays with the hope that they would have a better market value in the future. But no one was buying anything anymore. Selling and getting rid of everything they had was the main game of the day.

My brother and I put all the clothing and personal items we could find in the house on the front porch and whatever price those avaricious men put on the objects we accepted remorsefully. Mother sat in a corner supporting her head with her hands and watched the nightmare. Exhausted, I sat next to her and watched the men hard at work. The scene before us looked exactly like leaf-cutting ants scurrying about in a tropical rain forest as if they sensed a coming thunderstorm. Men moved in and out of the rooms carrying on their heads heavy loads of mattresses, bedspreads, wall pictures, pots and pans, radios, TV, tables, chairs, everything imaginable.

It was hard to believe this was happening to us. All these goods that Mother had obtained during her life were gone forever. It hurt a lot to watch my mother being stripped of her possessions. But there was no other choice. I was certain that the same scene was being enacted in my sisters' houses too. Everyone was selling their household items that day. My heart was heavy and I felt unreal. It was like a nightmare or a sad movie, but not real life.

By the end of two hours almost half of Mother's household belongings were gone. There was no question of bargaining or saving anything; the idea was just to get rid of the stuff. Then I remembered that she had not yet finished the paperwork on her house. It would require at least another full day to complete. She had a buyer for her house and had received a down payment, but the new owner would not pay the rest of the money till tomorrow, after he received the title to the house. Mother didn't have a full day ahead of her; she had to be at the airport by ten. How could she finish the paperwork on time?

Since all their beds were sold and nothing was left in my sisters' houses by that evening, they and their families, along with Mother, spent the night with us. Night came. They all arrived at my house. After dinner everybody got busy checking their village clothes and *chadaries* (veils), the ones they must wear in the morning. I looked at their clothes and wondered where in the world my sisters had found those old dresses. The clothing they had bought represented almost every sector of the Afghan community: Pashtuns, Hazaras, Uzbeks, and even nomads too! Several were wearing their maids' old clothing. Even the veils were old – used and wrinkled.

Everyone was warned not to carry money. Nevertheless, Mother had to take some for living expenses in Pakistan. Carrying money in afghanis was not a good idea because it had very low value on the international market. In order to meet expenses outside the country, my family would have needed huge bundles of afghanis, impossible to carry. On the other hand, transferring money through the bank was not allowed by the government.

So we exchanged the afghanis for German marks. The biggest notes available on the black market were the one-thousand-mark bills. For every twenty-four thousand afghanis, one big one-thousand-mark bill was bought. During the night I made a small pocket in Mother's clothes and tucked in a handful of German marks, thinking that was the safest place if they were searched on their way to Pakistan.

My sewing job was hardly finished when mortar fire began inside the city about eleven o'clock that night. It was the first time I'd heard the terrible sound of a mortar so close. Its magnitude is very hard to describe. The echo thundered against the mountains around the city and reechoed many times. The noise, reverberating from all directions, made the clock stop. It was so loud and ear-splitting that it gave me goosebumps. A cold chill ran down my spine; I shivered and my teeth chattered. The mortar fire went on for an hour. I thought we would be killed that night while we were all together – that this was the end of our world.

The mortars finally stopped close to midnight. By one o'clock everybody was asleep. Our minds were full of questions and terror, not knowing what tomorrow would bring. Other nights when we'd had an opportunity to gather and spend the night together, everybody had had a lot to say, but tonight no one said much. The next day everybody was leaving except my oldest brother, Khalil, and me.

Mother got up at six and went to her house to take care of final details. She was supposed to meet the real estate agent there at eight and they would go to court to get the judge's signature, which was required when a house was sold. My brother Jaan had already gone to the court to finish the preliminary work and get the papers ready for Mother to sign.

At nine, since I hadn't heard anything from Mother and Jaan, I left for the court and found Jaan and the agent there. When I asked where Mom was, he didn't have the slightest idea. I took a taxi in a hurry to Mother's house. She was still waiting for the agent there, while he was at the courthouse with Jaan! It was nearly ten by the time Mom got back to the courthouse. We asked the judge to hurry and told him that Mother had to be at the airport by eleven because she had an appointment for an eye operation in two days and must not miss her flight to India. The judge, a nice man, finished the paperwork and Mother signed it. Completion of some of the forms required more time and the judge let her sign blank forms. But before signing, we had to count the money, which was all in fifty-afghani bills, bundled together in large stacks secured with rubber bands. Counting those huge bundles required too much time, so we accepted the buyer's word that they contained what was due.

It was getting very close to eleven o'clock. Mother and Jaan were supposed to be at the airport, not in court, at this time. When the bundles of money were turned over to her, I asked Mother if she had a sack or something to carry them in. To my surprise, she said, "Can't you put them in your purse?"

"Should I take them?" I asked in perplexity.

My God, it was at least four or five times more than my purse could hold! Mother hurriedly took a few bills and gave the rest to me to take home. She didn't actually say a word about what I should do with the money, but under the circumstances it was her first and final order that

I should take it home. Now, what I was going to do with it I did not know. There was simply no time to discuss the matter. What if I hadn't come to the court that day? Then what would Mother have done with all that money?

Imagine! Here I am standing in the middle of a large crowd in Kabul's busiest courthouse with bundles of money overflowing my arms, falling on the floor, and me not knowing what to do with it! Mother was leaving for India right in front of my eyes and I couldn't even say good-bye to her as I would have liked, for fear of making onlookers suspicious of her departure. God only knew whether I would see her again someday or not. The family I always received moral support from was leaving me behind, maybe for good. Totally confounded, I stood there not knowing what to do next.

At this moment the person who had bought Mom's house realized my situation and brought me something like a grocery sack to put the money in. In a rush I said good-bye to Mother and looked at Jaan. It was my last farewell to him until – who knew when? I never said a word, nor could I put my arms around him, because others were watching us. How badly I wanted to tell him how much I appreciated all of the help and moral support he had offered me in the past two most difficult years of my life.

Jaan winked at me and took Mother's arm. They ran to a nearby taxi. I watched them, my heart pounding, thinking that I might never see them again. When they got about twenty yards away from me, my heart broke. I couldn't hold myself back any longer. I ran after them and called, "Mother . . . M – o – m! Hey, . . . Jaan, wait!"

My voice echoed back; they hadn't heard me. Mentally I felt the gap between my family and me. I saw a long tunnel of time and space between us. Swirling windstorms, fire, and smoke filled the tunnel, and I was standing at the far end of it and couldn't reach them. I stood watching mutely as their taxi disappeared into the swarm of vehicles in the street.

I don't know how long I stood there mesmerized. A beggar came up and pleaded, "In the name of God, give me something." His voice brought me back to this world. I started to walk toward the cab station with the sack full of cash still in my hand. As I walked faster to get away from the beggar he started running behind me, constantly begging for some money. Finally he pulled on my arm and said again, "In God's name, give me a few coins." I was outraged. His pursuit and holding my arm made me furious. I stopped, looked at him, and shouted, "Where is this God? I am looking for Him too!"

A colleague of mine from the chemistry department who was in the courthouse crowd heard me shouting, came up, and pulled the beggar away from me. I didn't even thank him but pretended I hadn't seen him. I was afraid he might ask what I was doing there. People knew that when somebody appeared in court and sold their house, they were leaving the country.

From the hundreds of detective and spy stories I'd read in the past, I'd learned that if conspirators planned to kidnap or rob someone, the first cab driver in the waiting line was likely to be their agent. Therefore, when I chose a cab to go home that day, I selected one that was not the first in line.

I arrived home at noon and saw that everybody had left and I hadn't had a chance to say farewell to them. As I entered the house, the phone rang. My brother Khalil was on the line. He asked where Mother and Jaan were. I told him they had left the courthouse at eleven and should be at the airport any minute now. Luckily, the plane to Kandahar was an hour late. Around two in the afternoon Khalil came to my house and reported that Mom and Jaan had arrived at the last minute.

At the airport Jaan and Khalil never said a word to each other. They were wary of the airport secret police. From behind the terminal Khalil counted twenty-one family members plus one child in arms boarding the plane. He couldn't recognize the women because of their veils.

I told Khalil about the events at the courthouse that morning, then we sat down and laboriously counted the money. One bundle was five hundred afghanis short, but I didn't know how much Mother had taken with her, because at the courthouse she had pulled some money out of the bundle without counting it.

After some time Khalil left and I went upstairs. Everything was in the mess left by my family that morning. Sacks and bundles of clothing, watches, shoes, and other personal items were scattered all over the house. Someone's underwear on the clothesline, a pair of slacks on the floor, a T-shirt on the fence, a wristwatch, a half-empty purse, coins, containers of makeup – it seemed that everyone had discarded their mundane possessions and, in the last-minute rush, abandoned them in desperation. This scene made me so sad that I sat there trying to figure out what things belonged to whom. After hours of this effort there were still items left and I didn't know who they belonged to. The realization of how little attention I had paid to my family made me even sadder.

The next morning when I entered the kitchen I found sacks, tin cans, and bottles all over the floor. Mother had brought all the food she had in her kitchen: a half gallon of cooking oil, a couple of sacks of sugar, an open container of dried beans, some half-used spices, ground powdered tomatoes and onion, a jar of coffee, powdered dry milk. These things made me very unhappy, since I realized that Mother had saved them for her own family so they would have everything ready for winter. I opened a few other boxes. My sister Sophia was expecting her first child. There were packages of expensive baby soap and lotions, new baby clothing, toys, milk bottles. They made me so sad, realizing she'd bought them to use later but now never would. I said to myself, "O God, I can't take it anymore. Please don't overestimate my patience and strength!"

I put my left hand over my eyes. I don't know how long I sat there. For two days afterwards I collected things from all over the house and packed them into boxes, hoping to mail them when and if everyone got to India. In the meantime, I told my children to avoid talking to our neighbors for the next few weeks until I heard from my mom. I especially advised my daughter not to talk to our tenant's old mother, who sat behind the windows all day long and watched us closely.

One week passed and I didn't hear from my family. Two weeks and finally the third week went by, and I began to really worry about them. I didn't know what to do. So far we had received only a tiny piece of paper, about one inch square, given to us by the man who took them across the border. On this tiny note my sister Sophia had written that they had crossed the border safely. These were the only words about them that I had received so far. I still doubted the situation and did not trust what I read on that piece of paper.

FRIDAY, OCTOBER 24, 1980 (AQRAB 2, 1359)

During this month I was busy selling everything I could. The departure of my family had further convinced me that there was nothing to do but hurry up and leave Afghanistan. I'd been planning this step for the past year and now I wanted to finish as soon as possible.

Things at work were discouraging. The new assistant I had been assigned a year ago turned out to be a government agent designated to report on my activities. A Parchami student of mine named Akbar said that during Amin's time, twelve different reports were made about me by one of the teaching assistants. He said that if Amin's regime had not fallen when it did, I would have been in police custody by the next week.

"Why? On what charges?" I asked him, testing whether his information was correct.

Akbar responded, "The notes said that you talked to your students about your family situation."

"Good; I talked about my own problems, not theirs," I replied.

Akbar continued, "Other reports said that you did not attend party meetings and refused to put the Great Leader's photo in your office."

I asked him, "What Great Leader? Did you believe in him?" Akbar smiled and left my office.

I knew Akbar was right. One of my old neighbors, an army general who had worked with Saleem in the same office at Khoja Rawash, had been missing like Saleem since the first day of the April 1978 coup. His daughter, Souria, was in my class. Once in a while she would come and tell me where she'd gone to look for her father. Often I noticed that as soon as we started talking, the assistant would walk out of the room. At first I didn't care, but one day Souria told me that she would not come to my office anymore. I asked her why.

"Last time when I left your office," Souria explained, "I saw a student listening to our conversation through the keyhole. As soon as I opened the door, he ran away." So it seemed that whenever the assistant left the room, he told someone else to come and listen to our conversation. Indeed, Souria was afraid.

Everyone knew that a huge, well-organized student spy network was established at the university by 1980. These spies reported everything they saw, most often interpreting things their own way. I had stopped seeing students in my office a long time before. I told them to ask me questions during the first ten minutes of the class period. I was tired of trouble and knew that my family simply could not tolerate another blast. Common sense told me to be very careful because I needed time to organize myself and my children and leave with as little notice as possible.

SATURDAY, OCTOBER 25, 1980 (AQRAB 3, 1359)

As I waited for a letter from my family in Pakistan, I began to finish up the last steps in obtaining a passport. I also had to correct the birth date on Omar's I.D. and try to sell our houses.

My passport required the approval of a senior official in the passport division of the Ministry of Interior, so one day I took it there and gave the half-completed papers to the director of that particular section. His secretary told me to come back in two days, but when I returned I found that the paperwork was not completed. The secretary said to come back next week. Next week arrived and I went for the third time to the Ministry of Interior. The passport papers were still not finished. This time the delay made me really angry. I went straight to the office of the director, Mohammed Alim. I didn't wait for him to finish his work, but walked right in and said, "Sir, I have a complaint. I don't know why my passport can't be finished on time."

Alim raised his head from the files he was reading and looked at me quietly. I continued, "It has been more than ten days, and still I am not able to get it back. In fact, this is the third time I've been here."

Alim, a skinny man in his fifties with white hair and mustache, stared at me a long time from behind his desk. Finally he smiled and said, "Sister, for God's sake, I want you to go! You people should leave as soon as you can. There is nothing left in this country that I should encourage anyone to stay." He offered me a chair and added, "I am not holding your passport. As soon as it is done, I will gladly give it to you and let you leave."

He paused for a moment as he arranged some papers on his desk. Then he turned toward me and said loudly, "If passports were given so easily to everyone, believe me Babrak Karmal would be the first to leave the country. I'm not kidding." He laughed and promised to finish my passport by the next week.

I heard Alim loud and clear but wasn't sure how he dared to say those words in the Ministry of Interior, where almost every employee was either secret police or a government agent. I didn't respond; I kept my mouth shut. I'd often got into trouble by opening my mouth. Today I tried hard to stay indifferent. No point taking any chances on making things worse. Early the next week I returned to Alim's office. He was as good as his word; the papers were signed and ready.

The final step in completing the passport was to put up a house or other type of property as collateral. It was understood that in case I did not return on time, the government would take the property. I didn't know what to do because I couldn't put our house up, with my husband's name on the title as the owner.

One day my brother Khalil told me of an old man by the name of Ahad who wanted to sell his house. I asked, "Are you sure he isn't a government agent?"

"I don't think so," Khalil replied. "He seems like a very straightforward man."

The next day Ahad came. I asked him how much money he wanted for his house and he answered that it was now estimated to be worth ten thousand afghanis. When I asked where the house was, he indicated that it was way outside the Kabul city limits. He had built it himself a couple of years before at a cost of about five thousand afghanis. This old man with his long, white beard and big turban seemed to be a very simpleminded farmer who had not learned the shrewdness of city folk. He looked very honest.

Khalil told him, "Please listen carefully. I want to buy your house for the price you ask. But it is a very different kind of deal. I buy your house but you still keep the ownership and the title. You can sell it in the future if you want to." Ahad nodded his head constantly, listening. Khalil went on, "The only thing I want from you is to put your house up as collateral for my sister's passport. Can you do that?"

Ahad nodded again and said yes.

Khalil, wanting to make sure Ahad knew what he was consenting to, explained, "Remember, you can sell the house. The worst thing that can happen to you would be if the government found out that the passport owner did not return. Then they would probably take your property."

The old man replied, "Yes sir. Only God knows what tomorrow may bring for us. I am sure these people" – he meant the Communists – "will not last that long." I paid Ahad two thousand afghanis and told him I would pay the rest tomorrow, as soon as the passport was completed.

The following day when Khalil and I went to the passport division, we found Ahad waiting for us at the front gate. He had with him all the papers needed to put his house up as collateral on my passport. Surprisingly, this innocent old man was very familiar with the passport offices and moved from desk to desk very easily. He knew exactly what to do next. We spent the entire day there and at the end of the day I paid him the rest of the money in cash.

Two days later Khalil and I returned to the passport division to get a couple of signatures from a clerk. There we saw Ahad again. He had another set of papers in his hand and was following a young man down the aisles, exactly the way he had for us, from one desk to the next. Khalil looked at him, smiled, and then whispered in my ear, "Are you thinking the same thing I am?"

"Yes. Well, he doesn't seem to be the simpleminded person we thought he was!" And we both laughed.

It seemed that Ahad may have sold the same house over and over again to many others who were trying to get passports. Or he may have had some connections with the passport clerks.

That day as I was leaving the office I heard another old man nearly crying with frustration: "I don't know who this damned person is who has put my house up as collateral for his passport. What's his address? I don't even know his name!" Apparently the man wanted to sell his house but could not. It seemed that someone who had access to his documents had put this man's house up as collateral for his own passport and may already have left the country. I thanked God that I still had my own property!

MONDAY, OCTOBER 27, 1980 (AQRAB 5, 1359)

I got rid of Omar's fake I.D. and, as Abdul had recommended, asked for a replacement copy from the Census Bureau in the Ministry of Interior. In the hall of the ministry I saw Samae, my former student who had helped me with my passport a long time before. He invited me for a cup of tea in his office and asked me about my passport – whether it had been issued or not. In fact, he was surprised to see me still in Afghanistan. I told him my problems, of not having any official documents on Saleem's whereabouts and not being able to sell my houses while my children were underage. "Why didn't you have one of your houses in your own name?" he asked. "I know half of that property must be yours, because you've worked all your married life."

"True. But I trusted Saleem, and I never thought that one day life would get so complicated. And then, I never liked courts and always thought they were for people who had a family dispute or had killed someone."

"Our rotten rules of the past must be changed. That's why we need a new system."

Samae asked if I had my sons' I.D.s with me. I told him I had only Ali's, that I'd lost Omar's and was there to get a duplicate. Samae laughed and said, "Well, you've come to the right place then. I'm in charge of issuing I.D.s."

Samae looked at Ali's I.D. carefully and said, "I'll give you two new I.D.s for your sons showing that they are of age, but I won't put the data in our records. You go ahead and finish the legal documents for the sale of your property." He pulled from his desk two I.D. booklets, filled in all the blanks, stamped them, and signed both. He kept Ali's original I.D. in his desk and said, "After you finish the court papers, bring these I.D.s back and I'll replace them."

This all happened so fast that I was shocked. I hadn't expected to find Samae there in the Ministry of Interior, nor I had dreamed that he was the final authority on issuing I.D.s or that he himself would change the I.D.s for me. I felt awful. Here was my student breaking the law for me. I think Samae knew of my discomfort. He said, "If anyone gives you trouble over these I.D.s, tell them to call me."

I stood up, feeling embarrassed and still undecided what to do. Should I accept his help or not? Samae looked at me and said, "Professor, I would never have done this if our system were fair for everyone. Till we change our corrupt system, honest people like you will always suffer."

I left Samae's office with the two new fake I.D.s in my hand. Although I now had Samae's support, I still was not able to go to court in person, fearing to be caught with the fake I.D.s. I asked Abdul, our friend, to finish the paperwork for me. Surprisingly, they never asked my sons to appear in person in court. When everything was completed, I went and signed the documents and Abdul returned the I.D.s to Samae, exchanging them for the real ones. Now that I had the legal documents to sell my property, I put both of my houses up for sale.

WEDNESDAY, OCTOBER 29, 1980 (AQRAB 7, 1359)

Yesterday my office phone rang. Someone on the other end of the line said, "*Ostad*, Anahita Jan, minister of education, wants to meet you. When is a good time for you to see her?"

"What? I'm sorry, I didn't understand. What did you say?" I asked.

The secretary replied, "There will be a Nationwide Conference of Afghanistan's Educated Women and you are invited to be a member of the executive committee."

After a brief pause, I said, "I am? Well, when is it going to be?"

"Dr. Anahita Jan" – Jan is a term of respect commonly used in our everyday conversation in Persian – "wants to see you before the conference. Can you come to the Ministry of Education tomorrow morning at eleven?"

I thought it was not wise to refuse Anahita's request, because she was very close to Babrak, Afghanistan's president. In fact, she was the second person from the top in the government. So I said I'd be there.

All day long after the phone call I felt miserable for accepting the offer even though I had no choice. Saying no to Anahita would not have been a wise move. I simply needed to buy some time, just a few more weeks, to leave the country, so I had to avoid attracting attention.

When I went to the Ministry of Education, Anahita put her arms around me and blamed the previous governments (Taraki's and Amin's) for all the unreasonable trouble and disasters created for many families. It seemed that she knew my family's history fairly well. She knew a great deal about Saleem and me. This was the first time in my life that I'd seen Anahita this close and I noticed that she had green eyes. She showed me to a chair and offered me a cup of tea.

At this point the phone rang. She politely apologized and took the call. While she was on the phone, my thoughts wandered back to the mid-1960s, when the constitutional reform stimulated the formation of many political groups in the capital city. The results were very obvious at Kabul University, since all the groups tried to influence the youth. University students gathered frequently on the campus and listened to political leaders. Anahita was one of those who made provocative speeches at that time. I had seen her once from a distance as she spoke to students, but I wasn't interested in politics or her speech.

Anahita's voice brought me back to her office as she hung up the phone and said, "Do you mind serving on the executive committee for the conference?"

"No, not if it doesn't interfere with my schedule at school."

"We should have several meetings before the conference. Most of them will be after three in the afternoon," Anahita replied. "I'll let you know the times and dates later."

SATURDAY, NOVEMBER 15, 1980 (AQRAB 24, 1359)
I sold the new house in less than three weeks. I wanted to sell the second house but found out that in the legal documents at court, Abdul had mistakenly asked permission to sell only one house. I didn't want to go through the unpleasant process again of securing authorization to sell the house, so I decided to lease it.

Six weeks had gone by and I still had not heard from my family. I didn't know where they were or what their situation was. My brother Khalil and I were the only ones left behind in Kabul. We felt closer than ever before. He came almost every day to visit us. We tried to support and give courage to each other now, but I was the one who needed it the most.

As Khalil and I sat every evening after work, we talked about the good times we'd had together. We talked about our family a lot and remembered the old-time stories. Khalil started, "When I was in junior high, Mizhgan hired Jaan and me to water Dad's willow trees in our backyard." He laughed and continued, "You know, that *kafir* [infidel] was taking advantage of us, because Dad gave her ten afghanis every week but she hired us to do the whole job for three afghanis. She kept the rest of the money for herself! You know, if she ever falls into my hands, I'm going to take all that money Father paid her!"

Khalil remembered the day that Mom and Dad planned to go and visit our uncle. Mom washed one of her fancy dresses that she wanted to wear and hung it lengthwise on the clothesline. Sometime during the day, the gate was left open and the neighbor's cow came in and chewed up her dress. In no time at all the cow had eaten exactly half of Mother's dress and left the other half hanging on the line. Khalil said, "Mother came into the room with her dress in her hand, and it had only one sleeve, half the collar, and half the skirt. It took us a few minutes to figure out what had happened. Mom was so upset we didn't dare say a word. But later, when she calmed down, we all broke into laughter and Mother joined in too."

I remembered the day that Mizhgan somehow lost the two hundred afghanis Mother had given her to buy some groceries. She didn't tell Mom that she had lost it but instead went and borrowed money from a neighbor and bought everything on Mother's list. She told the neighbor that she would return the money the next month. The next month came and Mizhgan hadn't been able to save the money, so she went and borrowed two hundred afghanis from a second neighbor and gave it to the first one. Another month passed by, Mizhgan went to a third neighbor, borrowed the money, and gave it to neighbor number two. The cycle went on and on for almost six months until all the neighbors had been approached for loans. Finally one day the last neighbor, who had not received her money, came and asked Mother if she had forgotten it.

Mother said she'd never borrowed the money. The neighbor said, "Well, Mizhgan came last month and asked for it, so I thought she gave it to you." Mother paid the neighbor and when Mizhgan got home that evening the whole story came out.

It was strange that when the family was around, we never thought about the past. Now we were remembering these stories one by one. I realized it is human nature that when we have all the blessings, we take them for granted, but once we lose them, we dearly miss those happy times.

TUESDAY, NOVEMBER 18, 1980 (AQRAB 27, 1359)

Last night one of our neighbors who called herself Mahgul and who had rented the house next door came with her husband to lease our house. Since I didn't know them, she introduced her husband as Rais Sahib. (Rais means a dignitary, or head of a commercial enterprise, and Sahib is a word of respect that is added to many other professional titles such as Engineer Sahib, Teacher Sahib, and so forth.) They looked at all the rooms and the yard and agreed to lease it for 400,000 afghanis. (Under normal circumstances it was worth three times that amount.) They put 10,000 afghanis down as a nonrefundable down payment and promised to bring the rest of the money by next Tuesday, when I would give them a notarized document that was not required to pass through the court. Such contracts were common and valid.

All this past month, not only did I need to comfort and calm myself down, but I also had to reassure my relatives. Some of them were related to the spouses of my sisters and Jaan – people whose names I had heard but whom I had not yet met. They thought I would be the first to get the news from Pakistan. Jaan's mother-in-law, who lived in Mazar-i-Sharif, came every week to ask for news. She returned home crying in disappointment when she learned that I was waiting for news too. The road between Mazar and Kabul was extremely dangerous, and because of the war between the Afghan people and the Russian soldiers, communication by letter or phone was impossible. All my sisters' in-laws came and inquired often and left in tears. I honestly didn't know what to do. I myself needed some support, and playing hostess to disappointed, tearful people didn't help.

On this day at school as I was standing with colleagues in the hall, I saw my sister Sophia's sister-in-law. I couldn't talk to her in front of the others, but I noticed her questioning eyes fixed at me. I knew she wanted news of her brother and his family, so I shook my head no. As soon as she saw my gesture indicating that there was no news, she began to cry. All the professors around me were confused. One of them asked, "What did you do to her?"

I laughed and said, "What parapsychological powers!"

I left my friends and took the young woman to my office, where I tried to calm her down. I told her, "Look, you have only your brother and his wife in that group. But look at me! Twenty-one members of my family are there. If something happened to them, then all my family is gone. I won't have anyone in this world!" I embraced her and kissed her and said, "Let's pray for their safety and wait courageously. As soon as I get news, you'll be the first to know."

SATURDAY, NOVEMBER 22, 1980 (QAUS 1, 1359)

As I was giving a test in class today, the office clerk brought me a letter mailed from West Germany. The address and the name of the sender were unfamiliar. I couldn't resist reading it right away. I opened the letter. Inside was a smaller envelope. It was from my brother-in-law Wali. The letter couldn't be mailed directly from Pakistan to us. Wali had sent it through his friends in Germany.

The letter did not carry good news. Wali said that they were very unhappy in Lahore and that if things didn't work out in the next few days they all would return to Kabul. He didn't explain what the problems were, but the message hit me hard. The more I thought about it, the uglier it looked. I knew that if they returned, they would all go to jail. They had sold everything. Where would they live? How would they live? They'd given up their jobs.

The whole classroom began spinning around me. The students' faces became a blur. I couldn't hold myself up; I was about to faint. I stepped back and leaned my shoulders against the blackboard and stood there for a while to catch my breath. Fortunately, the students were busy writing their test and didn't notice my condition.

My brother came in the afternoon and I showed him the letter. He said, "No way! They must not come back. It is too dangerous for them." He was as shocked as I was. He wanted to go to Pakistan and tell them not to come. It would not be easy for him to cross the border and return, so instead we tried to send a message telling Mother that I would be there very soon and please to wait for me. In the meantime, I decided to rush and finish my chores faster and meet them in India. I felt very responsible for them – I don't know why, but I always felt this way for my whole family. Since Mahgul would lease my house in three days, I went ahead and bought airline tickets to India for November 27.

I exchanged most of the money I had for American dollars through a Sikh merchant, from whom I received a check on the Wells Fargo Bank in New York. It was very risky and I didn't dare convert Mother's money in such an unreliable way. I also bought from him many one-thousand-mark notes.

I was very careful about the money the government would allow to be taken out of the country. At the Ministry of Foreign Affairs they told me that those with medical passports could take up to $600 per person covered by the passport. The passport owner could take an additional $200. I prudently converted 150,000 afghanis at the local government bank at the rate of 57 afghanis to the dollar, about 7 afghanis per dollar more than the open-market rate. I saved all the bank papers with my passport as a precaution. I would carry the maximum allowable cash with me to the airport. I was afraid that if I did not do so, questions might be raised about how I could support my family in India for the proposed three months of our stay.

WEDNESDAY, NOVEMBER 26, 1980 (QAUS 5, 1359)

During the past week Mahgul and her husband had brought an endless number of friends and relatives to see the house that she was supposed to lease. I was surprised by the way the couple talked to each other; somehow it didn't seem normal. For example, when her husband was talking, Mahgul would interrupt him frequently and say something like "Oh, Rais Sahib, director of such and such firm, excuse me for taking the words out of your mouth. . . . " Or "Pardon me, Rais Sahib . . ." Or "Forgive me, Rais Sahib . . ."

I didn't know if she wanted to impress me by being so polite or was just showing off. One week was gone and this friendly couple kept postponing the payment due on their lease, switching times and dates for it. It didn't take me too long to figure out that I was dealing with a couple of charlatans and the whole deal was a scam. Somehow this extraordinarily polite and sweet couple had figured out that I was leaving very soon. They wanted to own the house for the down payment they had made. I sent Omar to their house to tell them that if I didn't get the money by twelve noon today the deal was off. At ten in the morning both showed up. Mahgul and her husband were blaming each other for the delay. They started fighting in front of us. There were no more of those polite apologies. I didn't say a single word, but watched them patiently. Soon they realized they had set the show and we were the audience. Omar and Ali laughed frequently at what they said to each other. Finally Mahgul stopped and looked at me and said, "What do you suggest, *Ostad*?"

"Well, it's your problem. You decide now."

I had asked 400,000 afghanis for the house. Mahgul said, "Could you reduce the price just a le-e-e-e-tle bit?" She made a coy gesture with her fingers and facial expression.

"No!" I said firmly.

The couple sat for a while, whispering at times. I knew they wanted their money back, so I went in the other room and brought out 10,000 afghanis and put it on the table in front of them. Mahgul tried to grab the bundle of fifty-afghani bills, but it slipped through her fingers and the bills scattered about the floor. Both husband and wife got on their knees, collected the bills, and left apologetically.

In great annoyance I went to the airline and canceled our reservations for the next day. Then I went to the post office and sent my sister Mizh-

gan in India a telegram that said: "Arrival in Delhi Dec. 3 at 2 p.m. Flight
. . ." Later, in India, I heard that Mother became nearly hysterical when
she saw our telegram, fearing that something was very wrong.

SATURDAY, NOVEMBER 29, 1980 (QAUS 8, 1359)
The Nationwide Conference of Afghanistan's Educated Women (NCAEW)
opened today. It was the first of two conferences planned. The other, the
International Women's Seminar, was scheduled to begin on December
1, following the NCAEW.

I believe that when Babrak visited his masters in Russia on his last
trip, he was told that his government was not effective in attracting new
members to the party. Their target was those who were still undecided
and were not members of any of the existing political parties. Soon after
his return from Russia, Babrak's party started a big campaign focusing
on politically uncommitted public employees who were in contact with
many citizens. One such group was teachers. In Afghan society, teachers
were highly respected. A good teacher was always admired by the public, so bringing uncommitted teachers into the party was the main goal
of the government's policy, which in turn would serve the purposes of
Babrak and his party.

I was among the four or five nonparty teachers who were selected
to be on the executive committee for the NCAEW along with famous
Parchamis – national leaders and Politburo members. About a hundred
nonparty teachers and four hundred pro-Russian teachers from all over
the country were invited to attend this conference.

We, as members of the executive committee, were supposed to work
out the conference details. Before each committee meeting a message
was sent out by Anahita's office to the university informing me of the
time and date. Most often such messages were conveyed by a student in
my class who would stand up just before I started lecturing and would
say loudly, "Professor, Anahita Jan said that the next meeting will be on
such and such date."

For some people this type of message from the country's most author-itative woman was considered prestigious, but for me it was not. In fact, I was very unhappy about it, because some students would now con-sider me a member of the Parcham group, which in reality I was not – but I was being boxed into their political square with no other choice.

I didn't want to reject Anahita's invitation/orders completely because my family did not need any more trouble. At that time, during the first two weeks of November, I didn't know if Mom and the rest of the fam-ily were still in Afghanistan, or if they had crossed the border. The best thing was to keep my old policy of noncommitment – neither to join any of the political groups nor to give them the idea that I would oppose them directly.

Many of the committee meetings were held in the Shahr-i-Naw area, in a building called the Afghan-Russian Friendship Building. Of all the meetings, I attended only three, using my daughter's illness as a pretext for missing the rest. I thought this tactic would leave them still confused about my sympathies, something that would help buy time.

A short refreshment period preceded the first meeting I attended. Among the group of ten women I found three familiar faces from many years back. There was a short, medium-dark woman who had a thick lock of white hair and was named Zarghuna. People teasingly called her Zarghuna-e-Sar Sapheed, "the white-headed Zarghuna." She had been a student of mine in high school in the early 1960s when I talked a lot about women's rights and so forth. I also saw one of our neighbors named Mashal. She was a tall, beautiful woman in her mid-twenties. I couldn't remember the name of the third woman I recognized, but I think she was a relative of Mashal.

Besides me, there were, I believed, three others who did not belong to the Parchamis. One was Fahima Jan, the old principal of Malalai High School. Another, Jamila Jan, had been the well-known director of the Women's Organization Institute during the government of King Zahir Shah and probably in Daoud's time too.

After we had our tea, we left for the conference room. Since I was at the far end of the room, I was the last person to leave, and on my way out I noticed, in a corner, a small statue of Lenin. I had a sudden impulse to go over and give it a big slap on the face: "Damn it! Your stupid ideas have brought us all these troubles and miseries!" But I didn't do it. I thought they might have surveillance cameras watching us.

The conference room was not very large but had an expensive oblong table in the center. Books lined the shelves all around us. Most of the committee members were already seated when I arrived. As I selected an empty chair in the far corner I heard Zarghuna's voice, "Anahita Jan, where should I sit?"

Anahita, standing at the other end of the table, pointed to an empty chair just in front of her and Zarghuna sat down quietly. Anahita began her speech, which was well prepared and nicely worded. It emphasized both her high hopes for the country and its problems, the major ones of which were reflected in her talk. She discussed the uprisings of people everywhere and told us, "People are on one side of the river, and we" – she meant the Parchamis – "are on the other side. We cannot communicate and can't see each other. You" – she pointed to us – "you become a bridge and bring us together. You fill the gap that exists and let us communicate. You are the ones who can help us!"

The way Anahita spoke, it seemed that now the party in power really wanted to talk to the people. But on the other hand, I knew that the Afghan citizens were not ready to listen to them. The "bridge" that she emphasized so much was probably those of us who had not yet joined the party, because she looked straight into the eyes of the nonparty members whenever she said the word "you."

At another such meeting we talked about overnight arrangements for the teachers from the provinces and different options were offered. Some suggested that the guests stay in the Kabul Hotel. Others suggested the Speen-Ghar Hotel, the Marco Polo Hotel, and a few other hotels around town. They all had disadvantages, such as the lack of enough rooms or of an adequately large lobby. The only place we all agreed upon was the Inter-Continental Hotel, which was big enough and had better facilities.

Anahita suggested that using the modern facilities – elevators, television, toilet arrangements, and so forth – of the Inter-Continental Hotel would create some problems for the provincial guests. We must, she said, present some sort of orientation program for the guests to familiarize them with the surroundings and how to use the modern facilities. Now the question was asked how we could accomplish that. Many suggestions were discussed. At one point, when we were not able to find a good solution, Anahita turned to a Russian woman, probably her foreign adviser, who had been there from the beginning, and said, "Let me ask our *Mushkil Gushah* [ultimate problem solver] what to do."

Her action was very offensive, I thought. Here we were, born Afghans, proud of our education and heritage and gratified with the knowledge of knowing our own cultural problems. If we could not solve our problems, then how could someone from outside tell us how to train the provincial teachers to use those modern facilities! The second thing I did not like was her use of the term *Mushkil Gushah*, which in our everyday Dari-language conversation is most often used for God, the ultimate problem solver.

At the university just two days before the opening of the conference, Baba, the custodian, came and told me that someone was on the phone in the next office and wanted to talk to me. Apparently they had dialed the wrong number. I went there and picked up the phone. A person from Anahita's office was on the line and said, "Professor, you have been asked to read the conference's aims and purposes on television during tonight's news."

I asked her, "By whose order?"

"Zarghuna Jan's," she replied.

"Shouldn't she have asked my opinion first?" I inquired firmly.

"They decided it during our last meeting, when you weren't there."

Decisions concerning myself made in my absence always made me furious. I wasn't about to take orders from Zarghuna. So I said, "I don't care who told you this. I can't read the aims on television; because of our family's problems I'm a little disoriented. I'm afraid I would ruin the entire program."

Suddenly I realized that my direct rejection might create a lot of problems and I needed to smooth the edges of my words a bit. I added, "It's true that I am a teacher and can talk to a large crowd without any problem. But if the TV lights are focused on me, it psychologically disturbs me. After all, I'm not a very good public speaker to begin with."

So here I was, rejecting the government's honors again! The professor in whose office I received the call heard my conversation. He shook his head and laughed as I hung up the phone.

Whenever we left the meetings, Anahita always put her special car at our disposal to take us home. The license plate had no numbers but instead bore the party's special logo. All the windows were covered by shades. No matter how much I insisted on taking the bus, Anahita would not let me do so; her driver must take me. When I arrived home from a subsequent meeting, I found a visitor there, a close relative of ours who was a Parchami. Since I'd always trusted her as a good friend, I told her about my distress over attending the meetings and about my refusal to read the conference aims on television.

"Well, they're asking for your help. That's good; congratulations! I think you should not refuse it. Soon you'll be assigned to a big job," she said, to my surprise.

Her answer made me rather angry. I replied, "To tell you the truth, I don't like it. One day we are antirevolutionists, their foes, and the next day we are their friends." I recited for her the song written by Abul Qasim Lahooti in 1930 that I liked very much. The translation goes: "If showers of real pearls fall on your head in servility, / Tell the skies . . . go away . . . I don't need those rain showers / Life always comes to an end / Slavery and degradation are not needed."

"My pride and dignity are far more important to me than all the treasures that could come my way through shame and oppression. I don't want a job that would make me one of their puppets," I told my friend.

Skipping some of the meetings and not reading the conference aims on television probably served as a hint to Anahita that I was not willing to join the party. I didn't know what was going on behind the scenes or what was in store for me; all I needed was a few days more. I was getting close to the culmination of my plans for escape.

The NCAEW conference opened in the Salam Khana Palace, which was situated in a far corner of the People's House, the former presidential palace. As a member of the executive committee, I was seated right behind the Politburo members. When Babrak made his opening remarks, we were expected to applaud after every sentence. I was in a very awkward position. Sometimes out of fear I clapped. Other times I didn't clap at all, even when the cameras were focused on us. Next to me sat one of my high school teachers. After a few rounds of applause she whispered in my ear, "They say this is a gathering of educated women of Afghanistan. If someone is really educated, she shouldn't be here!"

I turned and asked her, "Then how come you are here?"

She replied, "What could I do? They forced me into it."

I whispered, "Same here."

We both laughed. Deep down I admired her courage in being so outspoken.

MONDAY, DECEMBER 1, 1980 (QAUS 10, 1359)

Today I attended the opening session of the International Women's Seminar. Around ten in the morning we had a break, during which I tried to leave for home without attracting anyone's attention. I went into the hall and stood in a corner, hiding myself behind the large white pillars. When the others went back into the conference room, I would sneak out and go home. Suddenly someone called my name from behind and said, "Salaam, *Ostad*! What are you doing here?"

I looked in the direction from which the sound came and saw

a pleasant-appearing, well-dressed young woman coming toward me. Since I didn't recognize her, I kept quiet. She approached and asked, "Do you want to leave?"

I mumbled, "Well, my daughter is very sick and I have to take her to the doctor."

She said, "Then hurry and come with me. I'm leaving too. Let's walk fast, behind these pillars so nobody can see us."

Silly me! Without further thought, I followed her toward the main gate. A military Jeep pulled up in front of us and she told me, "Jump in. Hurry! Let's go!"

We both got in and she asked where I was going. I told her the Karte-Parwan section of the city, where my mother-in-law lived. I didn't want her to know my address.

She ordered the driver, "Go to Karte-Parwan."

On the way we talked a lot, but about nothing important. From our conversation I found out that she knew me very well, while I didn't know her at all. She said, "I know they asked you to read the conference message on television and you declined to." At another point she said, "I also know you've skipped most of the executive committee meetings."

I told her that Sahar's illness had prevented me from attending the meetings regularly, but her words were a very real warning signal. "Who is this woman in this military Jeep?" I thought agitatedly. Military vehicles were for special important government officials. "How does she know all these things about me? What I am doing here with her in this car?" I was really frightened. I cursed myself. How could I have trusted her and got in the Jeep in the first place?

As she talked about my family I noticed that she didn't seem to know of my relatives' departure to Pakistan. That was encouraging. When she finished speaking, I inquired, "May I ask your name and how you know all this?"

She replied, "Yes, of course. I am Dr. Safia, Babrak Karmal's sister-in-law. I'm the director of the Children's Hospital."

I thought to myself, "Good grief! I've run out of the rain only to stand under the gutters!" I pulled myself together. "Well, it's good to know you," I said inanely. I looked her straight in the eye. She was smiling and looking back at me. We both laughed out loud as our eyes met. Perhaps she was laughing about surprising me, and I was laughing about my stupidity.

From here on, she was extremely friendly, and our conversation was warm and cordial. When we arrived at Karte-Parwan and I got out of the Jeep, Safia said, "If I can be of any help for Sahar, please let me know." I don't know why, but somehow I trusted her, so I answered, "Thank you! I'll keep that in mind." As the Jeep drove away down the street I saw that her hand was still waving behind the window. She was probably still laughing at my stupidity.

When I got home, I received a long, detailed letter from my sister Sophia and her husband, Daryush. It was brought to me from India by a friend, who said that he'd gone to their house in India unexpectedly. Since Sophia didn't have the time to write a letter, she'd cut pages out of her diary and given them to him. Here is a translation of her diary account, with a few explanations added for clarification:

As I left my beloved country behind, it all happened as in a dream and passed in front of my eyes like a motion picture. The more I thought about it later, the more it seemed like a nightmare.

The night before our departure we were all packed and ready to leave. There was nothing to be packed actually, because the guide had told us not to take anything with us except the clothes we wore. That night around midnight fighting suddenly began in Kabul. Cannons fired from all directions. The nerve-racking sounds were extremely close and deafening. The cannons and tanks fired constantly for two hours. Everybody was making some conjecture. Someone said the Rishkhor Army Base was being bombed. Others suggested that the Qargha Rocket Base was under fire. We tried the radio, but there was nothing on the news. After the shelling stopped, we all slept, scared and worried about tomorrow's trip across the border.

Morning came. We got ready to leave. The flight to Kandahar was scheduled for eleven. We wore veils and Pashtun tribal dress. The men had cut their hair short and had shaved their mustaches neatly. (Most Khalquis had long hair and mustaches; we didn't want to look like them.) They wore old turbans or round caps. We all had tribal shoes and sandals.

We left the house at 10:30 a.m. When in the airport we covered our faces. The flight was delayed for an hour. The big problem was to avoid the attention of the airport police and also the large number of government secret agents, who were all over the place. Although we didn't know who was who, we had to be careful, so didn't talk in Persian. The eastern border's language is Pashto, and since we didn't know how to speak Pashto, we kept quiet as much as was possible. Mom and Jaan had left early in the morning to finish the last few bits of paperwork for the sale of Mom's house. They weren't back yet and I was worried. At this point my two-year-old niece began to cry. She insisted that her mother remove her veil. She was crying loudly and pulling her mother's veil away from her face, which scared all of us. If the police knew that we didn't normally cover our faces and that's why the child was crying, we were all history! To discourage police attention we all swarmed around her. Finally after some time we managed to calm her down. Luckily, no one had paid attention.

That day we all pretended that we were going to attend a family wedding in the Spin Boldak area, near the Pakistan border. Close to noon Mother and Jaan showed up, Jaan in his blue jeans and Mother in her regular clothes. Apparently they hadn't had a chance to change their clothes.

At 12:30 in the afternoon we all got on the plane and two hours later we arrived at the Kandahar airport. The guide was waiting for us. He resembled a character in a French movie that I had seen recently on TV, so I called him Sherri Bibi. He took us to a house far from Kandahar city. We didn't know the hosts, but they seemed to be expecting us. After an hour we heard several gunshots, very close, from the direction of the entrance gate. It scared us all because we thought the Russians had discovered our location and were coming after us. The hostesses laughed and one of them said we needn't be afraid. It was their tradition. They were welcoming the honored guests and had informed the neighbors of our arrival!

We all sat quietly. Mother was busy talking with them in the Pashto language. At night they put a big white spread on the floor and brought us the best food they could provide, but none of us were hungry. We all were worried and waiting for tomorrow. After dinner we went to bed.

We had hardly slept for a few minutes when we heard a loud, persistent banging on the door. We all jumped out of our beds. All of us, including the hosts, were terrified and began to panic. Every one of us was trying to hide someplace, but there were not enough corners to hide all of us. Every corner I ran to in the dark, I found someone was already there. Falling on my face and stepping on others, I finally sat on the floor. A few moments later Sherri Bibi came in, laughing, with my six-year-old nephew, Karim. Apparently Karim had gone to the bathroom and couldn't open the door. He became frightened and knocked at the door very hard.

Night went by in fear and prayers. Early in the morning, when it was still very dark, we got on a big truck that was full of large sacks of grain. Sherri Bibi told us to find a place among the sacks. We had barely driven for an hour when Russian tanks appeared on the horizon. On seeing those armored vehicles, we hid ourselves behind the sacks. It took the tanks almost ten minutes to pass by. When the sound of their motors faded away, we came out of hiding. We were trembling with cold and fear. The sacks seemed to be filled with rocks, they felt so hard and uncomfortable.

For several hours we drove in fear and prayers. Finally the truck stopped next to an American Jeep. The guide came and told us to get in the Jeep. It was a small vehicle, probably big enough for eight people, but, surprisingly, all twenty-one of us got in, either from lack of options or from extreme fear. The Jeep moved very fast across the vast desert. There was no road. It often bounced high in the air as it crossed ditches. Very strange! – no one had complained so far. We were all silent; even the small children sensed the fear and didn't say a word.

After an hour the Jeep driver took us into a small hut. It was built beside a narrow road that looked more like an abandoned hiking trail. It was around noon and we were hungry. The people who lived in the house brought us a huge pan full of buttermilk, a dozen deep spoons, and several nans. Reluctantly we ate the food. Every bite of bread stuck in my mouth, and we gulped it down by drinking some buttermilk. We stayed in this house till the next morning.

Very early in the morning, way before sunrise, Sherri Bibi came and told us to get ready. We were all ready in two minutes because there was nothing to do. We'd slept in the same clothes that we had worn since Kabul, two days ago. As we were getting into yet another car, the guide said, "Please hurry. At a certain time at sunrise the Russian radars don't function properly. If we make this day safely, we'll be out of trouble soon." We drove in fear. It is so hard for me to describe those moments spent in fear and lassitude. It was like watching your death every minute in front of you!

A few minutes later the car stopped. Sherri Bibi told us to get into a different car, which was parked under a small tree. So far, this was our fourth vehicle. It was a little bigger than the Jeep. As the car moved forward, we were escorted by several large dark-haired men on motorcycles. At times a couple of them went ahead to check the road and see if it was clear and safe for our car to pass through.

A few hours later we arrived at a place where we found *mujahidin* (people who resisted the Communist government) all around us. They were on hilltops, on the road, and everywhere in the valleys too. This was comforting and gave us a little peace of mind. According to Sherri Bibi we were safe now. We drove for another half hour till we got close to the Pakistan border. There were another couple of hours to go. We now all began to cheer up and the normal color returned to our pale faces. The road ahead of us was paved. We stopped at a small bakery and bought a few hot breads.

After two hours the border came into view. Here we were supposed to get the Pakistan government's permission for refugee status. The completion of the paperwork was tiring and time-consuming. I spread my veil on the ground and lay down on the street corner. I thought that we had left our miseries behind, not knowing that it was the beginning of another time of struggle and many troubles.

After getting the documents, the guide, who still accompanied us, came and said we had to go to Quetta, which was another few hours away. At two o'clock in the morning we reached Quetta. We tried to find a hotel, but they refused to give us a room, rejecting us when they saw our tired faces and clothes with an inch of dust on them. Most hotel managers demanded passports and obviously we did not have them. Finally Mother talked to a hotel manager in the language of the region, Urdu. He gave us three large rooms. Mother, with her knowledge of various languages, was unquestionably a great help to all of us.

As soon as we got to our rooms and found the hot water, we began to bathe and clean ourselves up. I washed out my only dress, the one I was wearing. Then I tried to sleep. My eyes had hardly closed when we heard Sherri Bibi's voice as he knocked at the door: "The train to Lahore leaves in half an hour. You'll have plenty of time to sleep on the train."

We got up again and walked a few minutes until we reached the station. We got to the train just in time. I don't know what kind of train it was. The distance that was supposed to be covered in one day took us two days and two nights on this train. It stopped and started again almost every fifteen minutes. Screaming and crying belligerently, it rolled through the rugged terrain. At times I thought I could certainly walk faster than the train.

Sun came up two hours later and we were very hungry. At a station I went to a cart that people were crowding around and saw that many of them were eating dal (lentils or beans) and chapati (flat tortilla-like bread) with great appetite. After searching here and there I found a cart selling sweet cake. I bought several large ones. As we were eating, Mother's voice was heard saying, "Now you have to get used to Pakistani foods!" At noon Jaan bought a big tray of hot vegetable fritters called pakora, full of spices and hot peppers. With great appetite and with tears in our eyes we ate the pakora.

This disgusting, horrid train kept moving at the pace of a slow slug, day and night. I didn't know when we would reach Lahore. Our clothes were dirty and our faces covered with dust. It was hard to recognize anyone anymore. Another morning came. Now the weather was getting hotter and hotter as we neared Lahore. By noon it was intolerable. Finally the conductor told us that by four in the afternoon we would reach Lahore.

Lahore was very hot, just like an oven. Everybody who left the train had at least a bag with them, but we didn't have anything with us. In tattered, dirty clothing we headed for our relatives. When our hostess saw the condition we were in, she was shocked. It took my cousin and her husband a while to recognize us. Anyhow, we got inside her house. She offered us some tea and food, which disappeared in the very first few minutes. After tea we went one by one into the bathroom to take a shower and clean up a bit. We finished two twenty-ounce bottles of shampoo the very first night. It obviously made our hosts even more frightened than before.

The next day Mother said we would have to find a house of our own, but she soon learned that renting a house was impossible because of the mass movement of Afghans into Pakistan. The prices had gone up and the landlords would not rent their houses for less than one year at a time. They demanded that the tenants pay the full year's rent up front.

The first few days were spent in shopping. Lahore weather was as hot as hell and made us all sick. The change of place, weather, and food; the lack of enough clothing; and, above all, the lack of a definite daily program or work drove us all crazy.

People said that we must obtain an I.D. from any one of the Afghan political groups in Peshawar (a city near the Afghan border), so one member from each of our families went to Peshawar. In Peshawar there were about a hundred Afghan political groups, large and small. Each opposed the Kabul regime in power and some were in disagreement with each other too. The refugee camps there were in poor condition. The tent cities were overcrowded and the lack of space, the hot weather, and inadequate food and water made the living situation terrible. After obtaining I.D. cards our family representatives returned to Lahore.

Since we couldn't find a house of our own in Lahore, we had to live with our relatives, which was extremely hard. Because of stupid customs, the hosts felt humiliated and disgraced if we cooked our own food in their house. Yet, preparing food for nine persons (my two sisters and their families had moved out and lived with other friends or relatives) was costly and not an easy job for them. One day in their absence Mother went and bought some grocery items. As soon as the hosts found out that we had bought our own food, we faced their upset looks and the wife began to cry. She said people would blame her for not being able to support their guests. What an awkward and difficult odd situation for all of us! With tears and all sorts of words and tricks, she paid Mother the price of all of the groceries we had bought.

Two weeks later, on the return of my sisters from Peshawar, we decided to go to India, where our sister Mizhgan was studying. Going to India required passports, and passports for Afghans were issued only in Peshawar. A powerful single government did not exist in Peshawar. A friend told us that fake passports were issued to those who paid the price demanded. Almost every small shop in town had an illegally made government stamp and issued passports. The price of such passports varied greatly. At times one passport was sold and resold many times.

The decision to leave Pakistan was arrived at very quickly. In a couple of days we got the passports and left for New Delhi, India. At Palam Airport in New Delhi we applied for entry visas. When the applications were made, news spread among the airport officials that a large family from Afghanistan including teachers, doctors, two television directors, and a police officer were seeking asylum in India, so the officials tried to finish the visa work as quickly as they could.

While waiting for the visas, Mother looked in her purse and couldn't find her money. Soon all of us were searching everywhere for it. It was all those German marks, which we all depended upon. After nearly half an hour of searching and running up and down, Mother remembered that the night before our departure from Kabul, she had put the money in the pocket that my sister had made in her undergarment. She laughed and said, "Don't worry; it's with me! I found it!"

The visas were ready in an hour. The funny thing was, when the time came to inspect our luggage, we didn't have any. Some of us felt very embarrassed when we showed the airport inspectors only a small cloth-wrapped package in our hands. From the airport we went directly to Mizhgan's house. Mizhgan was shocked to see us all standing there with our cloth-wrapped "luggage" in our hands. In fact, she didn't know that we were coming to India.

New Delhi is beautiful. It doesn't have the problems of Pakistan. Women walk freely on the streets without attracting anyone's attention. Each of our families rented a place in a far northern district of the city called Ashok Vihar. In the afternoons we make up a football team and play with the Vietnamese and Indians of Ashok Vihar. Although we don't have the needed practice, often we end up winning, which makes the other teams very upset.

Mother is anxiously waiting for my sister and her family to come and join us here in India.

Sophia's diary-letter ended with the hurriedly written words "Please come soon; we are all waiting for you." I read it several times every night till we left. Although my family had gone through a lot of trouble before reaching India, they were safe now. That was all that mattered and it was comforting.

As soon as I got the news, I tried to send their clothes. I packed about ten large pieces of luggage and took them to the Kabul airport. There each item was inspected very carefully. When it came to Laila's "fur" coat they raised a lot of objections until I ripped open the corner of the coat and showed them the back, which was not real animal skin. After going to all that trouble I wondered why Laila wanted her coat in the hot weather of India.

While at the airport I saw several large Russian planes at the far end of the runway, which could not be seen from the terminal. Two long lines of soldiers were moving parallel to each other, one line toward the planes and the other away from them. Some twenty caskets sat on the ground near the planes. On top of each was a military cap apparently belonging to the soldier who had lost his life in Afghanistan. The soldiers who were boarding had worn-out, discolored uniforms and looked very tired. The soldiers who were entering the country had new uniforms and clean, shiny boots.

An airport employee approached as I stood and watched the planes from behind the barbed-wire fence. He laughed loudly and said, "See how clean they arrive and how ragged they leave! It seems they are not getting the hospitality they expect." The man laughed again and left while reciting a beautiful poem of Maulana Jalaludin Balkhi that can be translated as follows: "This world is like a mountain, / Our deeds are like sound waves, / Whose echoes will come back to us one by one."

TUESDAY, DECEMBER 2, 1980 (QAUS 11, 1359)

I spent my last few days in Afghanistan with mixed feelings. Sometimes I was very sentimental and emotional, at other times too busy and hard as a rock, with no feelings at all. My schedule at the university, getting rid of all the remaining household goods, feeling hopeless about Saleem, anticipating freedom for all of us, plus filling Anahita's demands to attend meetings at odd hours, and, above all, my love and ties to my country and friends left me lost in a maze of mixed and inexplicable feelings.

Every day I attended school and tried not to attract attention. As I walked alone between home and school, I found that those were the only moments I had to myself. I thought a lot about everything. I found that I still had deep ties to my homeland and it was not easy to let go. I tried to look around carefully to see all those tiny details that I had always taken for granted. I tried to grasp the beauties of my land, the sky, the clouds, the mountains, the mountainside houses too, that kept increasing in number up the mountains as years passed.

The majestic Aliabad and Sherdarwaza (Noon Cannon) mountains stood as proudly as ever. I could still see the place where the old cannon was. I remembered when it used to fire at noon and people timed their day's activities in reference to it. It was said that some years before, a visiting dignitary from a foreign country was passing along the road just below the cannon when it fired. The foreign guest didn't know our tradition of the noontime cannon and was terrified. After that the firing of the cannon was stopped.

Feeling miserable and homesick, I walked along the streets, among shops, houses, and people, and looked at every one of them carefully. This time I wanted to see them to treasure the memories for the future, perhaps for the rest of my life. One day I took a special trip to Karte-Parwan, to our first house, the one we'd built years before on the mountainside. I stood and looked at it for a long time. It was all the same; nothing had changed. Each room carried memories of our life – those happy days when we didn't have much money but were joyous.

One day after school I went to my parents' old house where I'd grown up. All the lovely farmland nearby was gone and now a complicated network of streets and houses had been built, with many small new shops. I dearly missed Mom's presence there. I looked at the gutter on the north side of the house, which had given us so much trouble. Father and I often climbed a tall ladder in the cold of winter to fix it. Dad's countless willow trees next to the water well stood taller than ever, proudly sheltering birds' nests in their arms.

During my last weeks in Kabul I visited almost every part of town that had been important in my life. I even went to visit two of my high school classmates who lived in the Microrayan area. Of course I couldn't tell them I was leaving, but I knew it was probably my last visit with them.

At home, the things that I couldn't sell were still everywhere, so I called KuKu, an old neighbor of Mom's, and told her to pick up whatever she needed. She came and took loads of clothes, pots, pans, cups, trays, and firewood. It kept the poor lady busy for several days.

I sent a message to the woman who used to do laundry for us. She had a young son who needed an operation. He had been injured long before when digging a well, but they didn't have the money for proper medical care. I told her I would pay the hospital bills if she hospitalized her son, and sent her some money.

Although I tried, I couldn't find Abbas, Rahmat, Rahim, or Sadiq, our servants of past years. I wanted to see how they were. Why was I doing it? I didn't know. I'd paid them well when they worked for us, but I still wanted to see them get through the upcoming winter safely.

Finally, just days before my departure, I went to see my uncle. Normally he came to our house every week, but this time he was late and I hadn't seen him for two weeks. Of all our family, my uncles and their families, he was the only one left in Kabul. He didn't have a wife or any children. In fact, he'd never remarried after his first wife died many years before. I found my uncle very sick. I tried to take him to the hospital, but he wouldn't agree. Finally my brother Khalil and I took him to the hospital, but his case was hopeless. The doctors said he wouldn't live very long and sent him home.

After we returned from the hospital I sat with my uncle. I wanted to tell him I was leaving for India very soon, for he didn't know yet. It took me a while to decide how to break the news to him. Time was running short; I had only two days left in Kabul and my uncle had to know. After some thought, I said, "Kaka Jan" – dear uncle – "I want to leave for India the day after tomorrow for Sahar's checkup. I'll be back in three months."

"No, you're not coming back," he replied. "Go! Everybody else is gone! I wanted you all to be with me when I died. Your mother is gone . . . everyone else is gone," he cried out like a child. My uncle was right. Of all his twenty-six nephews and nieces, only my brother and I were left in Kabul.

I knew my uncle would be dying soon, but, sadly, I couldn't help him. To give him moral support I told him, "Kaka Jan, don't worry; I'll stay by your side until you get better. Then we'll both go to India." I honestly was willing to do so, but he wouldn't agree. I gave him some money for his doctor bills. He took it in his shaky hands and began to count it.

That night at home I couldn't go to sleep until late. I thought about my uncle constantly. I remembered that two weeks before, he had come running to our house all out of breath. As soon as I opened the door, he said, "Thank God, you're here!" Without pausing he continued, "I don't know what I'd do if you were gone too!"

That day, he told me, he'd gone to my mother's place to visit her. As usual, he'd opened the door and entered without knocking. To his surprise, he saw that the living room decor had been changed. "So I rushed into the guest room," my uncle said, "and that had changed too. There was a strange woman there! A man came forward and saw me standing there, lost and confused. He asked what I wanted. I told him that this was my brother's house. 'Where are they?' I said."

The new owner told him that his brother's family had sold the house to them. My uncle, still in a shock, left the house and walked toward the bus stop. A few steps later he fell in a faint on the sidewalk. Passersby came to his rescue and helped him. He got a cab and rushed to my house. Now I realized my uncle had never recovered from that shock.

At school I requested a week of emergency leave. I told the office that I was going out of Kabul. In the meantime, since a few weeks were left until the end of the fall semester, I gave instructions to the teaching assistants to carry on the labs in my absence. I put all the student records and grades on my desk, clear and neatly printed. I wanted my students to get the grades they deserved.

Today, our last day in Afghanistan, I took my children to see their grandma, Saleem's mother. Grandma was surprised, because we never visited her before noon on school days. We spent the entire day with her. During all that time God knows how much I wanted to, but I never told her we were leaving. If I did, I thought, the poor woman would start crying and soon some relatives who were members of the Communist party would find out and we'd be in big trouble. When evening came we left her house. It was so hard to say good-bye forever. I loved her very much and always cherished those eleven years we'd spent together.

WEDNESDAY, DECEMBER 3, 1980 (QAUS 12, 1359)

Our plane to India was scheduled to leave at ten-thirty this morning. We left the house at nine o'clock. The streets were full of tanks and convoys running in all directions. My brother said, "Sis, when you fly safely out today, I'll be extremely happy. Don't worry about Uncle; I'll take good care of him."

As we approached the airport my heart beat very fast. I was afraid of seeing someone who knew me. I took my luggage to the check-in area. To my surprise, one of my present students, Halima, was behind the counter. She took my passport, looked at all the tickets, and weighed and labeled the luggage. I didn't know what my reactions revealed, but I felt rather foolish. Although I knew Halima was surprised to see me leaving, luckily she did not ask any questions.

There were still a few minutes left until boarding time, so I stood in an isolated corner right under the spiral stairways of the terminal, with my back toward the crowd that was entering the main gate. A few moments passed and suddenly I saw that a large group of university teachers, most of whom knew me, was entering the building. I said in a low voice, "Oh God, help me please. This is not what I need now!" Very nervous, I turned my back again and pretended to be looking out the window. Fortunately, the professors went into another room and none of them saw me. They were going to the various provinces to proctor the Kabul University entrance exam.

After they all left, I relaxed a little although I still worried about Halima. I didn't know what she might be doing. My relaxed mood ended abruptly when my brother came and asked me in an upset voice, "What is that stupid guy doing here?"

"Who?"

"Saleem's nephew," he replied. "He's in the customs area, searching the passengers' luggage."

Now I was absolutely afraid. I knew Saleem's nephew would do anything in his power to stop us. He was a long-time member of Babrak's party. He didn't know we were leaving, because I'd kept it a secret. I knew that when he saw us, he would call up everybody right away to tell them we were leaving. I wasn't sure what the consequences would be, but whatever the outcome, things didn't seem good. His family was still angry about past events; Saleem and I had stopped talking to them long ago.

Then things somehow began to fall into place. As we entered the customs area, the nephew went into the luggage area. I really didn't know why he left at exactly the time we entered. I thought that probably my brother tricked him and called him outside, keeping him busy there by pretending he'd come to visit him. Or maybe he just left. Anyway, the entire time we were in customs I didn't see him.

In the customs room an airport policeman with a hawklike curved beak and big pitch-black eyes asked us to open our bags for his inspection. I opened the first one. He looked carefully, removing almost everything. Then he began tapping and feeling the lining and sides. He even opened all the bottles of lotion and the toothpaste tubes. His actions were like those of a hungry wolf trying to scrape the last threads of meat from the bare bones of a carcass. His gestures were insulting. He probably thought he was the only honest man in Afghanistan and everyone else was a criminal. A policewoman came up. She looked at me and then started to inspect our other two bags. To my surprise, she opened one, didn't touch anything, closed it, and then ordered the man standing next to her to put them on the plane. She didn't even open the third one but said, "It's okay." She looked at me again, smiled, and said, "Thank you very much."

In the customs area there were only three police officers – the woman, the hawk, and one other. After inspecting the baggage all three gathered at the desk and it was time to check my purse and shoulder bag. One of them asked how much money I was carrying. I told them twenty-six hundred dollars. The rude hawklike officer heard and came closer. "No!" he said. "No way! You can't take that much money out – no more that eight hundred dollars for all of you."

I replied angrily, "Look, I'm not going to visit a relative who can pay for my room and board. I'm going there for medical treatment and I need the money for hospital costs."

The two other officers, who had listened to our conversation quietly so far, asked him, "How much does she have?"

The rude hawk told them. Then he said to me, "Give the extra money to someone you know in the visitors' room. Take only eight hundred dollars with you."

I protested. "No; I'll need this money in India. This is what the Ministry of Foreign Affairs told me I could take."

At this point things seemed pretty bad. Then the second officer who was watching us stepped forward and said, "Captain Rahim Jan, I think she is right. She can take about six hundred dollars per person if they are going for medical reasons."

I saw things were turning my way, but I was still upset about the situation. I said, "Okay, all right. I'm not taking more than eight hundred dollars. But give me a letter ensuring that if I run out of money in India, the Afghan embassy will help me. I can't sit there in the beggars' row on the streets of Delhi to collect money."

The woman officer added, "Rahim Jan, let them go; it's getting late. How can you send a woman with three children and no money to a foreign country? She tells the truth; where would she be able to get money?"

Rahim, still angry and upset, reluctantly agreed and left the desk. The two accommodating officers pointed me to the next room, where we were supposed to be searched. As I left, they gave me a salute, raising their hands close to their foreheads. The woman said with a smile, "Bon voyage, Professor!" I thanked them sincerely and we shook hands. Their actions made me realize anew that there were still many nice people left in the country who cared about others. It was delightful to know that under the government of those rude hawks there were still a large number of people who had that Afghani blood running in their veins and trusted you. Certainly I needed their good wishes. Those two officers were my nicest last memory from my country, and I will never forget them.

My sons were sent to a different room while I entered the special search area for women. It was separated from the main area by cardboard walls and was divided into small compartments about two meters square. These search rooms were new; I hadn't seen them on my previous trips. My daughter and I were almost strip-searched. The police checked inside my purse, all the hand lotion tubes, and even put a stick in the face cream to see if I was hiding something there.

Then they ordered me to go through the door that opened directly onto the tarmac. At a distance the Indian plane was being loaded. I waited for my sons to come out the other door. As they exited, I started walking toward the plane, but after a few steps I noticed that my younger son, Ali, was not there with us. I stopped, looked back, and saw that four officers were surrounding him. They were looking inside his pockets. One of them had a twenty-five-cent coin in his hand, flipping it around and looking at it.

Ali still had the small handbag with him that contained a check in American dollars. I had converted the rest of money I had into dollars and had hidden it inside the lining of the handbag the night before. Seeing Ali with those officers around him worried me. I thought they'd probably found the check and were questioning him.

I ran back to them, pulled out my passport and showed it to them, and said, "Here! . . . Here, if you want to see his passport, he's with me, on my passport."

My words made them let him go. They returned the coin and a piece of paper to him. A sigh of relief came out of my throat involuntarily. I silently said, "Thank God! Please don't let me down now."

We entered the plane after all this trouble. It was scheduled to take off at ten-thirty but was delayed for sixty minutes, which actually seemed like several hours to me. During the whole time I worried that they would come and take me off the plane. I was still concerned about my relative in customs and also my student, Halima – about what they were doing or where they might report.

After a few minutes Halima came inside the plane and asked me if I needed anything. I replied, "No, thank you." She looked very sincere in her offer of help. She went around and checked several other passengers and then came back to me and said, "*Ostad*, I know I might not be able to see you again in class. I want you to know that you were one of my best teachers. Thank you for being that way."

Her words came unexpectedly, and I opened my seat belt and stood up. I kissed her face and told her, "Good luck, my dear."

Halima left the plane and the doors shut. The engine revved up. However, we waited. I looked out and saw a large number of military planes and helicopters landing. My heart was still pounding. Every minute I thought they would come after us.

While we were still waiting on the ground, I asked Ali why he was called back after we'd started walking to the plane. He showed me the paper he carried and also the quarter. I didn't know he had them in his pocket; otherwise I wouldn't have let him bring them. The piece of paper contained the address in America of one of his former classmates. Ali had written underneath the address a big "USA," which attracted the attention of the police, who wanted to know where he got it. In the minds of government officials, anyone who carried coins, magazines, or letters from America or any other Western country was suspect as a foreign agent or spy. The police wanted him to say that no, he was not going to India; he was going instead to America.

Around noon the plane finally got off the ground. My children were happy, talking to each other excitedly and looking at the houses down below. The plane circled low over the airport and headed east toward India. I looked through the windows. The Khoja Rawash Air Force Base was in sight. Saleem had worked there. I heard a chanting voice from somewhere far away, among the engine noises. At first it was unclear, but slowly it came close and closer. I recognized it as it filled my ears: "Honey, if I die, would you come to my grave and pray for me!" This was Saleem's last request, made to me the week before his disappearance.

In great sorrow I looked around, searching for small bumps in the ground. The earth was covered with a low, off-green carpet of grass, camouflaged now by the December frost, which reflected the sun's bright rays back to me. It looked like there were thousands of stars twinkling down there. Every bump seemed so precious and holy to me. I couldn't help thinking that one of them might be holding in its heart my beloved one. My tears began to fall. The idea drove me crazy because I'd never been able to locate his resting place.

How dearly I wanted to get off the plane and put flags on every bump down there – the green flags placed on the graves of Afghan martyrs. God only knew how many of them contained the remains of innocent young people who died for the cause of freedom and whose relatives still faithfully stood outside Puli-Charkhi prison every Friday.

I closed my eyes in grief. I pictured . . . I pictured a land of holy shrines among green martyr flags swaying and flapping gently through the seasons to come, crying out for peace and justice. As Khoja Rawash headquarters disappeared behind the mountains, I kissed my land from far away for the last time, that holy land which carried my loved one in its heart somewhere down there.

EPILOGUE

In December of 1980 when I got to India I was pleased to see that my family was okay. The first thing I did was put my children and my young brother and sister in school to learn English. Then I went to the American embassy. There I discovered that all the documents of my visit to the American embassy in Kabul had been burned by the embassy personnel during the Kabul uprisings.

Several weeks went by and one day as I was talking to one of the embassy employees, telling him of my situation, he said, "Well, the fellow you had an interview with in the American embassy in Kabul, Tom, is here now. Why don't you talk to him?" He called Tom into his office. Tom remembered all the details of my interview about political asylum.

Christmas was getting close and I sent a couple of postcards to my friends in Omaha, Nebraska. This was my first message to them since I'd left Omaha at the end of 1976. In fact, I didn't write any letters from Kabul to any of my friends in the United States, just to be careful not to arouse the suspicion of government officials, even during President Daoud's time.

After six months in India, and with the help of our friends, my children, my mother, my youngest brother, and two young sisters who were not married came to the United States in May 1981. I was scared to death of my enormous responsibilities to my family and of the unknown future. My greatest fears were for my three teenagers, who had gone through very difficult times and now faced an unfathomed world full of many good and many bad things.

Fifteen years have gone by. Today I feel extremely lucky that not only my own children but the rest of my relatives who joined us later are very successful, each leading a decent life. All are trying hard to rebuild their own lives and to catch up on the things that they left behind. Although it may take years to heal, we are all hopeful for the future.

My three children have established their own lives. No signs of the hardship and stress they experienced are visible in them, but certainly the memories of our past friends and the scars of war will remain with them. Omar graduated from the university in 1988 and works in a local business. He was married in 1991 and he and his wife, who also graduated from the university, had their first child in March of 1993. Ali graduated from architectural school and completed his master's degree in civil engineering in 1989. He is is employed in an architectural firm. Sahar graduated from the university in 1991 and is working on her master's degree in psychology. She was married in 1991 and their first child was born in April 1994.

In the past few years, after several attempts to learn my husband's fate, I contacted Amnesty International in Geneva. Unfortunately, they found no records on Saleem in their files. The fate of some of those officers missing on the first day of the bloody April coup of 1978 may never be known in detail.

Today my happiness is complete but for the fact that I cannot share my joy with my husband, Saleem, the man who taught my children the values of life in their first few years – taught them so well that his inspiration kept them going with hope and strength through all those difficult times. Our prayers and heart go with those who live still in Afghanistan under even worse conditions. To those, the survivors of this never-ending war: Salutes to all who have died in the cause of freedom from political oppression!